"Historians usually dissect an event and then a[...] Souls Day the authors do the opposite. They s[...] families of soldiers killed under mysterious ci[...] and then work their way back in time to uncover what really happened and give those families some closure. It's an investigative masterpiece that exposes the horror of war on so many levels."

—BRUCE MOHL, editor of *Commonwealth Magazine: Nonprofit Journal of Politics, Ideas, and Civic Life*

"No family, no community, and no nation rests fully until its sons and daughters in arms have come home. In that spirit, we should all honor and encourage the work expressed in this book."

—DEVAL PATRICK, former governor of Massachusetts

"You might think that by now every story about World War II has been told. Think again. This book, based on in-depth investigative reporting, tells a compelling story that you've never heard about. It's a story that has needed to be told and is one you'll want to read."

—JOE BERGANTINO, cofounder of the New England Center for Investigative Reporting

"An impressive historical investigation into the battle on All Souls Day and into the men and the mystery of the lost battalion. . . . It is a remarkable and impressive effort to apply investigative journalism skills to bring to life a battle buried in the annals of World War II."

—BRETT ARENDS, author and columnist for Dow Jones publications

"Written in a style that is reminiscent of Tom Brokaw's *The Greatest Generation*, the authors tell a remarkable . . . story about the lives, valor, and sacrifices of select men from the 28th Infantry Division who fought in the Battle of the Hurtgen Forest but never came home. It is also a story of their families' search for closure. This is a story every American should read to remind them that our freedom and way of life have a high price if we intend to keep it."

—EDWARD D. JENNINGS, assistant professor in the Department of Command and Leadership, U.S. Army Command and General Staff College

"I attended the funeral of Staff Sergeant John J. Farrell Jr. out of respect for his service, courage, and sacrifice as an American soldier, and to show his family and fellow Hurtgen Forest veterans that loyalty and commitment between soldiers spans generations. In my mind he is an American hero. There is no nobler a cause than the preservation of a Soldier's life through the telling of his history."

—THOMAS SELLARS, Brig. Gen., U.S. Army (Ret.)

# ALL
# SOULS
# DAY

# ALL SOULS DAY

## THE WORLD WAR II BATTLE AND THE SEARCH FOR A LOST U.S. BATTALION

JOSEPH M. PEREIRA AND JOHN L. WILSON

Potomac Books

*An imprint of the University of Nebraska Press*

© 2020 by Joseph M. Pereira and John L. Wilson

All rights reserved. Potomac Books is an imprint of the University of Nebraska Press.

First Nebraska paperback printing: 2023

Library of Congress Cataloging-in-Publication Data
Names: Pereira, Joseph M., author. | Wilson, John L. (Military historian), author.
Title: All Souls Day: the World War II battle and the search for a lost U.S. battalion / Joseph M. Pereira and John L. Wilson.
Other titles: World War II battle and the search for a lost U.S. battalion
Description: Lincoln NE: Potomac Books, an imprint of University of Nebraska Press, [2020] | Includes bibliographical references and index.
Identifiers: LCCN 2020010711
ISBN 9781640122253 (hardback)
ISBN 9781640125643 (paperback)
ISBN 9781640124202 (epub)
ISBN 9781640124219 (mobi)
ISBN 9781640124226 (pdf)
Subjects: LCSH: United States. Army. Infantry Regiment, 112th—Biography. | Hürtgen Forest, Battle of, Germany, 1944. | United States. Army. Infantry Regiment, 112th—History. | United States. Army. Infantry Division, 28th—History. | Soldiers—United States—Biography. | World War, 1939–1945—Missing in action—United States. | Missing in action—Family relationships—United States. | World War, 1939–1945—Repatriation of war dead—United States. | United States Army. Infantry Regiment, 112th—Registers. | World War, 1939–1945—Regimental histories—United States.
Classification: LCC D769.31 112th P47 2020 | DDC 940.54/213551—dc23
LC record available at https://lccn.loc.gov/2020010711

Set in Arno Pro by Mikala R. Kolander.

In Flanders fields the poppies blow
Between the crosses, row on row
That mark our place; and in the sky
The larks, still bravely singing, fly
Scarce heard amid the guns below

> We are the Dead. Short days ago
> We lived, felt dawn, saw sunset glow,
> Loved, and were loved, and now we lie
> In Flanders fields

Take up our quarrel with the foe:
To you from failing hands we throw
The torch; be yours to hold it high
If ye break faith with us who die
We shall not sleep, though poppies grow
In Flanders fields

— Lt. Col. John McCrae MD,
Canadian Army, Ypres, Belgium, May 1915

# CONTENTS

# ILLUSTRATIONS

*Photographs*

# ACKNOWLEDGMENTS

There is an irony to the tale of *All Souls Day*, and it took me a while to see it. On its face it's a book about war, but its stories are really about love—a type that I was unfamiliar with, and perhaps that's why at first I didn't "get it." This is a love that has no bounds. It drives people to cross oceans, travel great distances, spare little expense, write letters for decades on end, and endure an eternity of pain.

Jack, the coauthor of this book, of course, has lived that life, and I thank him for sharing it with me. How can you love someone—I mean truly love someone—you've either never seen or, if you did, for only a brief time? I subsequently came to learn of so many others like Jack, some of whom made it into this book and some who didn't: Rosemary Farrell in Norwood, Massachusetts; Peggy Robinette in San Francisco, California; Eve Cunningham in Roswell, Georgia; Stanley Farrior in Burgaw, North Carolina; Linda Bepler in Sarasota, Florida; Nancy Eckel in Marlboro, New Jersey; Amelia Messina in Mays Landing, New Jersey; Charles Pecue in Hudson Falls, New York; Sheila Peterson Helmberger in Baxter, Minnesota; Leonard Greenway in Rolling Hills Estates, California; Judith Sullivan Crittenden in Birmingham, Alabama; Willie Fikes and Ed Howell, both in Hamilton, Alabama; Jean Sanders Mixon in Hawkinsville, Georgia; Ken Harbison in Xenia, Ohio; and Rebecca Detmer in South Norfolk, Virginia. Their numbers are many, and they walk among us, bearing this yoke upon them.

I'm also indebted to many others who have contributed, each in their own capacity, to the telling of this story: Sally Hughes, for mustering the energy to pore over every word in the manuscript and reminding me—more often than I sometimes appreciated—of their misplacement or misuse; Dylan Hughes, a computer whisperer, for creating a software application to help me catalog in tidy tables the sacred names, ranks, and serial numbers of the missing; Carole-Anne Tyler, a published author and university professor, for her lengthy late-night emails (after hours of correcting graduate dissertations) about academic press rigor; Rachel Luebke, a millennial fresh out of graduate school, for declaring what would (or wouldn't) resonate with a generation for whom the war is primarily a couple of chapters in a history book or the subject of a Netflix documentary; Anthony Grasso, a nonagenarian prodigy who remembers the questions on his high school exams from 1943, for tolerating such questions from me as "What did you have for supper the night before you left for the war?" (spaghetti and meatballs); Bette Miller, for showing me the vestiges of a town from the 1940s that linger in the pretty homes, yards, and roads that is the Spirit Lake, Iowa, of today; military historian Thomas Bradbeer, who, despite teaching full time, writing a book, and taking numerous government-business trips to Florida and the UK, made time for three long sessions to explain the U.S.Army's deployment in the Hürtgen Forest; curator Charles Oellig, for permitting me to enter his private study in a loft above the Pennsylvania National Guard Museum so that I could thumb through his neatly arranged stacks of unpublished manuscripts and obscure writings by soldiers who fought in the All Souls Day battle; Bill Snider, the grandson of the regimental commander of the 112th, who, without any coaxing, provided a trove of documents from his family's collection; Cindy Davis, director of Spirit Lake Public Library, who made available its carefully archived literature on the region's early beginnings and town history; Ed and Anita Tiebax, who, from their home fifty miles away from the Hürtgen Forest, in Maasbracht, Netherlands, have collected every scrap of information that has been recorded about four of the soldiers in this book; and five other Europeans, all German nationals—Ludwig Fischer in Schmidt; Achim Konejung in Muddesheim-Vettweiss; Pr. Axel Lautenschlager in Vossenack; Dr. Christoph Rass in Ossnabruck; and Manfred Jansen in Aachen—for their touching generosity with their time, writings, and research materials. Also, of invaluable help was the devoted staff at the National Archives and Records Administration, which helped locate aging files among two billion feet of documents in its glass-encased edifice at College Park, Maryland; Bobby O. Bell of Hombourg, Belgium; Paul Fowler and Jamie Harmon of Salem, New Hampshire; Deborah Hawkins of Pawlet, Vermont; Dr. Arne Esser in Germany; and Bill McCarthy of Arlington, Massachusetts.

My gratitude also extends to the University of Nebraska Press: acquisitions editor Tom Swanson; Editorial, Design, and Production manager Ann Baker; assistant editor Emily Wendell; the other staff members in the EDP Department; and Emily Shelton, whose deft editing improved the text and made it more readable.

Finally, I wish to remember the very reason for this book: the selfless love of the young men who willingly made the ultimate sacrifice for you and for me. About that, coauthor Jack Wilson had this to write:

> Searches for all our missing soldiers, sailors, airmen, and Marines from all wars must accelerate. The Department of Defense has an enormous task to recover and return to families more of the seventy-two thousand Americans still missing after our nation's wars. While some warriors are not recoverable—due to being lost at sea, in airplane crashes, and in other incidents—the difficult task of finding and returning our heroes must continue, and quickly. The National League of of POW/MIA Families is still active and encouraging the Pentagon to do more. In 2015 the two previous military search organizations, Joint POW/MIA Accounting Command (JPAC) and the Defense POW/Missing Personnel Office (DPMO), were evolved into a singular and improved organization called the Defense POW/MIA Accounting Agency (DPAA). We urge all Americans to visit their website, at https://dpaa.mil. There you will find more detailed and updated information on recovery actions. Our missing military still in the Hürtgen Forest are but the tip of the iceberg. Increased advocacy of American families of missing warriors to their congressional representatives and the DPAA will accelerate the return home of more of our missing warriors. They deserve nothing less.

Fig. 1. In November 1944 three regiments of the Twenty-Eighth Infantry Division
prepared to attack five towns in the Hürtgen Forest. National Archives
and Records Administration/U.S. Army.

# ALL SOULS DAY

# Introduction

*The Price of Bravery*

Eddie Slovik faced the morning of January 31, 1945, with surprising calm. After being driven all night for approximately 250 miles in a blinding snowstorm from Paris to Sainte-Marie-aux-Mines, a coal mining village high in the Vosges Mountains near the French-German border, Slovik stepped off the back of a military truck, cold and wet.

He was taken to a Roman Catholic chaplain who heard his confession and gave him Holy Communion. Then he was escorted onto the grounds of a stately house fronted by a heavy iron gate. The handcuffs that locked Slovik's arms behind his back cut into his wrists with every movement as he made his way to a courtyard, followed by a retinue of soldiers marching slowly. There, in the grayness of the morning, a hastily erected wall awaited him. In front of it, a wooden stake had been driven into the frozen ground. As much as fifteen inches of snow had fallen the night before.

Slovik was a handsome man. He had an angular face, his eyes were clear blue, and his eyelashes matched the color of his hair, which was a shade darker than the khaki of his uniform. In ordinary times he would be just a young man who posed little to no harm to anyone. But on this, the 1150th day of war since the bombing of Pearl Harbor, Slovik, a private and member of the Twenty-Eighth Infantry Division of the U.S. Army, was about to be made an example of. For the first time in more than eighty years, a U.S. military man was ordered to be "shot to death with musketry," which is army-speak for "before a firing squad."

Present was Gen. Norman "Dutch" Cota, commander of the division, his two silver stars and American Eagle patch glistening in the light reflecting off the freshly fallen snow. Also in the execution arena were fifty-two handpicked soldiers who had slow-marched into the courtyard to take their discreet positions off to the sides. They had been chosen to bear witness, a ceremonial role not unlike those at a swearing in of a U.S. president or government official.

There was silence in the courtyard. In a passionless voice, the execution director read the general court-martial order, a cumbersomely worded explanatory military canon. During the three minutes it took to read the entire document, Slovik appeared to be in prayer, his eyes closed, his lips moving.

"Private Slovik, do you have a statement to make before the order directing your execution is carried out?" the director asked.

"No," Slovik replied softly.

"Private Slovik, do you have a last statement to make to me, as a chaplain, before your death?" asked a Roman Catholic priest.

"No, Father," Slovik said.

The accused man was then strapped to the wooden stake in three places: across his shoulders, above his knees, and around his ankles. Just before an officer pulled a black hood over his head, the priest leaned over and whispered, "Eddie, when you get up there, say a little prayer for me."

"Okay, Father," Slovik responded. "I'll pray that you don't follow me too soon."

Moments later, twelve army men raised their M1 rifles and fired. Slovik slumped forward, his knees buckling under him. A total of eight bullets had pierced his chest: five on the left, two on the right, and one dead center through the breast bone. One entered his left upper arm, another his collarbone, and another his left shoulder. Blood and flesh had splattered onto the hardwood panel behind him.

Somewhat amazingly, about five seconds after the shots, Slovik tried to straighten himself, his head and shoulders rising about a foot before he slumped down. Approximately three seconds later, he raised himself again. Three medical officers shuffled through the snow, the crunch of their footsteps interrupting the rustic stillness of the morning. Everyone in the courtyard stood in agony, wondering whether the execution, as gruesome as it seemed, would proceed. The execution director nodded to his firing squad to reload their rifles and resume their positions. Then one of the medical examiners raised his hand. "We pronounce this man dead," he said. The riflemen lowered their weapons. The squad director spun on his heels and turned to the commanding general.

"Sir," he said. "The execution is completed."

"Dismiss the witnesses," Cota replied.[1]

What was Slovik's crime? He was accused of violating the Fifty-Eighth Article of War: desertion to avoid hazardous duty. In other words, he was charged with being scared. The army private had deserted his division twice in eight weeks. The first time, he found himself in his foxhole, unable to move after living through his first ever artillery shelling by an enemy. The second time, Slovik tried walking away from his unit after he failed to negotiate an assignment far from the frontline.

Is being afraid to die a crime? Fear is, after all, a biomechanism wired into us by evolutionary forces beyond our control, for the preservation of the species. So why was his behavior deemed to be so unbecoming? Paris and London, at the time, were full of Sloviks—GIs who had deserted their units, scared of dying on the battlefield or wanting to have nothing to do with the war. They blended in nicely with the thousands of servicemen that thronged the pubs and alleyways on forty-eight-hour passes.[2]

At the same time, there is another consideration, contradictory in essence but nonetheless wholesome and valid as an argument. The U.S. Army has established a code of conduct, an organizational norm for the probable success of a combat unit in its military undertakings. That code nobly calls for a soldier to be brave in the name of duty, honor, and country. Any violation of that code by an inordinate number of soldiers would jeopardize the safety not just of his comrades on the battlefield, but of the nation as well.

Therein lies a conundrum. How can one be scared and brave at the same time? This is a question I have struggled with ever since my high school days, when I had to write an essay on Stephen Crane's

*The Red Badge of Courage.* I turned in my assignment without really coming to a clear understanding of how Crane's fictional protagonist Henry Fleming was able to mightily transform himself from coward to hero within the course of a battle. Then one day I met my coauthor, Jack, who told me over coffee about a strange experience he'd had one spring morning a few years before. It had something to do with his uncle, who was a soldier in World War II. I was intrigued. Together we dug into the past, reviewing photographs, maps, journals, diaries, declassified military documents, and recorded interviews with men now long dead. As it turns out, Jack's uncle —Staff Sgt. John J. Farrell—was in the same infantry division as Private Slovik.

What we discovered was a small battle, approximately eight days long, that was waged by a group of men, including his uncle, at about the same time that the case of Pvt. Slovik was scheduled to be tried before a military tribunal in Germany, just a few miles away. The battle was horrific, the worst defeat the Americans suffered in Europe during World War II. Because of some flawed decision-making, these young men were sent into an unwinnable engagement. They were just kids, some of them still in high school. It was a military campaign that few today—even among the army elite—know much about, if anything at all.[3]

In one scene we reviewed, an armada of Panzer tanks and Wehrmacht troops had surrounded the Americans on three sides.[4] The U.S. Army was in panic and disarray. There was only one thing to do—run. Defying the orders of lieutenants and captains to stay and fight, the men fled. Even efforts to collar the retreating masses failed. Yet, amid the stampede, a hardy band of soldiers decided to be brave. They stayed. The blitzkrieg was inevitable, their deaths almost certain. In existential resignation they breathed their final breaths, every youthful fantasy of war about to be crushed by a wave of ugly reality. This was the defining moment of their young lives.

These men existed on the flip side of Pvt. Slovik's universe. Their tales are the same: they both ended sadly. The one was put before a firing squad, the other ordered to undertake a suicide mission. Is there a difference? While the one has been told in military history books and in a made-for-TV movie, the stories of these other few men have lingered silently like ghosts in that misty past, invisible yet ever present.

There's something else. Mysteriously, some of these men have simply disappeared. They didn't vanish in the middle of a jungle or the bottom of an ocean; they perished in and around three German villages where the terrain, for the most part, is easily traversed, with villages full of kind people to keep vigil. In a remarkable demonstration of compassion between warring armies, both Germans and Americans laid down their arms to tend to their wounded and carry off their dead during that brief conflict. When lives hung in the balance, the two sides even shared medical expertise. So where are the missing? One would think that under such mutually cooperative conditions finding missing soldiers would be easy. But the recovery of their remains has been one of the most frustrating endeavors undertaken by the U.S. Army.

Meanwhile, these mysterious disappearances have wrought on their families an anguish that most humans have never experienced. It has led them to do things quite unthinkable, that one would normally find in a work of fiction and not in historical nonfiction. Some family members kindly invited us into their lives to show us that indeed the surreal had imperceptibly moved into their everyday existences for good. Now three generations away from that war, the grief has been handed down like an ugly heirloom, from father and mother to son and daughter and from uncle and aunt to nephew and niece. These are their stories.

Fig. 2. Marjorie (*left*) and Peggy in Spirit Lake, Iowa.
Courtesy of the Weaver/Robinette Family.

# 1

## Molly and Peggy

"I've knet yeh eight pair of socks, Henry, and I've put in all
yer best shirts, because I want my boy to be just as warm
and comf'able as anybody in the army."
—Henry's mother in Stephen Crane's
*The Red Badge of Courage* (1895)

Peggy took a deep breath, her chest rising, and, gathering all the emotion a young girl could conjure, screamed, "You should never have remarried so soon."

Molly looked down in utter disbelief at her eight-year-old daughter. Her face had turned two shades darker. Peggy had no right to say what had just come out of her mouth. Molly paused, waiting for her anger to subside. The days, weeks, and months of pain that throbbed deep inside, punctuated by night after night of restless sleep, had caught up to her like a bounding beast in a dream.

Her eyes filled with tears. "What was I supposed to do?" she shouted back. The question sounded more like a confession. "What was I supposed to do?" Her voice had lowered to a whisper. "I have two little girls to feed."

Peggy remained unmoved. She faced her mother, her two skinny arms folded defiantly across her small frame. "Maybe you should have gotten yourself a job and gone to work." The staccato admonition was cold and tinged with a bitterness that rang beyond the capacity of most girls her age. All was not well in the house of Molly and Peggy.

Animus between mother and daughter only worsened with the passing of time. On the outside—and to most of the townsfolk in Spirit Lake, Iowa—Peggy was a sweet kid with doe eyes, narrow shoulders, wavy blonde hair, and a smile that curled up in perfect symmetry with the contours of her chin. What a cutie, some neighbors would note when they saw her golden locks straightened against the wind as she sped past them on her Sears Roebuck roller skates.

But, within the walls of their small lakeside log house, the feud between mother and daughter continued to undulate, the tension invisible but always there. From time to time Peggy would declare, with the boldness of an heiress, that she was her "daddy's girl." Invariably her mother would respond, "You're just a spoiled brat."

Peggy knew just what her mother meant. Quietly, she partially agreed. Her dad enjoyed being with his daughter so much that he obliged her many whims. What would normally be viewed as patience took on the appearance of indulgence. When Peggy rode on the merry-go-round and the ride came to an end, he would tenderly ask, "Do you want to go again?"

Peggy also liked to roller-skate but hated having to take her skates off to go see her father milk the cows in the barn. She couldn't skate as easily on grass and dirt, so he promised that he would build a sidewalk from the house to the barn to make her short trek less of a hassle. The problem was that he left before getting around to it.

ONE DAY WHEN PEGGY WAS TEN YEARS OLD, MOLLY TOOK her to the doctor, even though she wasn't sick. The doctor listened to her heart, checked her ears, looked inside her mouth, and tapped a reflex hammer against her knees. Then he asked her a few questions. How do you feel? At what time do you go to bed at night? Do you go out to play? Peggy told the doctor she wanted a horse. Both her mother and the doctor were taken aback. This had come out of nowhere. Neither could think of a quick response. But the physician deftly continued with the exam, pretending he didn't hear his young patient.

Peggy knew what her mother was up to. Molly was preparing to pack her daughter off to reform school. A medical evaluation was just the prelude, or perhaps even the grounds for it. After mother and daughter left the doctor's office that day, Peggy waited for the words: pack your suitcase, it's time to go.

A day passed, then a week; two weeks; a month. But the order didn't come. Molly never did send Peggy away. Peggy continued to live at home, go to school, do chores, visit cousins, attend church, take care of a sister four years her junior, and anguish. "I really wish I had been sent to reform school," Peggy said to herself often when alone with her thoughts. "My life would be a lot better." Few, other than Molly, knew of her daughter's torment.

Peggy's problem was this. She could never forgive her mother for what she had done. In her mind, her mother went out looking for a husband and found one, without even making sure that her father was dead. What if Peggy ended up with two fathers? She dreaded the thought. On November 21, 1946, Mrs. Sydney Weaver had become Mrs. Wiley Lambert. Molly, then twenty-seven years old, looked radiant at the Presbyterian parsonage where she was married in a double-ring ceremony. She stood slightly over five feet four inches in heels. Her dark brown hair cascaded over the back of her wedding attire: a black-and-white pin check suit. For a corsage, she wore a red carnation.[1]

It wasn't that Peggy begrudged her mother some happiness. Rather, the problem lay in a more fundamental question: Was Peggy's dad dead or alive? Molly believed he was dead, but Peggy wasn't that certain. In fact, she was quite sure that he was alive. There was no corpse, no casket, no funeral. It was just someone's word, without a shred of evidence, that her dad was dead.

But, if anyone was of the belief that this was just a case of wishful thinking by a little girl who loved her daddy very much, there was additional proof. Her grandfather Curtis Weaver, an upstanding citizen of Spirit Lake and a respected businessman in the community, also didn't believe that Sydney was dead. Curtis was Sydney's dad. In fact, Curtis was so convinced that Sydney was still alive that he bet the family business on it.

Spirit Lake, perched on the banks of one of the Great Lakes of Iowa, distinctively serves as the seat of Dickinson County in the open prairie that borders Minnesota. After recovering from its bloody beginnings, when a renegade group of Sioux Indians wiped out a settlement of white pioneers in 1857, the town revived itself with some down-home Iowa ingenuity. Two railroads passed through the area, and Spirit Lake metamorphosed into a hospitality way station for travelers. It also cleverly seized upon the natural bounty created by continental glacial activity fifteen thousand years before and became a fisherman's mecca. For the town is bounded by twenty-three miles of glittering freshwater: East Okoboji Lake to the east, West Okoboji Lake to the west, and, to the north, Spirit Lake, separated from the Okobojis by a thin strip of isthmus land effectuating an almost miraculous parting of the waters that would have made Moses proud. Teeming in their depths were small- and large-mouth bass, channel catfish, bluegill, black crappie, northern pike, walleye, and muskellunge.

Curtis owned acres of land that sat handsomely between the lake and a scenic recreational state park. He sold fish bait and rented out boats, but he had plans to expand his boat livery business into a resort facility as America began to rise from the ashes of the Great Depression into the world's largest manufacturer of aircraft carriers, battleships, cruisers, destroyers, submarines, fighter planes, bombers, tanks, jeeps, trucks, and cannons, all of which generated unprecedented prosperity.

Curtis had seven grown children on hand—four boys and three girls—but he was waiting for Sydney to launch the new Weaver enterprise. Curtis would on occasion say to family members that Sydney was "the best of the lot." Sydney helped his father immensely. He drove a 1930s pickup truck with a water tank on the back where he dumped the minnows that he seined from local rivers and that he and his father would sell for bait. He would roll up his pants and lower his six-foot frame gently into the water so the minnows wouldn't get spooked and scatter; then he would effortlessly drag his net across the riverbed, his knees bent and arms swung wide as if he were performing a choreographed dance. Sydney was also a jack-of-all-trades: a farmer, a homebuilder, and a repairman. Once he even installed a new roof by himself. For food, he caught frogs and fished and hunted pheasant. He also trapped muskrat for their fur, which he and his dad sold in town. In the winter he cut big chunks of ice out of the lake and stored it with straw in the basement of the boathouse, and when the hot months of summer arrived, he sold the ice. Peggy said her dad was a "salt-of-the-earth kinda guy," always outdoors, looking to help his dad and feed his family.

Curtis told everyone he was waiting for Sydney to cut the ribbon to launch the new business, not because he was a hard worker and a great business partner—both of which were true—but because Sydney was still alive somewhere. But where was he? That was the question. No one in the Weaver family knew the answer.[2] As Peggy grew from childhood to adulthood, she witnessed the devastation that her father's disappearance had on her grandfather. Darrell, Curtis's second-oldest son, was anxious to get the resort plan off the ground, lest someone else beat the Weavers to the idea. "Every time Darrell would say, 'Dad, we're going to do this and we're going to do this,' my grandfather would sit him down and say, 'No, we're going to wait for Syd,'" Peggy says today. "We're going to wait for Syd. We're going to wait for Syd."

But Darrell couldn't wait forever. He eventually became estranged from his father, went across the lake to buy a plot of land, and launched the business without his dad. Darrell made no secret of the fact that he was now in direct competition with his father, if he ever got started. Everyone could see Darrell's boat and resort operation prospering in plain sight from across the lake, where he once toiled for his father's business, like a good son.

In 1964 Sydney's mom, Sarah Emaline "Sadie" Guthrie Weaver, died. She was seventy-nine years old. Two years later her husband, Curtis Elmer Weaver, passed away, at eighty-one. "My grandfather waited and waited and waited for dad to show up until the day he died," Peggy says. "He never did expand the business." Spirit Lake, with its bucolic surroundings, became one of the most popular vacation spots in the Midwest. "My grandfather's business never did amount to anything," she says. "It just fell apart." Peggy's relationship with her mom also continued to be strained: "We never really bonded." After graduating from Drake University with a bachelor's degree in theater arts, Peggy piled her belongings into a small car and

Fig. 3. Michael Loncar, before his army days.
Courtesy of the Loncar/Bepler Family.

drove west in the middle of a snow storm to pursue graduate studies, first in Seattle, and then in San Francisco. In California Peggy got married, settled down, and raised a family. The years turned to decades and decades to a generation. During that time the feeling of not knowing hung around, silent and invisible. She once read a novel and a line jumped out at her. It described what she was feeling inside: "It lingered like a fog, impenetrable on some days, lifting on others, but it was always present."[3]

Then, on January 27, 2016, Peggy got a telephone call from a man in Massachusetts, identifying himself as Jack Wilson. "I believe I have some information for you," he said. "It's about your dad." Peggy pulled up a chair; she had to sit down for this. Inside, she sensed a rush of more than fifty years of sadness suddenly well like primordial matter beneath the earth's surface, and she felt a tug in her throat. For all these years the secret longing ebbed and flowed with no place to go, its melancholy movements rising and falling in intervals. Now it was coming back again. Jack said, "I think I know where he may be."

Surrounded by tree-lined golf courses, neatly manicured lawns, and handsomely paved driveways, Linda Bepler was sitting in her ranch-style home in Sarasota, Florida, when she, too, received a call from Jack Wilson. "Do you have an uncle or a dad who fought in World War II?" he asked.

"Yes," Linda said. "Michael Loncar. He was my mother's older brother. We never knew what happened to him." The call was welcomed because Linda often thinks about her mom, Mildred, who passed away in 2003. She was a small, skinny lady with big thick glasses and nerves of steel, which came in handy during her hard life. She had lost her father as a teenager; he took his life after he was laid off from a job in a town where work was difficult to find. After that her mother needed help, and the children pitched in, working odd jobs. But the biggest cross Mildred bore was the disappearance of her brother in the war. "Every day she had off from work, she went to the theater, just to look at those newsreels," Linda says. "All she wanted was to spot him in one of those newsreels. That was her goal in life. It was an overwhelming thing to try to think that you would find him among all those soldiers, all those wounded men being taken away by the Red Cross, but it would have made her so happy." If for only just a glimpse.

During World War II, five Hollywood Studios (20th Century Fox, Universal Studios, the Hearst Corporation, Paramount Pictures, and RKO Radio Pictures) worked together with the U.S. Office of War Information to film soldiers in various war activities. They were spliced together in the editing room with the frontline footage taken by military combat cameramen and organized into 1,506 newsreel stories, each about 10 minutes long. The clips were shown in theaters along with regular feature films made by the Hollywood studios. For the studios it was a win-win situation: they got paid by the government for making the newsreels, and the newsreels themselves were a major draw for their feature films.[4] Folks like Mildred flocked to them. The minidocumentaries depicted soldiers, sailors, and airmen in the middle of invasions, bombing missions, resting while awaiting orders, or traveling in trucks or on foot from one battlefield to the next; they also featured the wounded, with bandages on their heads and their arms in slings, some with their eyes shut, carried on stetchers by fellow soldiers to the hospitals and aid stations where Red Cross nurses waited to receive them. During all that time in the theater, Mildred never did spot Michael. When the show was over, she would linger for a moment to collect herself, then walk out of the movie hall without saying a word. While others happily chatted on their way out about Humphrey Bogart, Ingrid Bergman, Clark Gable, and Bette Davis, Mildred remained silent. She was there for a different purpose.

Mildred and Michael were very close. Michael was born in 1919, Mildred in 1921. They grew up in Weirton, West Virginia, a photogenic town with smoky steel mills, brooding hills, and the Ohio River snaking through its backyard. Factory whistles blew at regular intervals. Work crews filed in and filed out. Hollywood noticed the town's dutiful rhythms and sent film crews to shoot movies there, including Michael Cimino's *The Deer Hunter* and Steven Spielberg's *Super 8*.

"My mother did more research than anybody I know into what happened to my uncle," Linda says. She saw every single newsreel shown in a theater. Still, after a lifetime of searching, all they had of her uncle was a pair of eyeglasses that he had left behind. "They were like soda bottle bottoms, they were so thick," she says. "My mother could not believe that he was accepted into the military." There were also a few letters that he penned from a Texas boot camp, from England, and from somewhere in Europe. Also in the Loncar collection were a handful of family photos: a picture of Michael in his uniform, looking handsome, next to his sister, Mildred, and their mom, as well as another picture of him that had been published in a local newspaper. The caption noted that he was named salutatorian from among his 111-member senior class at Weir High School. And there was a brief telegram from the War Department in November 1944. It simply said that he was missing.[5]

Linda didn't know her uncle. She was born long after the war had ended. In a sense, her uncle Michael was just a story and a face in a photo because she never got to know him. But her mother talked about him all the time, as if he was alive. When Mildred died, Linda was by her side, but the pain of searching for her brother did not die with her. Like perfume in the wake of a houseguest, it continued to linger in Linda's home, and in her heart. Now Linda, the niece, needed to continue where Mildred, the sister, had left off; it became incumbent upon her to look for Michael. But how does one look for someone who disappeared a lifetime ago, thousands of miles away? With the passing of each year the task seemed to grow more and more impossible. Any chance she had of finding out anything about her uncle's disappearance was slowly fading in the fog of time. The phone call Linda had just received, however, could be a glimmer in the mist. The man on the other end of the line wanted to know if someone from her family fought in World War II. Linda held the phone close to her ear. She was hungry for information. "What can you tell me?" Linda asked Jack.[6]

GROWING UP IN MASSACHUSETTS, MAINE, AND CONNECTI-cut during the 1950s and 1960s, Jack Wilson and his four siblings would eagerly anticipate the arrival of Memorial Day. The singular occasion in May, when the nation honors the memory of those who died in the armed service of their country, had become a rite of spring for the Wilsons.

After attending the local parades, Jack's dad would open his World War II navy chest and tell the kids a story or two about its contents. Inside the wooden trunk, as wide as the foot of a twin bed and as high as the knees of a man, he kept rifles from four countries, helmets from three countries, beach sand from two countries, and part of an engine from one kamikaze plane.

Like many veterans, Jack's dad talked little about his war experience. It was years after he had passed that the family learned from a high-ranking naval officer that their dad had undertaken twenty-nine harrowing trips across the English Channel to Normandy. Months later his ship was attacked in the Pacific Ocean and sunk by a Japanese kamikaze plane at Okinawa, putting him in a select group of naval officers who had fought in both theaters of World War II. Despite his reticence to say much about the horrors he'd encountered, Jack's dad was truly proud of what he and his shipmates helped to accomplish. The navy box was a relic from that previous time, and the ritual of discussing its contents a soulful moment of reflection. There was no braggadocio, no love of war in his words. Afterward everyone settled in to watch *Victory at Sea* on a black-and-white TV.

Jack graduated from college during the Vietnam War. Upon graduation he enlisted in the army and was sent to six months of basic training and advanced infantry, followed by five and a half years in the reserves. While in the reserves, Jack got a job in the corporate world, married his college sweetheart, and earned a graduate degree in business. Life as a corporate executive took him overseas on numerous occasions. On one trip to Europe in the spring of 1985, as Jack looked out the window of the plane as it crossed the English Channel en route to Frankfurt, his mind wandered back to the early 1940s, when thousands of smaller aircraft had battled in these same skies during World War II. It was a conflict in which he had acquired great interest, not only because of his dad, but also because of how various war time advances in technology gave birth to a plethora of postwar peacetime accomplishments: V2 rockets from Germany helped launch NASA; jet aircraft from the German Luftwaffe spurred the commercial aircraft industry; the UK's effort to protect London from German bombers gave rise to radar science; and nuclear energy power was rooted in the atomic bomb.

The captain informed the passengers on board that they would be descending over Belgium and western Germany in their approach to Frankfurt. Jack peered out the window as villages, towns, rivers, and forests slipped by. He had another reason to turn the clock back forty years: somewhere down there was the battlefield where his uncle and namesake, Staff Sgt. Jack Farrell, disappeared during World War II. His family's long-standing belief, based on letters and news reports, was that he had been killed in the Battle of the Bulge in the Ardennes Region, but it was a continuing mystery.

After that plane trip to Europe three decades ago, Jack became increasingly intrigued by the mystery of his uncle's disappearance. On subsequent trips he would visit German cemeteries and museums whenever he had free time. Always in the back of his mind were the unanswered questions about his uncle. And then, in the late spring of 2009, it happened. He experienced something, although he couldn't say exactly what: a hunch, an intuition, luck, clairvoyance, the cry of someone from beyond the grave or the hand of God.

That something was triggered by a picture he saw on the internet. It was June 10, 2009. The day began much like any other Wednesday. After breakfast he went to his office on the first floor of his two-story home in Harvard, Massachusetts, to review the news and financial markets and to look at his emails on his computer.

The Great Recession was showing little sign of loosening its grip on the nation's economy. Korea was going nuclear. Swine flu was spreading. Amanda Knox, the controversial American abroad, was about to go on trial for murder in Italy. On a cheerier note, the Boston Red Sox had crushed the New York Yankees the previous evening by a score of seven to nothing. The legendary DiMaggio versus Williams bouts of the 1940s were playing out today with different stars: Jeter and Rodriguez against Ortiz and Pedroia. Boston eagerly awaited another slugfest at Fenway Park later that day.

As he pored over the online pages of the *Boston Globe*–affiliated website Boston.com, an image caught his attention: a black-and-white photograph of a single boot. Underneath was a short caption: "More U.S. Army artifacts from WWII found in Germany." Still caked with mud from more than half a century ago, the boot was made of light brown leather, which had become frayed and rumpled from heavy use. It had maintained its original shape for the most part, and its laces were firmly tied. The right front of the boot was torn open, possibly from flying shrapnel, possibly from a bullet. It had clearly taken its share of abuse on the battlefield. World War II matériel is frequently discovered in Europe, but Jack was fascinated; there was an intimacy to this particular photo. He couldn't get it out of his mind, that it had once belonged to a soldier.

Having other business to attend to, he clicked off the computer. When he logged back on about an hour later, the photo of the boot was gone. In its place was another story. Jack swallowed hard. Carpe diem. He had failed to seize the moment. Overcome by regret for not printing a copy, his mind started racing.

"Who knows," he thought. "Maybe it could be Uncle Jack's boot."

Jack had never met his uncle, who had gone off to war in Europe and never come back. Despite not knowing what had happened, the memory of Jack Farrell always held a special place in the Wilson family. As a child Jack had heard so many stories about his uncle's intelligence, joviality, athleticism, and wit. He also happened to be named after him, at the request of his mother, who was one of his uncle's two adoring sisters. For years his mother's family had tried to find out what happened to his uncle Jack. The government provided little information. There was almost no way to track him from the military camps in the United States to which he was stationed, his journey overseas, the battles he fought in, or the name of his regiment or division. For strategic reasons the GIs were instructed not to divulge any information that could be used against them by the enemy. All the family had to go on was a letter from Jack. All they could deduce was that it had been written somewhere in Belgium with a Waterman fountain pen. Returning to his camp late one night, his uncle had noted in the letter how amazed he was by the demeanor of the local townspeople. Ecstatic about being liberated by the Allied Powers from Nazi occupation, they were washing and sweeping their streets long after dark. The village, his uncle wrote, was "the cleanest place he had ever seen."[7] This was Jack's last letter to his family in Arlington, Massachusetts. It was dated October 1944.

Molly and Peggy

As he sat at his desk on that late spring morning in 2009, Jack Wilson wondered how he could even venture a guess about whether that boot belonged to his uncle. Sixty-five years had gone by, and his family still didn't know much more than the fact that Jack Farrell was at one time alive in October somewhere in Belgium. If he was in Belgium, how could a boot in Germany possibly be his? Jack Wilson is a numbers guy, a businessman who, for his entire career, centered his decisions on hard facts and figures. But he had this strange feeling that he couldn't ignore.

In the growing anthology of war stories, a handful of similar experiences have been told by otherwise quite rational folk. Pat Scannon, a physician and CEO of a biotech company in California, was wading in waist-deep water one afternoon off the beaches of Koror Island in the Pacific Ocean when suddenly he "felt a chill wash over his body—as if the temperature of the water had plunge to nearly freezing." The sensation began in the lower part of his legs and moved all the way up to his scalp, making him feel as though his hair was standing at attention. The inexplicable experience set Scannon off on a self-funded, multimillion-dollar expedition that resulted in the discovery a B-24 Liberator, a World War II bomber, carrying fourteen U.S. airmen.[8]

On the night of November 4, 1944, Ruth Lynn, mother of two small children, was awakened from her sleep by the sound of someone whistling on her front porch. It sounded very much like her husband who was away at war in Europe. As the story is told in a memoir written by her granddaughter's husband, "She jumped out of bed and hurried to the front door, but there was no one there: the porch was empty, and the road in front of their little house dark and deserted." Until the day she died, Lynn believed that was her husband. Not long after that, she received news that he had been killed in battle.[9]

On that bright spring day in June 2009, Jack Wilson resolved to find out the identity of the owner of the boot that flashed on his computer screen before disappearing. It was the beginning of an obsession that took over every spare moment of his life from then on.

# 2

## They Can't Find Jack

> Still when he had looked back from the gate, he had
> seen his mother kneeling among the potato parings. Her
> brown face, upraised, was stained with tears and her
> spare form was quivering.
>
> —*The Red Badge of Courage*

It was Thanksgiving Day, 1944. The holiday was celebrated a week earlier than usual due to Proclamation 2629 by president Franklin D. Roosevelt, which granted the nation's retailers an extra week of holiday shopping, in part to help offset any lingering economic impact from the Great Depression.

In Arlington, Massachusetts, the weather was a cool forty-two degrees with a trace of rain as the door at 8 Field Road was opened. The two-story white colonial was nestled in the town's Arlington Heights section, a heavily Irish middle-class neighborhood, where families faithfully went to mass on Sunday mornings, people followed the rosary broadcast on the radio every evening at seven, and children attended the local parochial school. Climbing up three concrete steps and entering the Farrell's front door were Katherine Culhane and her daughter Marian.

The Culhanes and the Farrells were close—Katherine Culhane and Elizabeth Farrell were sisters—and they both had sons in the army. James was Katherine's only son and Marian's brother; Jack was

Elizabeth's son. Also at the celebration were Jack Farrell Sr., Jack's dad, and his two sisters, Barbara and Rosemary.

As they embraced at the door, Elizabeth glanced at her sister Katherine. "Heard anything?" she asked softly. "No," Katherine replied with a quick shake of her head. It was not a happy time for the Culhanes. They had recently received a telegram from the War Department reporting James missing in action in Europe. He was twenty-one years old and had been fighting the Germans and Italians in Italy.

At the meal John and Elizabeth tried to sound hopeful. They said that the telegram the Culhanes received would soon be replaced by another, happier one letting them know that James had been found safe. "You know, Katherine," Jack said, "'missing in action' means just that. Missing in action. It doesn't mean killed in action. Just hold tight. I'm sure James is fine. We're winning the war."

"My father was very positive and upbeat at the Thanksgiving dinner," recalls Barbara Farrell, Jack's sister. "He buoyed the spirits of everyone there," pointing out that the Allies had reclaimed France with unexpected ease after a rough beginning in Normandy. The Germans were in full retreat. The war would be over in a few months, he predicted.

The Farrells had reason to be more cheerful that day. They had received a letter less than a month before from their son, Jack Jr.. The letter was short and contained no information about where Jack was, per U.S. Army orders, but it provided enough clues to let the family deduce that he was doing fine somewhere in a village safely in U.S. hands. He was most likely in Belgium.

Thanksgiving dinner that day—roast turkey, mashed potatoes, and gravy—was topped off with pumpkin pie and ice cream. The Culhanes thanked the Farrells for the delicious spread. "I'm glad we came," Katherine said. The two families hugged goodbye, and the Culhanes left as evening set in and more rain clouds blew in from the south. Three weeks later, in mid-December, Elizabeth Farrell heard a knock on her front door at about midday. A Western Union courier stood on the doorstep with a telegram in his hand. Elizabeth's heart began to pound. Upon opening the door, she was given an envelope. She opened it with trembling hands. It was from the War Department in Washington, DC. The telegram was brief:

> The Secretary of War desires me to express his deep regret that your son Sergeant John J. Farrell, Jr., a soldier in the U.S. Army, has been reported missing in action in Europe. If further details or other information are received you will be promptly notified.
>
> George F. Herbert
> The Adjutant General Chief, Casualty Branch,
> Washington D.C.

Elizabeth started to cry as she closed the door behind her. Her throat tightened. Her body felt weak. To keep from falling over she lowered herself to the living room couch. No one was home at the time. Elizabeth's husband and two daughters were at work in Boston. She telephoned each of them at their offices. "They can't find Jack," she said. John, Barbara, and Rosemary rushed home immediately.

Upon arriving home each took turns reading the telegram. Word had spread through the neighborhood as well; an observant neighbor had spotted the Western Union courier and alerted others. Neighbors poured into the house to offer support. It was an indelible moment in Farrell memory, like a photograph. The birch, oak, and maple trees outside had shed their leaves for the winter. The red glow of autumn had passed to make way for the chilly gray hue of winter. Only a few houses in the neighborhood had put up their Christmas lights; most could not muster the cheer. Many of the boys who once played noisily in the street were no longer around. They were all away fighting a war.

Christmas and New Year's came and went quietly. Laughter in the Farrell household had all but disappeared. In the spring the Culhanes received a second telegram: James, who was missing in action, had been found. He was being held as a war prisoner at Stalag 18A Wolfsberg, a German prison camp in Carinthia, Austria, and he would soon be released and returned to Boston. Other than injuries suffered to his chest and leg, he was said to be in good shape. Also that spring a care package arrived at the Farrell's address. It didn't have to be opened; Jack's mom was familiar with its contents. She had sent it in the fall to her son. Now the army was returning it, unopened. It contained rosary beads and woolen socks to help him make it through the winter. A pall descended on the Farrells' home. No one knew whether Jack was alive or dead.

Jack Farrell Sr. was beside himself. He felt an illness coming on. It wasn't like the flu or a cold, but something was not right. A red scaly blotch appeared on his neck. He felt weak and itchy. The stress caused the rash to spread over his entire body. The painful skin condition, diagnosed by doctors as psoriasis and caused by anxiety, remained with him for the rest of his life.

But there was a more urgent task at hand. Putting aside concerns about his health, Jack Sr. immediately began to make inquiries about his son. He telephoned and wrote letters to Washington seeking information about Jack Jr. He couldn't find out anything. He tried asking Elizabeth Farrell's sister, Alice Harrington, to help; she was working in Washington at the time. Perhaps the important people she knew in the nation's capital could get some answers. She too failed.

A year passed. On November 9, 1945, the Farrells received another telegram. This one was more ominous. The message from the adjutant general in Washington said that S/Sgt. Jack Farrell was killed in action. Jack Farrell Sr. who had served in the army in World War I, knew that the term "killed in action" (KIA) was standard military protocol and not always meant to convey actual reality whenever it was preceded by another term—"missing in action" (MIA). When KIA follows MIA by a year and a day, it only means there is an assumption of death without any actual evidence. KIA in these cases could mean any number of possibilities. A soldier had become disoriented, wandered off, and taken in by a protective civilian family; had suffered a nervous breakdown; ran away and lost his bearings; was suffering from amnesia (not an uncommon phenomenon in war); or may have found a new life somewhere in Europe, possibly with someone special, and was quite content to maintain a low profile. He could also be dead.

The Farrells didn't know what to think. Just in case Jack was no longer alive, the Farrells, who were staunch Roman Catholics, decided

Fig. 4. S/Sgt. Jack Farrell. Courtesy of the Farrell/Wilson Family.

to hold a religious service. A week later a requiem mass was held at Saint Agnes Church in Arlington. At the altar stood a group of Jesuit priests from Boston College, where Jack Farrell Jr. had completed his freshman and sophomore years not long before. After the reading of the Gospel, Jack Farrell Jr. was eulogized as a devout Catholic, a loving son and brother, and a young man always seeking to help others.

At the end of the mass, a soldier in crisp khakis slow-marched to the family seated in the front pew and presented an American flag folded in a triangle. He uttered the words: "On behalf of the President of the United States, the United States Army, and a grateful nation, please accept this flag as a symbol of our appreciation for your loved one's honorable and faithful service."

The church was filled with mourners, including members of Jack's family, friends from college, neighborhood friends from childhood, their families, and a few others who knew Jack as an altar boy. Almost everyone who came to mass knew not just Jack's family but Jack himself. After the service, everyone went home, because there was no funeral. There was no one to bury, no casket, and no hearse to follow to the cemetery.

The Farrells, too, went home. Those were awkward moments. They wanted to talk about Jack, but they couldn't speak of him in the past tense. Even though they had just sung his requiem and extolled him in eulogy, they were, in a way, still waiting for him to show up at any moment. Had the service been a goodbye or a prayer for his safe return? Could it have been both? They felt a confusing patchwork of undefined feelings. Should they be sad or hopeful? One emotion was dark and the other light, or at least glimmered with light, like approaching dawn. The Farrells didn't know if Jack was dead or alive.

To Elizabeth and her husband, the days that followed were like the times they waited up at night for their son to return from Boston, where he worked at a bank late into the evening after a full day of classes at Boston College, or when he went out with friends after a college football game. They would stay awake until they heard him bound up the stairs and he came into their bedroom to say goodnight—something he would always do, knowing how his parents worried. They say waiting when you're not quite sure what you're waiting for is a strange thing. It isn't an activity, and it isn't a lack of activity. It isn't doing something, and it isn't doing nothing. Waiting is vigilance mixed with hopefulness and perhaps a bit of anxiety and impatience. But, for the Farrells on the day of Jack Jr.'s ersatz funeral, the waiting was also clouded by a hopelessness that they tried to ward off as one does with negative thoughts.

One day in 1946, nearly a year after the war was over, Jack Farrell Sr. received a call from a military chaplain at Camp Edwards on Cape Cod, Massachusetts. The military base had been converted into a hospital and convalescent facility where many of the returning wounded were treated. Jack and Elizabeth drove down to meet the chaplain, a Roman Catholic priest who said he was well acquainted with their son. Since Jack was so versed in Latin, he had been able to assist the priest at many religious services, which were then celebrated, in the vulgate. The priest, however, said that he didn't know what happened to Jack after he headed to the battlefront. But, he added, there was another soldier at the camp who was in Jack's unit. He might have additional information, if he was well enough to talk.

He was. The soldier told the Farrells that he had fought alongside Jack, and in the haze of battle he thought he saw him at one point near a barn with wounded Americans. He heard the Germans call for the Americans to surrender. They refused, so the Germans destroyed the structure in which they hid, with artillery fire. But the soldier said he didn't know if Jack had escaped or was killed from the blast. The Farrells thanked him and left. On the way home, Elizabeth asked her husband, "Did you believe him?" Jack said, somewhat somberly, "No." As much as the serviceman tried to be helpful, he wasn't that coherent. His memory of events, dates, and places was vague, his account somewhat disjointed. If it wasn't for the war, he would have sounded like any number of homeless people on the street talking to themselves. He may have been shell-shocked or suffering from amnesia; for all the Farrells knew he could have made up the whole story. If only there was a military report to back up his account, the Farrells would have been able to come to some terms with their emotions and move on with their lives.

They Can't Find Jack

Elizabeth and Jack returned to Arlington that day with as many questions about their son's fate as they had when they left. For Jack the toll of not knowing soon took on an ugly appearance. The itch that came on more than a year before had worsened. Over the months it grew redder and spread slowly from his neck to his chest, belly, lower torso, and feet. The doctor diagnosed a severe case of psoriasis. The cause was internal: Jack's own immune system was attacking his entire body. The physician gave him calamine lotion to soothe the itch, but the itch never went away. It was always present, both when he was awake during the day as well as at night, as he tossed and turned. Whenever Jack looked in the mirror, he noticed his wrinkles deepening, as if a dark shadow were cast upon his face. He knew that the disfigurement on his skin was merely an outward manifestation of the pain he suffered inside his soul. The itch would remain with Jack Sr. for the rest of his life.

In 1968—twenty-four years, nine months, and four days after the Western Union messenger appeared at the Farrells' front door—Jack Sr. passed away. The agony of Jack's mom, Elizabeth, was more silent and less visible. She once confided to a family member, "When Jack was reported missing, I lost two people that day—my son and my husband." She died in 1982. Both she and her husband had spent their entire lives trying to find their son. They died not knowing for sure if he was alive or dead.

IN DOROTHY, NEW JERSEY, THE MERLOCKS ALSO STRUG- gled with the frustration of not knowing. The army was of little help. The story of Pvt. Joseph Merlock was very similar to that of S/Sgt. Jack Farrell. Both of them were discovered missing on the morning of November 8, 1944, and none of their cohorts could say with any certainty what had happened to them when questioned later by their superiors. Joseph's parents, Phillip and Amelia, decided on a different tactic to get answers: they sent notices to New Jersey newspapers asking if anyone had seen or knew where their twenty-year-old son was. The handwritten note read:

To the Editor:

I would very much like to contact any serviceman who knew Pvt. Joseph Merlock 42080273 Co A 112 In. 28 Division. He was reported missing in action in Germany as of November 8, 1944. No further information has been available. I do not know the name of even one of the men in his outfit.

Any news at all would be appreciated.

Please contact
Mrs. Amelia Merlock
Box 170
Dorothy, New Jersey

The Merlocks didn't get a single reply, which sent them back to square one. In their minds no response meant that their son could still be alive. They held on to that hope for the remainder of their lives. It wasn't just an idle hope, though; the Merlocks truly believed in the possibility. In dividing up their estate, the family farm, prior to their deaths, they set aside two acres for Joseph, just in case he returned from the war. The property is nestled in a pretty part of southern New Jersey, heavily wooded with black spruce, red oak, and American holly. Millie Messina, a real estate agent for the area, says the two-acre estate is still there for Joseph, if he ever comes back. She has no plans to sell the land. Millie is eighty-four years old and Joseph's niece, raised by Phillip and Amelia for part of her childhood and lived in the same home as Joseph when he was drafted. In Millie's mind her uncle Joseph isn't dead. "I mean, how do I know for certain that he's dead?" she asks. "It may be hard to understand, but I don't." Millie is far from the type that hallucinates—quite the contrary. Even though most people her age have long since retired, she still needs to be constantly on the go. She sells homes and remains active in the civic and political affairs of the area. As a former mayor and deputy mayor of the township of neighboring Weymouth, she is well known around town.[1]

In 2001, long after Joseph's parents had passed, Millie wrote to the army again:

Re: Joseph C. Merlock
Private, U.S. Army 42080273
112th. Infantry Regiment
28th. Infantry Division

To Whom it may concern,

I, Amelia A. Messina, am the niece of the above named individual
who was reported missing in action during World War II.

Private Merlock entered the military service from New Jersey.
Died: November 09, 1945, his name appears on the Tablets of the
Missing at Henri-Chapelle American Cemetery, Henri-Chapelle,
Belgium.

The only other information I have is that he was awarded the
Bronze Star and the Purple Heart.

I would appreciate any other information or records regarding my
Uncle that your office might be able to provide.

Thank You !!

Very truly yours,
Amelia A. Messina.

UNLIKE THE FARRELL, LONCAR, AND WEAVER FAMILIES,
who received no information about their relatives from the army,
the Wilsons of Hampton, Tennessee, did. The news, however, raised
more questions than provided answers.

The wait time with servicemen who are MIA is typically a year.
After the whereabouts of a soldier is unknown for that length of
time, the military declares the person dead, or KIA. The government didn't wait that long for Pvt. Mark P. Wilson. They reported
him dead on May 25, 1945, a few days short of seven months, since
he failed to answer to his unit's roll call on the morning of November 8, 1944. The army didn't have Mark's body as proof of death;
all they had was the word of a fellow soldier who said he saw Mark
get killed. But if someone witnessed his death on the battlefield,
why didn't the army report Mark as a KIA instead of an MIA? Why
did they wait seven months? Were they unsure if the eyewitness's
account was accurate? If so, how did the army then become con-

vinced that Mark was dead? Why didn't they wait until a year had passed before changing his status? And if the eyewitness was so sure of Mark's death, why wasn't there any kind of narrative of how he died? The military's correspondence with the family contained zero details about the circumstances under which Mark's life was taken.

The army did come into possession of a few of Mark's personal belongings, including two copies of the New Testament, a cigarette lighter, a wallet, a pipe, a ring, nine British pence, forty U.S. cents, and a picture of his younger sister, Eve. But, for the Wilsons, that also raised a question: If Mark's body was blown up somehow by a bomb or heavy artillery fire—which could explain why they didn't have a body—why where these items in pretty good shape when they arrived in the mail at the Wilsons' residence in Hampton, Tennessee? Soldiers always carried their belongings with them on the battlefield, since they never knew from day to day where they would spend the night. How did Mark's belongings get separated from him? Why was there was no explanation in the files about how the army came into possession of Mark's things? Did the eyewitness find them on the battlefield? Could that be the reason he thought Mark was dead? When the family asked, army officials just said they didn't know.

The Wilsons were also troubled by another possibility: in addition to post-traumatic stress syndrome (PTSD), which is common among soldiers, some also suffer from amnesia or acute memory loss. The neurological condition can be caused by head injuries, ear-piercing noise, extreme emotional trauma, constant flashing of explosions, sleep deprivation, and other vexations that result from extreme stress of war. Among other things amnesia victims experience disorientation, confusion, and an inability to recognize familiar faces and places. Could Pvt. Wilson have suffered a bad case of amnesia and gone on to start a second life with a new identity?

There was something else in Private Wilson's personnel file that greatly upset Mark's sister Eve, the one whose photo was among his possessions. On November 19, 1951, the U.S. Army sent a set of fingerprints to FBI director J. Edgar Hoover asking that his agency compare them to those they had on file for a Mark P. Wilson of Hampton, Tennessee. "Why would they want to do that?" asks Eve. "Why did they send the fingerprints to the FBI? It sounds like they felt he had abandoned them and slipped away or something. I just thought that was really strange."

Today Eve is eighty-nine years old. Her married name is Cunningham. She is still sharp and fit, walking and doing stretching exercises on a daily basis. She vividly recalls the childhood she spent with her brother, who was eleven years her senior. In Hampton the townsfolk had little choice but to walk the straight and narrow. "Everyone knew every one in Hampton," she says. "If you did something, everyone in town would know." For any type of socialization, Hamptonites had only one place to go, and that was Hampton. The town is tucked away in the recesses of a series of submountain ranges connected on the one side to the Blue Ridge Mountains and the Appalachians on the other. No matter which way you looked, there were mountains. The Wilsons had ten children and lived in a six-bedroom farmhouse with a big backyard where they raised cows and pigs. Their street and address, Route No. 2, no longer exists. Mark had a wonderful disposition. Not once did he get angry with Eve, who would pester him for rides on his back. Despite their age difference, they played basketball, football, badminton, and horseshoes together. Every time Mark said he was going somewhere, Eve would say, "Wait, I'm coming with you."

In high school Mark was voted the friendliest; it says so in his yearbook. After high school he worked a part-time job to pay his college tuition. He had never been arrested or fingerprinted by a law enforcement agency, or by the FBI. To Eve the request for his fingerprints was quite baffling. He was living a typical life of a young adult in a small town where the big jobs were at a company called the North American Plant, the local silk factory. Then, one day when Mark was a sophomore in college, the draft notice arrived in the mail. He had to leave in a hurry, and everyone in the family was upset. "I remember the day he left," Eve recalls. "It was a terrible dark day. My sisters were all standing there. They didn't want to see him go."

Life was never the same after that. Eve thinks of him every day. "I want to know what happened to him," she says. "There's no closure. It's every day, just pondering what could have happened. I'll do anything you tell me to. I want to know, I really want to know what happened to Mark. I'll dig in the dirt if you show me the location."[2]

# 3

## If You Were Young and Strong and Male

As he basked in the smiles of the girls and was patted and
complemented by the old men, he had felt growing within
him the strength to do mighty deeds of arms.

—*The Red Badge of Courage*

America, as it wheezed its way out of the Great Depression
years of the 1930s into the 1940s, exhaled a New Era air of
optimism. The Jeep was the talk of Detroit; its sexy small
hood—relative to a sedan, whose front protruded like the nose of an
aardvark—dazzled the motoring crowds. Surreal toys like the Slinky,
which could miraculously walk downstairs, tickled grownups and
children alike. Velcro, the wonder fastener that made buttoning up
coats and jackets a tedious task, was a new fashion statement. And
Tupperware, a marvel in food preservation because it could "burp"
contaminating air out of containers with the mere press of a thumb,
sent housewives into rapture.

Men wore suits and ties everywhere, even when they reported
to work as masons, plumbers, and housepainters, changing into
dungarees or overalls at the job site. Animal skins and furs, alliga-
tor purses, and crocodile shoes adorned the status-conscious. Envi-
ronmental correctness was not yet a notion. Scarves were called
"mufflers," which women wore on their heads; moviegoers went
to the picture show; and the term "sex symbol" had not yet been
invented—the closest in meaning was a pin-up girl. In music and

dance, swing was in. Hemlines were below the knee, except on the dance floor, where flares could fly, as when you did the Lindy Hop. And any man who could toss his partner up in the air and catch her just before she crashed to the floor, her knees exposed, was a handsome knight of the night. If you were young and strong and male and born any time in the 1910s and 1920s, it was your time to shine. If you were young and strong and male, they were also terrible years in which to be born.

In Needham, Massachusetts, a small town of mostly farmland about ten miles west of Boston, Anthony Grasso was finally going to get to play baseball for his high school varsity team. For years he had existed in the shadows of two older brothers, in the awkward reticence of early adolescence. He was now winding down his junior year, and he knew, with the quiet confidence of an able athlete, that he would make the team as a senior. Spry, sturdily built, and with a full head of dark hair, it was likely that this "guinea," as he was sometimes called (the derogatory name for Italian Americans in those days) would earn some respect and perhaps even admiration from his schoolmates. His senior year was upon him; his moment had come. All he had to do was make sure that he answered the questions on his final exams correctly. He knew he was going to do okay in U.S. history. Mr. Frost, one of his "cool" teachers, taught the class, and Anthony had memorized the preamble to the U.S. Constitution: "We the People of the United States, In Order to form a more perfect Union, establish Justice, insure domestic Tranquility, provide for the common defense, promote the general Welfare, and secure the Blessings of Liberty to ourselves and our Posterity, do ordain and establish this Constitution for the United States of America."[1] He smiled when he saw that it was one of the questions. He aced his other exams as well: English, geography, woodworking, and math. He liked math, which he characterized as "a fun class," because of the low-cut blouses its young instructor wore.

After turning in his math exam, Anthony walked down a gentle slope, satisfied by what he had accomplished. In a town of clapboard homes and ranch houses, Needham High loomed stately behind him on top of a hill, its three-storied, red masonry structure stretching longer than two football fields; bookend balconies extended out on each side, and in the middle, under a weather vane and a shiny dome, six white Greek Ionic columns rose from the ground to seemingly hold the entire edifice together.

The smell of cut grass wafted across the school's wide lawn in an ode to spring. Anthony's thick black hair glistened in the sun. Little did he know that he wouldn't be returning in the fall. Anthony was born on October 13, 1924.

IN MARION COUNTY—A LAND OF PEANUT, HAY, CORN, AND cotton fields tucked away near the Mississippi state line in rural Alabama—Robert Wiginton had a premonition. For over a decade since graduating from high school, Robert, a sixth-generation descendant of Anglo-Saxon immigrants, had diligently worked his way up from a clerk in the local hardware store to a position as a banker in the town of Hamilton. At six foot three he cut a dashing figure. "Robert was very handsome," recalls Bill Fite, himself a Hamilton resident. "I can still see him now as he walked down the street. He carried himself erect like a banker and was always neatly dressed." Bill went on to become a lawyer and, now in his nineties, is still practicing. "It hardly seems as if it was seventy years ago," he says wistfully.

Robert married Norma, a young woman who also worked at the bank. One day in June 1943, Robert purchased a house for them. The next day a long envelope arrived in the mail. It read: "Greeting, Having submitted yourself to a local board composed of your neighbors for the purposes of determining your availability for training and service in the armed forces of the United States, you are hereby notified that you have now been selected for training and service in the Army." Robert Wiginton didn't really like the news. He was recently married. His career in banking was about to take off. He also had a bad feeling. In front of Norma and his parents he tried to look upbeat. But, as he prepared to report for basic training at Fort Wallace in Galveston, Texas, he told his uncle, "I do not think that I will return from this war."[2]

IN NEEDHAM, MASSACHUSETTS, ANTHONY GRASSO RECEIVED a similar envelope in the mail. He was asked to report to Fort Devens in Devens, Massachusetts. Anthony was sad that he wouldn't be able to complete his senior year in high school, that he'd be leaving a younger brother and sister behind and a house that he loved. It sat on top of a hill, and his backyard edged up to a brook and a small bridge, where members of the National Guard took turns standing watch because it emptied into a reservoir from which the surrounding community drew its water. Around dinnertime his mother, who was as Italian as they came, would ask Anthony to take a couple of plates of spaghetti and meatballs down to the guardsmen. Now the task would fall to his brother, Joe, who was two years his junior.

To get to Fort Devens, Anthony had to leave on an early morning train from a station that was smaller than his house. His dad, dressed in a dark suit, drove Anthony to the Needham train station on his way to work as a housepainter. The drop-off was done hastily; the engine of his blue Ford pickup truck was running. "Bye, Dad," Anthony said as he slipped off the passenger seat. His father seemed preoccupied. "Good luck, son," he said, "hope to see you come back," and drove off to pick up his business partner. Some Italian men prefer to hide their emotions, Anthony said to himself as he waited for his train. For a moment he'd thought his dad was going to cry. But he didn't. He just drove off. He didn't even wait to watch his son walk toward the station.

On the chipped cement platform, two other young men took their places that morning alongside Anthony. They acknowledged each other's presence, briefly introduced themselves, and continued in their silent thoughts. One of them said, his voice tinged with pride, that he had recently signed a contract to pitch for the New York Yankees. Neither of his draft mates questioned the veracity of that declaration; they were absorbed in the sobriety of the moment. It's hard sometimes, to leave a life behind. The heat from the morning sun pressed their backs through the fabric of their shirts. In a few hours the mercury would climb to a sizzling ninety-one degrees. The train pulled into the station without a whistle. The men climbed aboard and sat in separate seats.

Young and Strong and Male

IN 1939 THE UNITED STATES HAD THE EIGHTH LARGEST army in the world behind Romania—about 190,000 soldiers. They were armed mostly with guns from World War I. The navy had 60,000 fewer men and the Marines just 19,432. Congress and president Franklin D. Roosevelt agreed that its combined armed forces needed to be much larger. The buildup also had to be quick.

On September 16, 1940, FDR, dressed in a white shirt, black tie, and dark suit with wide lapels cut in the fashion of the day, sat before a microphone and announced in his fusion Yankee (half-American, half British) accent: "Now therefore, I, Frank D. Roosevelt, president of the United States of America, under and by virtue of the authority vested in me, by the aforesaid Selective Training And Service Act of 1940, do proclaim the following: First. The first registration under the Selective Training and Service Act of 1940, shall take place on Wednesday, the 16th day of October 1940, between the hours of 7:00 a.m. and 9:00 p.m."[3]

Thus the United States instituted its first peacetime military draft. On the appointed day, every male between the ages of twenty-one and thirty-six registered himself at his local precinct. On October 29 secretary of war Henry Stimson put on a blindfold, reached into a ten-gallon glass bowl, and pulled out a piece of paper from a plastic capsule. On it was a number. He then passed the paper to President Roosevelt, who announced on national radio in his distinct accent, "The numba is 158." In a matter of seconds, 6,175 men across the country holding that number found out that they had to report for military service. Many more numbers were called later that day, and the in days, weeks, and months to follow.[4]

The theatrics were deliberate, in order to underscore the urgency of the call to arms. The United States was in catch-up mode. Germany boasted an armed forces unit of 22 million; Japan, 2.4 million; and Italy, the third Axis power, 2.6 million. The United States had 320,000 men in the military; its marketing campaign had better be effective. A poster of a goateed man in a stovepipe hat, pointing a finger at the viewer, appeared everywhere. The caption read: "Uncle Sam Wants You." The body language of the man in the James Montgomery Flagg sketch was unmistakable. Uncle Sam looked angry and determined.

The country needed strong young men to rise to the occasion. Still, there appeared to be some reluctance at least on the part of a few. One ploy to get around the draft was to have children. Statistics from the Center for Disease Control and Prevention show that this possibly happened in some circles. The U.S. birth rate in 1937 to 1939, just prior to the war, remained steady at approximately 2.45 million newborns a year. The birth rate following the Selective Training and Service Act of 1940, however, during the draft years, jumped 23.4 percent, to 3.1 million, from 1940 to 1943.[5] Curiously, the number of births increased, even though the number of males in the country dropped dramatically as millions of GIs were shipped off to war. In 1940 the size of the combined armed forces climbed to about 460,000. In 1941 it grew to 1.8 million, and to 3.9 million in 1942.[6]

ON NOVEMBER 2 OF THAT YEAR JACK FARRELL JR. GATHered together a group of his five closest college buddies at Boston College. They decided to cut classes, take the trolley from their campus in Chestnut Hill on the outskirts of Boston to the city's downtown district, and enlist in the U.S. Marine Corps. At the enlistment station, Jack's friends were quickly signed up; men in their prime were prized U.S. Marines material. Jack, on the other hand, wasn't. He was told that, at five foot six, he was an inch too short for the corps. He returned to his home in Arlington that night and said nothing to his family about his day.

He had a plan. Anyone who knew Jack sensed a determination about him. He had green eyes and shortly cropped light red hair that took on a blondish sheen under bright lights or in the sun. His face was angular with a tapering chin and a straight nose. Though small in stature, he possessed the lean build of an athlete. There was a quickness to his movements that served him well on the athletic field. Jack played varsity baseball and basketball and ran track when he was in high school. He also loved tennis.

One thing that was unusual about Jack was his gaze, which was strangely both serious and jocular: two seemingly contradictory qualities that at once reflected an intensity about life and a playfulness bordering on mischief. In his eyes was a "gotcha" kind of glint.

　　　　　　　　　　Young and Strong and Male

It was little surprise that he was elected to the student council in high school and characterized in his yearbook as a "prankster at heart." His friends described him as a "bon vivant." At the same time, Jack was an altar boy and a Boy Scout. The more serious side of Jack was manifested in his dress, which was almost always impeccable: a sports coat, slacks, and shined shoes wherever he went.

Starting in junior high school, Jack developed a passion for languages. He took four years of French and five years of Latin. He read Homer, Cicero, Ovid, and Virgil. He was able to recite all of the liturgical responses of the Roman Catholic Mass in Latin, including the Lord's Prayer, the Apostles' Creed, the Gloria, and the Confiteor Deo. To others in church, the prayers were a litany of mumbo jumbo, but Jack understood every single word as he answered the priest on behalf of the congregation in sync with the Latin that was read from a missal at the altar by the liturgical celebrant. *Pater Noster qui es in coelis, santificetur nomen tuum . . . Gloria in excelsis Deo et in terra.* Jack's love of languages ultimately led him to major in Greek and Latin in college.

Under his neat manner and cheery exterior, however, Jack harbored a secret. He was a diabetic, a condition that required him to keep to a strict diet and abstain from alcohol, sweets, and bread. Many diabetics of the day were put on low-calorie diets. Insulin injections were available, but there was a stigma associated with their use because they had to be extracted from the pancreases of cows and pigs. Diabetes at the time was mistakenly thought to be a terminal illness. It was also one of the medical conditions that could get you an exemption from the draft. But the thought of getting a draft waiver never crossed Jack's mind.

After he was turned down by the Marines, Jack went to see a doctor. He asked the physician if it were possible to stretch his leg muscles so he could gain an inch in height. It could be done, he was assured by the doctor, who put him on a daily regimen of bananas and mile-long runs. Jack did as he was told. One week later he returned to the Marine station to reapply. He stepped up to the height measuring stick. He had failed to gain the required inch.

Jack promptly walked across the street and enlisted with the U.S.

Army. The minimum height requirement there was five feet. When he broke the news later that day that he had joined the army, his parents didn't seem surprised. Jack Farrell Sr. had also served during World War I. His parents said, however, that their preference would have been for him to have joined the U.S. Navy. Aboard a ship, he would be assured of a bed and a hot meal.

On the night of November 28, 1942, Jack received what some members of his family took as a good omen. He and his buddies from Boston College were preparing to attend a victory celebration scheduled at the Cocoanut Grove Club in the city. BC was playing its archrival Holy Cross College in divisional NCAA football. A victory would automatically secure a bid to play in the Sugar Bowl. But Holy Cross trounced BC that afternoon, 55–12, and the Cocoanut Grove Club celebration was canceled. The loss proved to be a blessing in disguise. That night a fire broke out at the restaurant and dance hall, killing 492 people in what remains the deadliest nightclub fire in American history.[7] Had BC won the game, Jack would probably have been trapped at the Cocoanut Grove. A few weeks later on January 8, 1943, Jack Farrell Sr. drove Jack Farrell Jr. to the train at North Station in Boston. Jack Jr. reported for army duty at Fort Devens in central Massachusetts.

In 1943 enlistment in the Armed Forces had climbed to about 9.2 million, but the number was still short of what the War Department thought it needed. So the Selective Service began to dilute its qualifying criteria and cast its recruiting net to a broader demographic. To be admitted into the U.S. Army today, a candidate must be able to perform a minimum of thirty-nine pushups in two minutes; forty-five sit-ups in the same amount of time, and run two miles in under seventeen minutes. The requirements during World War II were much more relaxed. A man had to have at least half his teeth, weigh 105 pounds or more, and be between five and six-and-a-half feet in height. Teeth were important; in case of death, they are one of the main ways the army identifies a soldier, and teeth take hundreds of years to decay. There was one other requirement. It pertained to the morals of an individual, which was judged by the answer to one question on the Selective Service application: Do you like girls? Males who answered "no" were disqualified.

Young and Strong and Male

To expand the size of the selective service pool, the army dropped a previous requirement: the ability to read and write. It also eliminated the requirements for perfect twenty-twenty vision with or without glasses and to have a clean criminal record. Congress also lowered the draft age from twenty-one to eighteen and allowed seventeen-year-olds to enlist, if one parent consented.

BOY RIVER, MINNESOTA, A TOWN OF ABOUT 450 PEOPLE, became embroiled in a battle for the mind of Otto Peterson, or Ott, as some folks called him. He was a wide-eyed seventeen-year-old looking for adventure, and, like many youths his age, Ott felt invincible. On the one side were the adults of Boy River, including his parents, who wanted to temper Otto's adolescent enthusiasm to join the war, and on the other side was a persuasive local army recruiter whose mission was to find all the young blood available for America's war.[8]

While the U.S. Navy and Army Air Corps, the predecessor to today's U.S. Air Force, had more than enough men to fill their available slots, the army had much larger quotas to fill. It aggressively eyed the seventeen-year-olds. They were full of energy, could stay up late, were as strong as many adults, and were malleable. There were an estimated 120,000 of them nationwide. Ott was one of them.

One afternoon Ott came home and told his mother, Margaret, that Fred Anderson, the gentleman who worked in the local grocery store, thought he would make a good soldier. Margaret disagreed and quickly ended the discussion. She had already given one son, Dale, to America; he was in the army stationed in the Pacific. But Fred repeatedly kept whispering in Ott's ear that the army needed more men if there was any chance of winning the war. To Ott those were inspirational words. He begged his mother to sign a slip of paper that would allow him to join. Margaret fought hard to hold on to him. Her boy had quit school following his sophomore year in high school to help with the family finances. He held three jobs, driving a school bus and working as a mechanic and a woodcutter. In the tug of war between mother and the recruiter, the recruiter ultimately won. With much misgiving, Margaret signed the papers, but not before paying Fred a visit at the grocery store, to give him a piece of her mind. Boy River wasn't happy either. Fred had already succeeded in signing up another seventeen-year-old in town.

On February 4, 1944, Otto Peterson travelled two hundred miles to enlist in the U.S. Army at Fort Snelling in Minnesota. Before leaving, Otto built an oak desk as a gift for his mom. In addition to the underaged, the military also began calling up family men—men who were married and married men with children.

IN OCTOBER 1940 THE SPIRIT LAKE BEACON, THE IOWA town's daily newspaper, posted on its front page the draft lottery numbers of males residing in Dickinson County. The numbers had been picked by the War Department in Washington DC, following the enactment of the first peacetime conscription in the nation's history. The names of about 1,000 Dickinson County men appeared on the list. Sydney Elmer Weaver was no. 681.[9] At the time Sydney was twenty-nine, married, and with a seventeen-month-old baby girl named Peggy Jogene Weaver.

Sydney did not want to go to war. He had a wife and a family to take care of. The Weavers hoped that there would be a large enough pool of younger and able single men to placate the pooh-bahs of the war. But hope was dashed to the ground in February 1944 when a long brown envelope was delivered to the Weavers' mailbox. The typewritten yellow notice inside read: "You are hereby directed to appear before the local board for physical examination. Failure to do so is a misdemeanor punishable by not to exceed one year's imprisonment." Watching her mom and dad that day, Peggy felt a chilling fog of emotion swirl into the room. The news, she knew, was not good. She saw the sadness on her parents' faces.

Spirit Lake prepared a farewell to arms for yet another of its sons. The Milford Mail reported on Thursday, February 24, that a dinner party was held in Spirit Lake in honor of Sydney Weaver, who was about to head off to army training camp. In early March Sydney hugged his two daughters, Peggy and eleven-month-old Meg, kissed his wife goodbye, and walked out the front door. The pain of parting with her father branded that moment in time in Peggy's memory forever.

On Saturday, March 4, Sydney boarded a train bound for an unknown destination. The journey took four days, during which time he wrote five letters with a shaky pen, filled with expressions of how he missed his family and how he longed to be home. Each passing day took him farther away from "my darling girls," he lamented in one letter. "How are my girls?" he wrote in another. "Hope you are all fine. Seems like a long time since I've seen you."

From the direction of the train Sydney knew he was headed west. By the third day the train had reached Las Vegas. He noted snow in the distance on the mountaintops, presumably the Sierra bordering California and Nevada. "I would rather be home with you tonight (more) than anything," he wrote.[10] In another letter he indicated that his train had just reached California, where he thought it noteworthy to let his family know that he had just seen his first palm tree. The days were sunny and warm in Southern California, he noted. The comfortable climate prompted another soldier on the train to opine about how wonderful it would be to be stationed in California. Listening to him, Sydney wrote, "Wish I was back in Iowa. . . . I'm getting so I don't miss my girls so much. For a while I couldn't even think about you without almost crying."[11]

On the morning of Wednesday, March 9, the train pulled into Monterey, California. It was only then that Sydney learned where he was going to be spending the next seventeen weeks training to become an infantryman—Camp Roberts. The training camp, sprawled across forty-four thousand acres in Central California, midway between San Francisco and Los Angeles, was at the time one of the largest in the country.

For Molly, the pain of separation was too much to bear. She packed a suitcase and hopped on a train to Nebraska with her two small girls. Apparently the train from Iowa was late arriving in Omaha. There the Weavers found themselves staring at a Union Pacific pulling out of the station. Peggy grabbed her mother's suitcase with two hands as Molly pressed little Meg to her hip with one arm and toted a heavy bag with the other. Mother and daughter gave chase, running on the tracks, shouting in the hope that someone on the train would notice them and get it to stop. But no one did. The locomo-

Fig. 5. Molly and Sydney Weaver in prewar times.
Courtesy of the Weaver/Robinette Family.

tive rolled ahead and sped away. Molly and Peggy spent the night in the station. The next morning they boarded a train to the West Coast. In California they found a place that rented cabins near Sydney's boot camp. The family got together on weekends.

Sydney had a good life in 1944. Together with his dad, he was preparing to launch a new lakeside vacation resort business. He was also basking in the joys of fatherhood, with two young daughters and a loving wife. Word among the recruits at training camp was that fathers would probably not be sent abroad to fight.[12] But in training camp Sydney began to sense a new feeling inside him. The change had started—perhaps subconsciously—when he was alone with his thoughts riding the train in early March from Iowa to training camp in Monterey. It surfaced when he penned a line that seemed out of place at the time. Amid his protestations of love for his family and how he wished he were back with them in Spirit Lake, he wrote, "This life is not good but the war has to be won so it has to be. . . . I don't like it here but I'm not going to try to get out."[13]

The words revealed the beginnings of a transformation in Sydney that would weigh heavily one day in a decision on a battlefield thousands of miles away.

# 4

## Under the Gaze of a Zen Master

To the youth it was an onslaught of redoubtable dragons.
He became like the man who lost his legs at the approach
of the red and green monster. He waited in a sort of a
horrified, listening attitude. He seemed to shut his
eyes and wait to be gobbled.

A man near him who up to this time had been working
feverishly at his rifle suddenly stopped and ran with howls.
A lad whose face had borne an expression of exalted
courage, the majesty of he who dares give his life, was, at
an instant, smitten abject. He blanched like one who has
come to the edge of a cliff at midnight and is suddenly made
aware. There was a revelation. He, too, threw down his
gun and fled. There was no shame in his face.
He ran like a rabbit.

—*The Red Badge of Courage*

On the battlefield in every war there are inevitable moments of truths, such as this classic account from Stephen Crane's *The Red Badge of Courage*, of a panicked retreat by an army in the Civil War after finding itself overwhelmed by the enemy. Infusing infantrymen with a spirit of "exalted courage" during onslaughts of "redoubtable dragons," however, is an undertaking that would require years of tutelage under the gaze of a Zen master. The U.S.

Army during World War II typically had about seventeen weeks to do it. This was called "boot camp."

The task was overwhelming. Between 1940, when the Selective Service Act was passed, and 1944, at the height of the war, the military had to train more than eleven million civilians.[1] To do so, it bought up large tracts of land, ranging between sixteen thousand to more than fifty thousand acres apiece, and built training centers on them in just a few months. Construction costs alone exceeded $10 million per site—$180 million in today's dollars. In addition, the government had to purchase the homes of residents, whom they relocated to suitable housing in nearby towns. Home acquisition and relocation costs pushed the War Department's tab up by hundreds of millions of dollars. The Army operated 119 mobilization-training camps in World War II, 66 of which were built during or just prior to the war. An estimated 48 of them were shut down after the war, as they were no longer needed.[2] Many were located in states like Florida, Texas, Georgia, Arkansas, Louisiana, New Mexico, and California, where land was cheaper and the weather generally warmer.

Thus, almost overnight, the training centers became minicities, each with their own hospitals, dental clinics, movie theaters, post offices, chapels, fire departments, and shopping districts. Which camp you were assigned to often depended on where you lived. To eliminate the temptation to sneak home to the family in moments of homesickness, the army sent recruits to campuses in locations hundreds or thousands of miles away from their hometowns. Men who lived in the north were ordered to facilities in the south; those who lived in the east had to report to bases in the west, and vice versa.

Another factor in determining where you were sent was the way you ended up in the army—namely, did you volunteer or were you drafted? Approximately 6 million volunteered; 11.5 million were drafted.[3] Many from the latter group were assigned to what was known as Infantry Replacement Training Centers. IRTCs, as the name suggests, specialized in training soldiers to replace servicemen who were killed or injured on the frontline—the military equivalent of professional football or basketball players who get traded to a team just before game time and are placed into the starting lineup without a minute of practice. It was not unusual for replacements to be sent to a foxhole in the middle of the night, to fight the enemy at dawn. The only difference between the ballplayer and the replacement was that if the athlete didn't perform well, he'd probably be benched. If the soldier failed on the job, he got killed. IRTC graduates usually became privates, the lowest rank in the military pecking order. They got paid $72 a month, compared to officers who on average received $203 in monthly pay—in today's dollars, the equivalent of $1,063 and $2,998, respectively. In the social fabric of the army, replacements were persona non grata.[4]

Anthony Grasso, after getting his uniform and a haircut at Ft. Devens, about thirty-five miles from his hometown of Needham, Massachusetts, was put on a train and taken to Camp Croft outside of Spartanburg, South Carolina, more than nine hundred miles away. One of the largest IRTCs at the time, Camp Croft was built in a hurry in the winter of 1941, amid bad weather, a lumber shortage, a major flu outbreak, and a truck-driver strike. The army put a construction crew of 12,000 to work, and, within three months, a brand new military base—sprawled across 16,929 acres of what used to be cotton and tobacco farms and home to 263 families—opened its gates to train loads of khaki-clad infantry novices, most of them hailing from New England and Pennsylvania. Brown lettering adorned a plain rectangular wooden sign at the site's entrance:

Camp Croft Military Reservation
Speed Limit Autos 30 mph
Trucks 20 mph
Strictly Enforced

Behind it, a cylindrical checkered water tank towered so high above the tallest trees that it looked as if it touched the clouds. The tank provided all the cooking, showering, and sanitation needs of a population of about twenty thousand trainees, in addition to an auxiliary community of medics, nurses, and German prisoners of war. The training center was comprised of row after row of yellow barracks with brown shingles, two hospitals, a dental clinic, movie theaters, a post office, several chapels, a fire department, a shopping district, a welcoming center, and acres of training and exercise space that included climbing walls, obstacle courses, and rifle ranges. Trainees Henry Kissinger and Zero Mostel were among those who went on to become famous in their own right.[5]

Anthony Grasso didn't like it at Camp Croft. Reveille sounded before daylight, and the lights were turned out at night by eight. In between, cadets spent their time doing jumping jacks, push-ups, and sit-ups; endlessly marching; attending classroom lectures on venereal disease, safe sex, and sanitary bathroom practices; digging foxholes; living outdoors; making their beds; and learning how to crawl on their bellies in the training camp's notoriously soupy red clay. To hammer home the value of self-preservation, field instructors shot real bullets, which whizzed by about a foot and a half above the heads of the crawling cadets. Just raising yourself on your knees could get you killed.

One night, just as the camp was about to call it a day, Anthony's training unit was told to lace up, strap on forty-pound packs, fall in line, and hike fifteen miles to Alabama. Anthony was eighteen years old. With the daytime temperatures hovering near one hundred, broken up by torrential downpours and thunderstorms, his thoughts often floated back to the tree-shaded cool stream that ran along his backyard in Massachusetts, the joviality of his close Italian family, and the varsity high-school baseball he would now never play. Anthony and two other buddies from camp once walked into town on a weekend pass and struck up a conversation with a young woman, who invited the three of them to her home. Anthony was taken aback when he saw the rural austerity in which she lived and appreciated the big-city amenities he had come to take for granted back home. The men had to use an outhouse that evening. For water they had to pull a bucket out of a well.

To Anthony, Camp Croft was seventeen weeks of purgatory for sins that were not his.[6] The men with the flat-brimmed hats barking out not-so-nice things about you in drill-sergeant-speak tried their best to push their trainees to the edges of their cliffs, to use Stephen Crane's metaphor. On paper, the concept makes sense: by simulating the extremely stressful situations of war, the bosses of boot camp were, theoretically, programming the brains of the recruits to say "been there done that" and not throw down their guns and flee under the duress of a real battle. The verbal abuse was to toughen the mind, and the interminable marching, jogging, and hiking to strengthen the body. Add to that some knowledge of how to read a map, use a compass, recognize enemy aircraft, fire a weapon, and keep it clean at all times for optimal efficiency, and a soldier should be good to go. That was the basic idea of basic training.

The drillmasters, however, weren't always successful. The evidence of failure was copious, marked in the annals of history—in battle-field reports, morning-after analyses, and comprehensive recounting of events by military historians. This is the dark and seamy under-belly of combat, not always discussed openly but preserved none-theless in the records, which show that, during the war, hundreds of thousands of soldiers "blanched," to quote Crane. They inflicted wounds on their legs, feet, or arms; they feigned insanity, babbling like madmen; they openly defied the orders of officers, with the aim of being trucked away for some sort of disciplinary action—all of this in veiled and not-so-veiled efforts to be removed from the frontline.

The daring of soldiers, including the resolve to fight to the death, is a perennial subject of discussion in military circles. "We talk about it all the time in the Army," says Lt. Col. Thomas G. Bradbeer, who comes from a military family that proudly traces its bloodline back to the time of William the Conqueror in the tenth century, when a Bradbeer forebear served as a knight in King William's army. Brad-beer is also the leadership studies chair at the U.S. Army Command and General Staff College in Fort Leavenworth, Kansas, an elite train-ing center for military officers from around the globe. He maintains that naturally born brave people are rare, if any exist at all. "Every-body's scared, everybody's afraid," he says. Humans are genetically wired to flee in the face of danger. A soldier, however, can be trained to choose the former when presented with a fight-or-flight moment; bravery, in other words, is something that can be taught. Such a war-rior is capable of carrying out unbelievable acts of courage on the battlefield almost instinctively, and the driving force behind them is the band of brotherhood. "I think when it comes down to bravery," says Bradbeer, "they're fighting for one another. And if they understand the mission, they realize, 'I cannot let my buddies down. It has to do with pride and esprit de corps. I cannot embarrass my unit.'"[7]

Ironically, therein lay a weakness in the U.S. military system during World War II. The mistaken notion was that a soldier could be trained as a replacement to jump into a spot on the frontline vacated by a comrade who had just been knocked out by the enemy. The U.S. Army viewed itself as a war machine and GIs as replacement parts. The replacement thus sometimes found himself fighting on a front where no one even knew his name. The British system, on the other hand, was markedly different: it trained soldiers to fight as cohesive groups, and when military units on the frontline were weakened by injury or death, the entire band of brothers would be replaced by a new band of brothers.[8]

For his basic training, Pvt. Eddie Slovik was sent from his hometown of Detroit, Michigan, to an Infantry Replacement Training Center: Camp Wolters, about 80 miles west of Dallas, Texas, and 1,200 miles away from home. While he was there, Pvt. Slovik was inconsolably homesick; he deliberately underperformed at various tasks, hoping to be discharged and sent home. In one letter to his wife he wrote: "I'm going on the rifle range Sat. and I am going to foul up. I'll try to have a poor score so they won't send me overseas. If I am dum on everything they might send me home cause I won't be able to fight." The plan failed. Slovik didn't get his discharge papers.[9]

Unbeknownst to many, trainees were constantly under a sea of watchful eyes. From time to time, cadets were pulled aside by the staff for private conversations, many of them reprimands for failing at one thing or another. But some were soldiers like Julian Farrior. He was special, loved at boot camp by his superiors. That, in a strange way, became a problem for Julian's family, particularly for his older brother Edward.

Edward and Julian grew up together in the wide-open flats of southeastern North Carolina. The summer rains would roar down on to the chafed earth as if a celestial floodgate had been jarred open by a heavenly prankster. Then the downpour would abruptly trickle to an end, and life would return to normal—katydids, grasshoppers, and crickets chirping and the two brothers pedaling their bikes off in the shimmering heat to Burgaw Creek or the nearby Northeast Cape Fear River to cool off. Those were idyllic days for Ed and Julian, their lives filled with Huckleberry Finn moments. They were only two years apart. Julian admired Ed for his no-nonsense wisdom, and Ed always looked out for his little brother. In almost every aspect of life, Julian would seek his advice and pay close heed to his words. The siblings often thought alike, except for the one rare occasion in the winter of 1942.

Edward was twenty-eight years old and operating a retail clothing business that he owned with his dad. Julian was twenty-six and working at Fort Bragg. They had a disagreement that made Ed mad. Julian was quite a physical specimen: fit, muscular, and six feet tall, he had little trouble drawing the attention of his army commanders at basic training. The top brass at Fort Bragg in North Carolina also liked something else about Julian. For a number of reasons, including the hard days of the Great Depression, men who trained at the army base didn't have the luxury of a solid education; many lacked a high school diploma. Julian, on the other hand, held a master's degree in forestry science with a specialty in genetics from North Carolina State. In matters of the mind, he was head and shoulders above his peers.

After Julian finished his seventeen weeks of boot camp, his superiors asked him to be part of the cadre at Fort Bragg. It was a prestigious assignment that made him part of an select team charged with the training of some of the top military units for overseas combat at the sprawling 250-square-mile military base. You had to be smart, strong, and a heck of a soldier to be asked to join. Julian did it for a few months and liked it a lot. Then, one day, he sought his older brother's advice, asking if it would be a good idea to apply to the army's Infantry Officer Candidate School. Ed's answer was quick. No, he said. During a war, infantry officers are sent to the frontline. It was a bad idea, especially given the highly coveted position to which he had recently been appointed. In Ed's thinking, by remaining at the cadre Julian would be magnificently serving his country during a world war. But, more to the point, the task of preparing a group of soldiers in the skills of warfare on U.S. soil was a much safer job than commanding a group of soldiers with the enemy shooting at you from all directions on the battlefield.

Julian listened to his brother but respectfully disagreed. He applied, and, to no one's surprise, was accepted. On New Year's Day, 1943, Julian reported for training at Fort Benning's Infantry Officer Candidate School in Georgia. Unlike boot camp, where almost everyone passes—partly reflecting the extreme demand for bodies during World War II—officer school at Fort Benning was quite selective. In a letter to his mom and dad, Julian described the rigor of training, expressed amazement at the capability of the then-state-of-the-art weaponry, mentioned his fiancé and a probable wedding, and revealed a little-known practice of the military that has since been deemed illegal.

Dear Mamma and Daddy

Another week is passed and I'm still in school. There'll be a mass exodus of students Tuesday of next week—about 25% of our class will be kicked out for first one thing and then another. Any slight delinquency and you are out. Some classes flunk out 50% of their men during the thirteen weeks.

I have a 90 average on all of my exams thus far. The requirements have been raised academically, so now anything below 85 will flunk an O.C. (Officer Candidate) out. My command on the field has been average and my IQ grades were the highest out of 200 fellows in my class. [10] My speed on the obstacle course for the exam' grade was 10 seconds faster than that allowed, so my physical training grade will be alright.

I have qualified with all weapons thus far, M-1 rifle, Browning Automatic Rifle, Light machine gun, and Heavy machine gun. I qualified as 1st class gunner on the Heavy machine gun and expert or the Light machine gun. I can really shoot those machine guns— the heavy one is capable of delivering 525 bullets to a target in one minute and its accurate range is 2000 yards. We have what we call direct and indirect laying. In direct laying you can see the target and can sight on it. In indirect laying the gunner gets information as to direction and elevation to target from an observer at an observation post, and with this information he can lay on the target in just a few seconds without ever having seen the target. I can completely set up an MG and be in position to fire in ten seconds after the command is given "enemy to your front."

All the week we have been taking up bayonet training and I mean this is stiff training. The first thing that the instructor does on the bayonet field is divide the class in two parts, then every fellow has to grab the one next to him and throw him on the ground. This goes on for fifteen minutes until everyone is warmed up then we fix bayonets on the guns, covered with scabbard.

We are taught the thrusts, that is actually sticking the opponent. The coach places a dummy in different positions and you have to cut his throat. We are taught butt strikes, which are designed to crush your opponent's skull. Those strokes are used when you clash and both your opponent and your gun goes straight up in the air. When this happens, the one who comes around with a butt stroke first is the one who lives. Once you knock your opponent off his feet you are supposed to slice him in two with a slash of the bayonet, and then finish him off with a butt stroke.

We also took up hand grenades, when to use them, and how to use them. It is a very dangerous but effective weapon. . . .

Grace will probably come down to see me in March. She'll be busy all next month getting her sister, Helen, married. . . . If I'm successful down here, Grace and I will be married in April. . . . Write whenever you can.

Love
Julian.[11]

Julian survived officer school and was made First Lieutenant. He never explained why he went against his brother's advice. Family members thought it unusual and certainly out of character. Was it the pay raise, the career advancement, or a desire to impress his family and girlfriend that led him to apply? Or was he sensing within him the flames of patriotism that lashed in the soul of Henry Fleming, the hero of *The Red Badge of Courage*?

Under the Gaze of a Zen Master

One night, as he lay in bed, the winds had carried to him the clanging of the church bell as some enthusiast jerked the rope to tell the news of a great battle. This voice of the people rejoicing in the night had made him—and bravehearts like Julian—shiver in ecstasy. Later, he had gone to his mother's room and said, "Ma, I'm going to enlist."

"Henry, don't you be a fool," his mother had replied. She then covered her face with the quilt. That was the end to the matter for that night.

Nevertheless, the next morning he went to a town near his mother's farm and enlisted in a company that was forming there. And so it was that

Julian Farrior of Burgaw, North Carolina;

Anthony Grasso of Needham, Massachusetts; and

Eddie Slovik of Detroit, Michigan

would soon board ships along the Eastern Seaboard headed to Europe. Also boarding ships were

Jack Farrell Jr. of Arlington, Massachusetts;

Edward Jones III of West Pawlett, Vermont;

Michael Loncar of Weirton, West Virginia;

Robert Wiginton of Hamilton, Alabama;

Otto Peterson of Boy River, Minnesota;

Gerald Wipfli of Nekoosa, Wisconsin;

Joseph Merlock of Dorothy, New Jersey;

Mark Wilson of Hampton, Tennessee;

Ernest Temper of Toledo, Ohio;

Sydney Weaver of Spirit Lake, Iowa;

Leonard Greenway of Philadelphia, Pennsylvania;

Carl Harbison of Xenia, Ohio;

Edward Jones of Pawlet, Vermont; and

Waverly Lane of Virginia Beach, Virginia.

Upon completion of their respective Army training, these men had one thing in common: they were destined to join the Twenty-Eighth Infantry Division of the U.S. First Army. In World War II the United States fielded 20 armored divisions, 2 cavalry divisions, and 106 infantry divisions. Not many of these units would get tagged with a nickname by the Germans. The Twenty-Eighth, however, did. It was called *Der Blutiger Eimer*—or "The Bloody Bucket" in German.

The moniker wasn't exactly a compliment. To the Germans it was actually kind of a joke. Members of the Twenty-Eighth wore an emblem of a keystone on the sleeves of their uniform that looked like a bucket and was the color of blood.[12] Neither the Germans nor the Americans knew it at the time, but in a couple of months the significance of the name would become apparent to both sides, and the emblem would become, symbolically and literally, a red badge of courage for the Twenty-Eighth Infantry Division.

# 5

## In the Stillness of a Predawn Hour

> "We're going't movie t'morrah—sure," he said pompously
> to a group in the company street. "We're going way up the
> river, cut across, an 'come around in behint 'em."
>
> —*The Red Badge of Courage*

Like a grizzled warrior, the Twenty-Eighth Infantry Division has a storied past that hearkens back more than 250 years, to the days when soldiers wore tricornered hats, had to keep their gunpower dry in small pouches, and the United States of America was not yet the United States of America. Its beginnings are traced to a conundrum faced by Benjamin Franklin. Back in those days, America was up for grabs; the French, the Indians, and the early settlers were all claiming tracts of land as their own. Courts, of course, are useless in such disputes. What helped win territorial disputes instead was a mighty militia. Herein lay Franklin's dilemma: as a leader of a group of colonists living in the Commonwealth of Pennsylvania, he had to create an army capable of defending the commonwealth against its assailants. But Pennsylvania was the home of Quakers, the Amish, and other pacifist groups who eschewed the concept of war. How could he persuade some of the able-bodied men in those groups to take up arms? Astutely, Franklin named his army the Pennsylvanian Associators, which made it sound more like a civic association than a group of warriors.

Over time, as Pennsylvania grew in size, the army's name was changed to the Pennsylvania National Guard. As an insignia to be emblazoned on its uniforms, the militia picked the keystone: a wedge-like piece of material used by masons to hold together structures such as doorway arches. To ordinary folks who aren't masons, a keystone looks like a fancy bucket. The original thirteen colonies spanned from New Hampshire to South Carolina, and Pennsylvania, nestled at the center, became known as the keystone state, because of its central location and people like Franklin, who were linchpins in the founding of the nation.

Despite its Quaker lineage, the Pennsylvania National Guard has played a major role in the defense of the United States through a long succession of wars. It provided three companies of bodyguards to protect George Washington in the War of Independence, and it bravely participated in the War of 1812, when the United States was once again on the opposite side of British guns in a battle to maintain commercial trade with France. Some thirty years later, the Pennsylvanians answered the nation's call to arms when U.S. president James Polk declared America's "manifest destiny" to lay claim to the West. As a result Mexico surrendered thousands of miles of land that subsequently became the five U.S. states of New Mexico, Arizona, Nevada, Utah, and California. Fifteen years later, in 1863, the men of the Philadelphia Brigade took up a position high on a hill called Missionary Ridge at Gettysburg to thwart a desperate charge by the Confederate Army. In retrospect their valiant stand proved pivotal to victory in that historic battle.

At the turn of the twentieth century, when the United States went after the Philippines, the Pennsylvanians were once again an armed presence to help subdue the islands' ruling Spaniards. A half century later, the Keystone troops, now also called the Twenty-Eighth Infantry Division, were strategically dug in at the Marne River, sixty miles east of Paris, to hold off a fierce onslaught by the German Army. Its feisty defense came at a critical point in World War I. It paid a price, however: in a little over four and a half months, the division incurred casualties of more than fourteen thousand—approximately eleven thousand wounded, and three thousand dead. The unit's stand was so impressive that U.S. Army General John J. Pershing was prompted to dub it the "Iron Division."

The National Guard technically answers to a state's governor, who is its appointed commander in chief. But the U.S. government is also authorized to federalize it for active service, in times of national emergency. That's exactly what happened in early 1941, amid rising fears that the United States would soon be drawn into the then-raging global struggle that was World War II. And indeed it was, following the attack on Pearl Harbor on December 7, 1941.

Dutifully answering the call to prepare for war, the Twenty-Eighth Infantry Division—which is headquartered in Harrisburg, Pennsylvania—spent the next two and a half years training in five states. It moved to Louisiana to practice fighting in swampland; to the beaches of Florida to learn amphibious warfare; to Texas to get accustomed to the hot desert; to West Virginia for mountain maneuvers—rappelling down cliffs, climbing rugged trails with heavy packs, and driving various vehicles on winding roads in black-out conditions. In Virginia it joined the U.S. Navy in the Chesapeake Bay for assault landing drills. Over the course of two and a half years, the Twenty-Eighth Infantry Division lost sixteen men to drowning: fourteen at sea during a storm that struck in the middle of the night, and two more in the sticky swamps of Louisiana. In the fall of 1943, as the foliage began to change color, the division's stateside training finally wound down. The soldiers boarded a train to the frontier climes of New England and disembarked at Camp Myles Standish in Taunton, Massachusetts. It was a final checkpoint in preparation for an Atlantic crossing.

On a chilly October morning in the stillness of a predawn hour, a band assembled by the train station in Taunton and played George M. Cohan's the "Yanks are coming" fight song "Over There." Approximately 12,500 men of the Twenty-Eighth Infantry Division stepped on to a long locomotive and headed north to a seaport in Boston. At the Boston Harbor, the Red Cross handed out coffee and doughnuts as the men walked the gangplank onto the ship. As the USS *Santa Paula*, a Caribbean cruise liner converted into a naval transport, pulled away, some of the soldiers were teary-eyed, watching as the Massachusetts shoreline slowly faded out of sight. Marion Bedford Davis, a physician soldier who sailed that day with the division, noted that the departure was nothing like in the movies. "There were no wives or sweethearts bidding us farewell," he wrote.[1] Also on board was 1st Lt. Julian Farrior. He thought about his family in North Carolina, his new bride, Grace, and how fortunate he was to have spent the past few months with her in Florida. Farrior was assigned to the division as a last-minute addition shortly before it traveled to Massachusetts.[2] No one knew in advance, not even the soldiers themselves, what the division would be doing next, except the top tier of higher-ups. With German U-boats lurking in the dark waters off the Eastern Seaboard, secrecy was of paramount importance to any mass movement of troops. About a week later the USS *Santa Paula* dropped anchor three thousand miles away in a harbor at Cardiff, Wales.

Compared to the marathon training the Twenty-Eighth had been put through on U.S. soil, England was a Sunday stroll. The training camp was a mere mile and a half from the bustling town of Carmarthen. 1st Lt. Robert C. Nelsen, a historian with the division, filed this report to headquarters: "Many of the men have found homes for themselves. The men are always talking about the women and how sociable they are. There are three or four dances in town every week and shows every night except Sunday."[3] London was a four-hour train ride away, and, in the interest of keeping morale high, the army issued forty-eight-hour passes on a regular basis. But socializing came with a small problem. Britain at the time was in the middle of a draught; the King of England was on record as taking a bath just once a week. Hotels insisted their guests fill their bathtubs to no more than three inches high.[4] At the base the servicemen were limited to one shower every five days.

Thanksgiving and Christmas passed pleasantly. A Santa Claus party was thrown for the children of Carmarthen. Nearly a thousand kids showed up for cookies and candy. For the next few months the division trained by day and relaxed by night.[5] One of the more difficult chores of training was sitting through French and German classes.

D-DAY, JUNE 6, 1944—A FATED DAY FOR MANY—WAS JUST another day at the office for the Twenty-Eighth Division. Some of the more observant in the unit did comment about how there was more than normal activity at a nearby airport and in the English Channel.

"Many persons at breakfast time remarked at the size of the 'maneuver' that must be going on," wrote Capt. Richard Dana, another division historian. It wasn't until later in the day that the servicemen learned that the hustle they'd noticed wasn't really another military drill but a real invasion of France by the combined Allied Forces.[6] The news broke in a radio broadcast quoting reports coming out of Germany that the Allies had launched an attack on Hitler's defenses. The announcer said solemnly: "It is now official. We know that the long delay, the anxious days and weeks through which we have all past are over. The great adventure has begun. The final chapter in the history of the Second World War is being written." The news was received by the men with "mixed feelings of relief in that the job had finally begun, and regret of not being able to participate in the great event," Captain Dana reported.[7]

That day the division held a dress parade, marching in their handsome uniforms for a good part of the afternoon, while the band played on. The parade was unscheduled and came as a surprise to many. The marchers didn't know whether they were celebrating a major invasion or if the fanfare was just a gimmick to divert their attention from the wounded and the dead being brought back in ships from Normandy.[8]

For the Twenty-Eighth Infantry Division, its time came six weeks and four days later. On July 22, after receiving a payment of two hundred French francs each (the equivalent of about seven dollars in U.S. currency today), the men set sail across the English Channel for Omaha Beach. They left behind memories of British hospitality, a good many broken hearts, and promises to girlfriends, in at least a few cases, that they would come back to marry them.

War is not a good time to fall in love. Pvt. Michael Loncar knew that in his heart, as did his mom, dad, and older sister, Mildred, back in Weirton, West Virginia. Nonetheless, there's no avoiding Cupid's arrow, and fate has a way of overruling reason. When Michael saw a young British woman that his family came to know as Joan, he was smitten. In his letters home, he mentioned her with much affection and hinted at a future for the two of them. To his family, Private Loncar wrote, "By the way I've been an acting sergeant and so if you see Joan referring to me as sergeant you'll know why."[9]

Three things can happen when love and war get intertwined, and two of them are usually bad. A soldier can go off to war and never come back. A second scenario—also bad—is not going to war and staying behind with your sweetheart. The latter usually results in a court-martial on absent without leave (AWOL) charges. There were quite a few of those. Investigators with the U.S. Army Criminal Investigation Division, or CIDs, prowled the streets and hung out in bars, hotel lobbies, and nightclubs looking for deserters. The CIDs even continued their vigilance long after the war ended.

On the evening of December 15, 1945, thirty jeeps encircled a block in a downtown district in London, and a bevy of law enforcement officials squeezed through the front door of one of the city's largest dance halls. The music stopped, and its some two thousand patrons turned their gazes to the entrance of the establishment. A posse of British and U.S. police officers, clutching nightsticks, streamed through the door. They slowly walked among the merry-making crowd, paying special attention to the faces of the males in the room. Some were asked to produce identification cards. The ones who didn't have any were driven to the police station for questioning.[10] The CIDs were also dispatched to Paris. By the government's estimate there were forty to fifty thousand GI deserters.[11]

It really wasn't all that difficult to desert. For Pvt. Wayne E. Powers of Chillicothe, Missouri, it was actually a cakewalk. One day a few months after the Americans had landed in France, Private Powers struck up a conversation with a young French woman in a bar in Mont-d'Origny, a village near the French Belgian border. The girl's name was Yvette Beleuse. "Parlez-vous Français?" she asked. He shook his head. "Parlez-vous Anglais?" he asked. She shook her head. Then Yvette gave Wayne "a woman's smile."[12] That's all it took. Without words he and she knew that amid the carnage that surrounded them they had sensed in each other's presence a separate peace, away from the madness that the war had wrought.

Private Powers drove a truck for the U.S. Army's quartermas-

The Stillness of a Predawn Hour

ter unit, hauling clothing, food, whiskey, and cigarettes to other units at the battlefront. A month later, while making a delivery, his truck was hijacked by a hitchhiker he had picked up. As the story goes, the hitchhiker drove off, leaving Private Powers on the side of the road. Having no transportation, the U.S. serviceman walked to Mont-d'Origny and rang the doorbell of the house where Yvette lived. She let him in, and he stayed for the duration of the war. Fearing he would be court-martialed if he returned to the United States, Powers remained in Mont d'Origny. Three years after the war ended, an American wife he had left behind in Missouri divorced him.

In France, Powers avoided detection by never showing his face in daylight. He stayed at home and tended to housekeeping chores while Yvette worked in a local factory. The couple, meanwhile, had five children. When the family needed to visit Yvette's relatives in Paris, or go for an outing somewhere private, they left before dawn and returned after dark. When visitors came to the home, the American would hole up in a hiding place underneath the stairs. A few neighbors and fellow factory workers did wonder how Yvette managed to have five children without signs of a man in her life, but for the most part they minded their own business.

During all that time, the army hadn't a clue where Private Powers was. One day an observant gendarme investigating an automobile accident in Mont-d'Origny noticed a man looking out a window. He appeared nervous, so the policeman decided to investigate and found the secret space where Powers was hiding. The French police called the U.S. Army. Shortly thereafter Private Powers was taken into U.S. custody and court-martialed for desertion in a U.S. court in Verdun, France. In August 1958 a jury sentenced him to ten years in prison. But, because the trial triggered an international outcry, Powers was released in October of that year. Media in the United States, France, and Germany had covered the trial, and the U.S. embassy in France received sixty thousand letters from sympathizers pleading that Powers be allowed to return to his family.[13]

The thought of desertion never crossed Pvt. Michael Loncar's mind. He was intent on completing the mission for which he had crossed the ocean. In one letter home he wrote:

Dear Sis,

I received the first package that you sent a long while ago and another. There isn't much I need. I still have a lot of that gum you sent me. And some of the candy. But I'd like some hard candy, especially peanut brittle. Don't worry about me.

As for getting married that will be a long time yet. It takes at least three months for a G.I. to get married here. There's a lot of paperwork ala Washington style. We don't know whether we want to wait until after the war to get married. At that rate we may never get married. But that's the Army for you.

Your brother Mike.[14]

In addition to Private Loncar, Pvt. Anthony Grasso had also been assigned to the Twenty-Eighth Division. He had been with the division since Christmas, his first away from home. For Grasso, England was less about love and more about war. The nightlife and weekend passes were fine, but life in the moment was fleeting. It was life in the future—the future just up the road—where, for Anthony, the real living lay. The regular bombing raids by the Germans over the isle at night would remind Grasso why he was there and not back with his classmates at Needham High School in Massachusetts. Getting drafted into the army during World War II was a fast train out of childhood. "But, hey, but such is life," he thought. Sometimes it made him sad. After waiting most of his adolescence for his time to shine in high school, he would never get those lost days back again.

After setting sail from Wales, the Twenty-Eighth Infantry Division was on the water for two days before landing on Omaha Beach. Normandy quickly turned into a crucible for them. Britain may have suffered from a drought, but in France it rained for three days in a row. The foxholes where the men took shelter filled up with water as if they were plugged bathtubs. Helmets were given another use: as buckets for bailing water. The men also learned a trick of the Luftwaffe, the German Air Force, of setting off flares in the night and taking aerial pictures of Allied positions, returning to bomb them shortly thereafter. One night Pvt. Anthony Grasso didn't have a foxhole to hide in. In the panic of the moment, he dove under a truck and remained there for the entire night. The next morning he was informed by a fellow GI that the truck he was under was a munitions wagon full of TNT. This was his first experience of war. All he could do was thank his lucky stars for being alive for yet another day. It was to be a mantra that he adopted as his unit fought its way further into France.

In Normandy the Twenty-Eighth was introduced to a new type of warfare: fighting in the bocage. *Bocage* is French for the unique terrain that from an airplane looked like a checkerboard: acres of farmland marked off by hedgerows that are tall mounds of dirt covered by decades-long growth of shrubbery. Hedgerows made for excellent hiding places. You couldn't tell whether a German or an American was waiting on the other side with a machine gun. Grasso and some of the men he was with developed a secret code. Using the metal noisemakers that came inside the Cracker Jack boxes the army served up as snacks, Grasso and his buddies decided that they would identify themselves by clicking their noisemakers. If they didn't hear the other side clicking back, they would shoot through the shrubbery.[15] For many, walking through the hedgerows was an unnerving experience. 1st Lt. Julian Farrior wrote in a report, "We came so close to the enemy that hand grenades were tossed back and forth across the hedgerows and we opened fire at point blank range."[16]

One of the first major engagements for the Twenty-Eighth came about forty miles inland, near Saint-Sever-Calvados. It suffered more than 700 casualties in a firefight with German tanks and machine gun nests. The Americans also discovered that the countryside was flecked with snipers hidden in trees, hillocks, and the tops of bombed-out buildings and barns. In one corner of the battlefield the unit's crew of medics found themselves tending to 150 wounded Americans lying side by side in a field.[17]

A big problem the Americans faced was the impenetrable steel with which the German tanks were built. The Americans blasted .47 mm anti-tank cannons at line after line of attacking Tigers and Panzers, but the explosives merely splattered or bounced off their hard shells of steel, like ping-pong balls. In its arsenal the Americans also had .105 mm howitzers. One blast, unfortunately, landed on members of the Twenty-Eighth instead of the enemy, killing eighteen Americans.[18]

The month of August was not good for the Twenty-Eighth. The division lost 2,630 soldiers, including 404 deaths; the rest were wounded and had to be taken from the frontline. The division performed so badly that it was put through a revolving door of three commanding generals in less than forty-eight hours. Its first commander, Maj. Gen. Lloyd D. Brown, who had shepherded the unit's training for a year and a half, was relieved of his post by his boss, Gen. Omar N. Bradley, because of the high casualty numbers in his division under his command.[19] His replacement, Maj. Gen. James E. Wharton, was killed by a sniper just hours after taking over, as he visited his frontline units to introduce himself to the troops and assess their preparedness. German sharpshooters were constantly watching from concealed positions, their rifles fitted with Carl Zeiss telescopic lenses capable of picking out the smoke from the cigarette in a GI's mouth hundreds of yards away. Major Wharton was shot in the head. He was fifty-nine years old.[20] He was replaced by a third leader, Maj. Gen. Norman D. Cota, who was still recovering from injuries suffered during the invasion of Normandy. August marked the unit's first stream of replacements—new recruits finishing boot camp back in the U.S. boarding ships headed for Europe to fill posts vacated by the wounded and the dead.

Among the August replacements was a recruit from Detroit, Michigan: Pvt. Eddie Slovik. That year, after completing his training at Camp Wolters in Texas, Private Slovik was shipped overseas via England to the beaches of Normandy. From there he was transported by truck to join the Twenty-Eighth Infantry Division at Elbeuf, a town about seventy-five miles miles outside of Paris. At around dusk on August 25, just as a group of twelve replacements for the Twenty-Eighth reached the outskirts of the town, the division came under heavy shelling by the Germans. Everyone got out of the truck and scrambled for cover. Eddie dug himself a foxhole and remained there for the entire night.

In a handwritten confession that included misspellings and grammatical errors, Slovik later explained what happened: "At the time of my Desertion we were in Albuff in France. I come to Albuff as a Replacement. They were shelling the town and we were told to

The Stillness of a Predawn Hour

dig in for the night. The following morning they were shelling us again. I was so scared nerves and trembling that at the time the other Replacements moved out I couldn't move. I stayed their in my fox-hole till it was quiet and I was able to move. I then walked in town."[21] It was that easy for a soldier to slip away from his unit. Roll call is taken typically every morning, but if you're not present, the head-counters assume that you were injured or killed. Instead of report-ing to the Twenty-Eighth, Slovik found a group of Canadian Army men—the Thirteenth Provost Corps—who didn't seem to mind his fear of combat. Slovik spent the next two months with the mil-itary police unit in noncombat roles, which included meal prepara-tion for the Thirteenth Corps.

Unbeknownst to Private Slovik, the next few days were quite peaceful for the Twenty-Eighth. The division attended church ser-vices that Sunday, August 27, and motored to Versailles, the sprawl-ing estate of a number of French kings that featured a 2,300-room palace surrounded by gardens and an even more expansive pastoral compound. After bivouacking there for the night, the Twenty-Eighth Division moved to a park in Paris in preparation for the parade of the century down the City of Light's widest boulevard, the Champs-Elysees, with all of Paris welcoming their liberators. 1st Lt. Julian Far-rior, who kept an army journal for his battalion, wrote this of that resplendent hour in the war:

> Our division was given the honor of being the first Americans to
> parade in Paris for which we were very proud. The crowds went wild
> with joy, some crying, some singing, and others shouting at the top
> of their voices, Vive-Le-Americain or merci! Every time the column
> halted, hundreds of bottles of wine and cognac were passed out, and
> many beautiful girls came out with one objective in mind to kiss as
> many Americains as possible. Our effort to beat them off failed and
> the column was completely overrun.

Not every soldier felt as chaste. Pvt. Anthony Grasso was eigh-teen at the time, single, and had never been kissed. "Over here, over here," he said to the madames and mademoiselles delivering kisses. Unfortunately for Private Grasso, he was riding on an artillery wagon;

Fig. 6. The Twenty-Eighth Infantry Division of the U.S. Army at the Liberation of Paris. National Archives and Records Administration/U.S. Army.

it would have taken a high-jumping athlete to reach him. Pulitzer Prize–winning war correspondent Ernie Pyle described the scene as "a pandemonium of surely the greatest mass joy that has ever happened." German general Dietrich von Choltitz, finishing lunch in the elegant Hotel Meurice, said to the military leaders dining alongside him, "Germany has lost the war," and prepared to give himself up to the Allied leader. Large contingents of German soldiers streamed out of buildings, their shirts unbuttoned at the neck, their hands on top of their heads and their fingers interlocked. Anticipating this day, Cholitz had previously instructed his army to surrender peacefully wherever possible. By doing so he was defying Hitler's orders to fight to the last bullet. Cholitz also refused to comply with another of the Fuhrer's directives: destroy the city rather than hand over its immense treasures to the Allies. The Nazis' reign over Paris, which had lasted for four years and two months, had come to an end.

In somewhat of an anticlimax, Farrior wrote, "After the parade we marched to an airport ten miles Northeast of Paris where a defensive position was set up for the night."[22]

# 6

## The Autumn of Its Reign

> The trees began softly to sing a hymn of twilight. . . . There
> was silence save for the chanted chorus of the trees.
>
> —*The Red Badge of Courage*

It took the Allies eighty days to fight their way from the beaches of Normandy to Paris, a distance of about 160 miles. Getting from D-Day to the City of Light was a slow, gory grind. But, following its historic march down the Champs-Élysées, celebrating the liberation of the people of Paris, the Twenty-Eighth Infantry Division managed to pull off an astounding feat: it covered the roughly 270 miles from the French capital eastward to the German border in just ten days. Traveling both by foot and by truck, it stopped sporadically along the way to break up—mostly with rifles and machine guns— pockets of German resistance. In a war where progress was measured in yards, occupying that stretch of territory in that short a time was considered an amazing accomplishment for an infantry division.

Nazi Germany was on the run. As the Allies steadily but surely reclaimed the French cities of Caen and Saint-Lô near the coast of Normandy and then moved further inland to cities like Elbeuf and Falaise, Hitler realized that France was lost and ordered his troops to quickly retreat to the fatherland. As summer ended and the leaves began to change, the Third Reich also appeared to be entering the autumn of its reign. In addition to France, the occupied worlds of Belgium, Luxembourg, and parts of Holland were handed back to the Allies, with the exceptions of a few resistant pockets. In the east the Russians also had the German Army backpedaling from the Baltic to the Black Sea. A wide front encompassing Estonia, Latvia, and Lithuania in the north and Poland and Romania in the south was freed from German occupation. The momentum of the war had turned. For all of the Allied nations, it was a proud moment. In a press conference in London, Gen. Walter Bedell Smith, chief of staff to U.S. Army Gen. and Supreme Allied Cdr. Dwight D. Eisenhower, boldly declared, "Militarily, this war is over."[1]

The prophetic word on both sides of the Atlantic was that the war begun five years before by Imperial Nazi Germany would be over by Christmas 1944. History would prove, however, that the prediction was far from correct. Operation Market Garden, which followed immediately upon the celebrations, was a sobering reminder that the euphoria was premature. The massive failure of a combined Allied effort of British, Polish, and American soldiers to penetrate German defenses inside the Netherlands was brought to a halt by the German Army on September 25, just eight days into its execution. All that it took for the Germans to get the upper hand was a delay on the part of the Allies in reaching a bridge in Holland. The missed deadline was enough to thwart the plan of its British mastermind, FM Bernard Montgomery, to invade Germany's industrial interior. In his autobiography, A General's Life, Omar Nelson Bradley, a top military leader in World War II's European Theater, also notes that it didn't help that the Germans seized a Market Garden battle plan "that had been stupidly taken into battle by an American officer."[2]

If the United States didn't know the real truth about the war in Europe, at least a few GIs on the ground did. In a letter written from Luxembourg dated September 23, 1944, 1st Lt. with the Twenty-Eighth Infantry Division Julian Farrior wrote to his wife, Grace: "Don't be lured into too much optimism about the end of the war. The American public does incline to be that way but quite often they are mistaken. I wish I could give you my first hand information." But the censors of all outgoing mail from GIs would have either deleted this information or destroyed the letter.

The debacle of Operation Market Garden is now well known. It

The Autumn of Its Reign

was chronicled in dramatic detail in both a best-selling book and a star-studded Hollywood film by the same name, *A Bridge Too Far*. But, curiously, an even bigger failure—a military campaign undertaken exclusively by the United States almost simultaneous with Market Garden—has by and large escaped the general public's notice: the worst defeat suffered by the U.S. Army in Europe during World War II, a fact that probably explains at least in part the military's reticence about the offensive.

Then came U.S. Army Lt. Col. Thomas G. Bradbeer. Trim and muscular with a strong jaw, the bespectacled lieutenant colonel looks like both a soldier and an academic, which he is. He earned a doctorate in history from the University of Kansas and holds two master's degrees: one in adult education, the other in military arts and sciences. He also served in Iraq in the mid-2000s. Bradbeer learned of the existence of the battle at a military officers course at Fort Still in Oklahoma in the summer of 1980. During one of the military history lessons on World War II, the instructor mentioned that the Fifth Corps Artillery—a military unit—had done an excellent job neutralizing the German artillery in a battle he had never heard of before: the Battle of the Hürtgen Forest. With his father a veteran of the Pacific campaign in World War II, Bradbeer grew up reading all he could about that conflict and was surprised to hear of the Hürtgen Forest. He headed to the library and found two books on the subject, both of them written by Charles MacDonald, the army's chief historian. Then, rather boldly, Bradbeer approached his instructor and informed him that, according to MacDonald, the premier authority on the battle, the U.S. Field Artillery did not neutralize the German artillery.

Bradbeer was intrigued, not only by the misinformation about the field artillery, but also by the quiet surrounding the battle. From then on he was on a mission: he wanted to find out everything he could about the battle. Six years later he personally visited the forest, walked the terrain, and interviewed German war veterans as well as the local townsfolk. The lieutenant colonel found out that, contrary to what he had been taught in class, the Germans had fought superbly in that battle, even though heavily outnumbered. When

Bradbeer returned to Germany for a second tour of duty in the late 1990s and early 2000s, he realized that the secret of the Hürtgen Forest still lingered. Leading tours of the battlefield, he discovered that almost no one among the U.S. military brass knew that a battle had been fought there.

Upon his return to the United States, Bradbeer was assigned as a professor to the U.S. Army Command and General Staff College (CGSC) in Fort Leavenworth, Kansas. There he spent four years further researching the battle, and, while digging around the archives at the Dwight D. Eisenhower Presidential Library in Abilene, Kansas, he discovered something else: a diary kept by General Cota had been tampered with.

Bradbeer had wanted to know what was going through the mind of the general as he was directing thousands of men through that ignominious battle in the fall of 1944. "Guess what," he says. "The entire month of October and November is missing. Got torn out. What we (he and an archivist) surmise is that somebody must have removed the pages because there was damning stuff in there about what took place."[3] The diary was donated to the library by General Cota's wife, Alice. It was part of a 3,500-page volume of notes, correspondence, newspaper clips, photographs, award citations, and documentation of various disciplinary actions, including the execution of Pvt. Eddie Slovik, who, as a soldier in the Twenty-Eighth Division, was under his charge.

But what was the motivation behind ripping out those pages? It couldn't have been the deliberations behind the decision to send Private Slovik before a firing squad, which were made during those two months; that material was in the dossier, untouched. It couldn't have been about private family matters that someone wanted kept from public knowledge, because, for one thing, the general was stationed in Europe and too occupied with the war at the time. In all probability, the ripped pages had to have been about the decisions that Cota made on matters involving the lives of the ten thousand men in his unit.

The problem with being a general is that you have to use lives in order to achieve your objectives. And when those goals are mixed

The Autumn of Its Reign

with ambition, prejudice, and military politics, directing armies can become a dirty business. When dealing with life-and-death situations, residents and interns working the emergency room in teaching hospitals have their learned professors hovering nearby, steering them clear of fatal mistakes. Generals basically have themselves. They receive input from subordinates, but they are subordinates, not experienced overseers. What can't be ignored is that, when the smoke clears, a general is rewarded not by the lives of men he saves, but the battles he wins.

In the spring of 2010, Bradbeer published a ten-thousand-word case study in the professional journal *Army History* titled "General Cota and the Battle of the Hürtgen Forest: A Failure of Battle Command?"[4] It outlines all of the missteps and strategic errors made by the generals and commanders involved with that battle. Bradbeer isn't the only critic; other military historians also take issue with many aspects of the planning and preparation of a campaign that was ultimately dragged out over five hellish months for more than one hundred thousand U.S. servicemen. From September 1944 to February 1945, a dozen divisions—nine infantry, two armored, and one airborne—fought in a forest that was likened to an angry green "monster, an ice-coated moloch with an insatiable capacity for humans," in the words of Gen. James M. Gavin, who fought there as the commander of the 82nd Airborne Division.[5] Casualties exceeded 33 percent. In comparison, the rates of loss at the Battle of the Bulge and at Normandy were 13 percent and 7 percent, respectively.[6] The Twenty-Eighth Infantry was the division that spilled the most blood.

"You can't put a smiley face on this," Bradbeer says. "We had bad leadership, bad tactics, against a smart enemy. You can't say the division did a great job. I say they used poor tactics." But Bradbeer has taken it one step further: he has turned the failed tactics of the Twenty-Eighth Division into an academic course that he teaches at the CGSC.

Bradbeer, who is chairman of leadership studies and an assistant dean at the graduate school in Fort Leavenworth, Kansas, likes to start off the course with a question: "Has anyone heard of the Battle of the Hürtgen Forest?" Most of the time his students stare at

Fig. 7. Lt. Col. Thomas Bradbeer, leadership studies chair at the U.S. Army Command and General Staff College in Fort Leavenworth, Kansas. Courtesy of the U.S. Army Command and General Staff College, Fort Leavenworth, Kansas.

him blankly. Sometimes a bold student will verbalize what the class is thinking.

"No, sir, never heard of it."

"Has anyone been to Germany?"

A few will raise their hands.

"Has anyone heard of the Ardennes?"

A good many raise their hands. That's where the famous Battle of the Bulge was fought.

"Well, guys," Bradbeer says, "the Hürtgen Forest is only twenty-five to thirty miles north of there."

Why, if the two battles were fought in the same mountain range more or less at the same time, is the familiarity differential so big? That was the question Bradbeer posed to his administrative superiors in making the pitch to include his class in the curriculum. At least part of the answer is because the battle was an embarrassment.

The story of the Twenty-Eighth Infantry Division and the Battle of Hürtgen Forest starts not at the forest itself but about forty miles south near the Siegfried Line. The Siegfried Line, called "the West Wall" by the Germans, was a daunting barrier of mines, barbed wire, and minifortresses built close to the ground. They were called "pillboxes" and were made of reinforced concrete, some of them big enough to house twenty to thirty soldiers. In the walls they had holes for machine gun fire. The Germans also cemented into the ground their infamous "dragon teeth," so called because they look, from an airplane, like rows of white teeth: concrete blocks shaped to stop tanks in their tracks, much in the manner that traffic spikes work against the rubber tires of vehicles at entrances and gates. When tanks tried to go over dragon teeth, their treads fell off.

ON SEPTEMBER 12 THE TWENTY-EIGHT INFANTRY DIVISION was tasked with the mission of taking the small town of Uttfeld, about four miles from the German Belgium border. At an elevation of 1,700 feet, Uttfeld would provide the Americans a decent view of what lay beyond and a good launching point for further advancement into Germany.

Getting up the hill to the town, however, was quite a challenge. It loomed over the Americans like a citadel, and in front of it was a sea of dragon teeth, miles of pillboxes, and a creek with a muddy bed that could sink any tank attempting to cross it. The Twenty-Eighth had a couple of other problems as well, one of which was manpower. Another division, fighting German resistors in neighboring Belgium and Luxembourg, needed to borrow a regiment, consisting of about three thousand men, from the Twenty-Eighth. That left the division with just two regiments, or about six thousand soldiers. The question that Gen. Cota now had to answer was: How many men do you send up against the Germans? If he sent the entire group and they all got mowed down by machine gun or blasted by artillery fire, he would have no army left. Because of poor reconnaissance, the U.S. division commanders didn't really know the size of the German force that lay in wait. Cota decided to play it safe and line up just two thousand men for the fight, one battalion from each regiment. That would be considered a relatively small army of fighters in large-scale warfare such as World War II. Under the plan the 110th Regiment would make the approach from the north, and the 109th would attack from the south.

There was yet another problem. The battalions were to attack the Germans without two of their most effective weapons against pillboxes: flamethrowers and explosives. The flamethrowers—guns that can spew flames from ninety feet away—forces the pillbox occupants to close their machine gun windows. This allows GIs to run up to the pillboxes and place their TNT dynamite next to the walls. All the Americans had instead were mortar and artillery shells. But the shells were ineffective; most of them bounced off the concrete walls like ping-pong balls. At best they dusted off the camouflage.[7]

The only option left for the Twenty-Eighth was to move in close enough to fire their guns or launch hand grenades at the narrow openings in the pillboxes. The Germans responded with their own firepower from inside their redoubts as the Americans closed in. The counterattack pinned the U.S. servicemen to the ground; in that position, they became prey to mortar and artillery fire from German launchers looking down on them from higher ground. Meanwhile, the contingent of GIs attacking the pillboxes from the south—the 109th—got mired in a mile-long stretch of morass leading up to the creek. All the while, artillery and machine gun fire rained down on them. After an entire day of fighting, they couldn't even reach the creek, which was a few hundred yards away from the pillboxes. To make matters worse, the Americans had very little ammunition—just enough for brief exchanges and not for a prolonged firefight, which Uttfeld was turning out to be. U.S. officers were fully aware of the shortage, because, in racing at breakneck speed from Paris to the German border, the Twenty-Eighth Infantry Division had outraced its own supply convoys delivering gasoline and ammunition to the troops.

After darkness fell and the fighting ceased, a group of ten men from the 110th Regiment were ordered to fetch a cache of TNT explosives stored in the rear of the 28th Division encampment. The U.S. Sherman tanks, which had burned their engine parts out racing to the Siegfried Line from France, were now repaired, and the plan was to blow up a strip of dragon teeth to create a pathway for them to pass through. The explosives, however—all fifty pounds of it—inexplicably blew up at 3:00 a.m., killing the GIs who were carrying them. For the infantry, that meant another day without tank support. A second effort the following day (day three) by another group from the 110th was successful: they were able to remove a sufficient number of dragon teeth to allow a few U.S. tanks to pass through and provide fire support for members of the 110th to capture a handful of pillboxes and take fifty-eight German soldiers prisoner. But the Germans counterattacked and soon decimated the Americans, and a company of 193 troops was reduced to a mere fighting force of 18. The rest were either killed or injured. A number of them also fled.[8]

The next day Cota used all the manpower he had; the regiments were permitted to have all three of their battalions take part in the battle, since the Germans' counteroffense had been overwhelming the day before. The Americans encountered more problems, though. For one thing, their tanks got stuck in the mud. Unable to get them out, the infantry had pressed forward on its own, doggedly, until it was able to flank a mile-long row of pillboxes and capture their occupants. The seizure of the German bunkers came at great risk to the Americans, who had to run through minefields and face a barrage of enemy fire to reach the bunkers. After all that, they were still two miles away from the town of Uttfeld.

The Germans' clear advantage was that they owned the real estate at the top of the hill. From their lofty position, the 2nd Panzer Division of the German Army could see, with the aid of binoculars, the 109th Regiment's movements beneath them. Their tanks fired away at the men crawling up the hill. Pounded by German shelling, members of the 109th found themselves stranded out in the open, and some retreated without waiting for orders from their commander. Disobeying or acting without an order is a court-martialing offense in the army; that goes for the regiment commander as well. Cognizant of the rule, Col. William Blanton, commander of the 109th, was waiting for General Cota to give the command to retreat. That command never came. As the shelling increased, the men on the hill decided they could no longer wait and abandoned their positions. The stalemate continued for two more days. Had Pvt. Eddie Slovik not deserted the U.S. Army a month before, he would have been fighting here, as a member of the rifle platoon with the 109th Regiment.

Two miles to the north, the 110th Regiment also found themselves similarly stymied by persistent enemy shelling, machine fire from the pillboxes, and the nearly indestructible dragon teeth. Uttfeld was not going the way the Americans had hoped. The task of the 28th Division was to forge a gap in the Siegfried Line so that the 5th Armored Division, a fighting unit of about forty tanks, could move in. When it became apparent that the 28th was not going to be able to move the Germans out of the way, 5th Corps commander Gen. Gerald Gerow—who outranked Cota—called off the effort, and Cota and the 28th were ordered away from the frontline. The infantry division had suffered casualties of more than 1,500 men.[9]

The bloodbath proved to be the crucible that earned the division the German-given nickname of *Der Blutiger Eimer*—the Bloody Bucket. The characterization would stick with the division until the end of the war.[10] The informal title was far more humbling for the division than its previous nickname: "Iron Division." That was the name bestowed on the fighting unit by General Pershing for its defiant stand against the Germans in World War I.[11] It was at Uttfeld, a town the Twenty-Eighth couldn't take, that its image transmogrified to the less flattering "Bloody Bucket."

"My Darling Grace," wrote First Lieutenant Julian Farrior to his wife in Atlanta:

> Today doesn't seem like Sunday at all; however, we are going to pull a limited number of men out of the line for a little church service. I hope German artillery doesn't find our group. We'll all take our weapons and plenty of ammunition with us to church because Heinie may attack at any time and anywhere.
>
> I didn't tell you but I went through Versailles and Compiegne which were famous from World War I. I'll long remember Compiegne and so will Lt. Mills and I'll tell you why later. The people of Versailles gave us a tremendous reception.

The Autumn of Its Reign

Sometime ago when we were more or less in a static position, suddenly from an adjacent field came a blood-curdling yell. The (commanding officer) and a half a dozen of us grabbed our rifles and went over to investigate. We saw a Belgian boy on the ground by his wagon bleeding and yelling. After searching out the hedges around the field to prevent possible German ambush, we examined the boy and found that he had stepped on a booby trap and had gotten a foot pretty chewed up. Our aid men got him to the station for treatment and he'll be processed through our hospitals just like an American soldier. All wounded people, civilians, soldiers, friend or enemy are given the same treatment. I will write again today if possible. I am thinking of you always. I love you. Julian.[12]

Approximately ten miles away from the Siegfried Line in Verviers, Belgium, Gen. Courtney Hicks Hodges was following the movements of his U.S. First Army juggernaut, of which the Twenty-Eighth Infantry Division was an element. He had just recently established his headquarters in the elegant chateau de Maison Bois, which was owned by the Belgian Count and Countess De Pinto, and had set up his war room in a new trailer in the chateau's compound. The war room was spacious and featured a large plexiglass-top map table. Despite the new surroundings, the mood was turning somber. Maj. William C. Sylvan, an aide to Hodges, kept a running diary of the general's day-to-day thoughts and actions and wrote in his Sunday September 17, 1944 entry: "Supply both of POL [petroleum, oil, and lubricants], ammunition, and food continues to become more critical and that we are not now even holding our own. . . . It is not improbable that we shall have to slow up, even altogether halt, our drive into Germany and this in the very near future."[13]

The Germans had outsmarted the Americans at Uttfeld. In reality, the German Army was much less formidable than the U.S. commanders had thought. This became apparent after the Americans interviewed some of the German prisoners they had captured. The Germans, too, were understaffed. Many of the pillboxes were unmanned, the prisoners said; some of them contained only "two or three men." They were armed with rifles, a few machine guns, and

Panzerfausts, which were small shoulder-mounted rocket launchers. Desperate to fill their ranks, the Germans recruited men regardless of their age or background, many of whom came to the front with little to no training. One German soldier, a forty-year-old cook, was taken prisoner by the Americans just two hours after reporting to the frontline at Uttfeld. He complained bitterly about having to fight. He, like many of the prisoners, had snuck into their pillboxes just the night before. All the while the Americans thought that the pillboxes were robustly defended with units of well-armed Germans. The revelation led Maj. James C. Ford, who was assigned to the 110th Infantry, to comment later: "It doesn't much matter what training a man may have when he is placed inside such protection as was afforded by the pillboxes. Even if he merely stuck his weapons through the aperture and fired occasionally, it kept our men from moving ahead freely."[14]

No one needed to say it, but, at least in the eyes of some, Cota had failed in his job as general at Uttfeld. At that battle Col. William Blanton was fired from his position as commander of the 109th Regiment. In the army, of course, a firing meant reassignment. The cause for reassignment was the unauthorized retreat of members of the 109th from their positions during battle.[15] Uttfeld was one of the first major battles General Cota faced as a division commander. He had only been in the position for about a month, having received the appointment after his immediate predecessor was shot in the head by a German sniper just hours after he was named leader of the Twenty-Eighth, as he surveyed conditions at the frontline. That incident prompted rampant speculation in the community of commanders whether generals were told, explicitly or implicitly, to stay away from the front. In the hard-boiled world of the military, it is easier to replace a foot soldier than a general. For Cota, who was known as a "fighting general," that directive, if it was issued, took away one of his more notable talents. He made a name by fearlessly positioning himself at the "tip of the spear," in military parlance; he directed not by issuing orders from the rear, but by leading his men to battle from the front, inspiring the rank and file in the process to extraordinary heights of bravery.

The Autumn of Its Reign

On D-Day, Cota landed with his division on Omaha Beach at 7:30 a.m., an unlit cigar dangling from his mouth. At age fifty-one he was one of the oldest soldiers engaged in the fight on that bloody morning. To those nearby it was hard not to notice his piercing grey eyes, deeply set next to a beaked nose in a weather-beaten mien, among the fresh, young, terrified countenances around him. A slight hunch in the broad shoulders of the one-time high school football star was another giveaway that his days of youth had been left behind. Nonetheless he moved on the beach with the energy of men half his age. Wading through the icy waters of the English Channel, he clambered onto the soppy sand, as many of the men in his division—the Twenty-Ninth Infantry—were felled all around him by German artillery.

Then Cota went into action, leaning on one of his battlefield skills: on-the-ground improvisation. He scaled a seawall, helped direct a Browning Automatic Rifle attack on the Germans to provide cover for his men, and ordered a group of army engineers to set up an explosive made of piping material called a "Bangalore torpedo" and place it under a barbed wire mesh to blow a hole through it. The opening allowed his group—and, behind them, a long train of other soldiers—to squeeze through and run up a beach road to a strategic bluff. To a group of rangers waiting behind a dirt wall, he barked, "Goddamnit, if you're Rangers get up and lead the way."[16] That exhortation has undergone a small edit since then. The phrase "Rangers, Lead the Way" is a slogan now used by the U.S. Army Rangers to underscore its elite leadership status in the armed forces.

A few weeks later, Cota's up-tempo derring-do took on a legendary flavor while leading "Task Force Charlie" in a push to take the French city of Saint-Lô. Trying to set an example for his men, he stood defiantly upright on a open road as the enemy shelled the area around him. This time he got hit in the arm by a piece of flying metal from a nearby explosion. Though the wound was serious enough to hospitalize Cota for two weeks, he sought treatment only after his task force team was out of harm's way.[17] His extraordinary heroism and meritorious conduct on the battlefield netted him a wall full of medals, including the Distinguished Service Cross, two Silver Stars, two Legion of Merits, and an Army Distinguished Service Medal.

What had happened to General Cota? How did he go from being a superstar in a historic battle to a failure in a battle almost no one has heard of? The two battles were just four months apart. Born in 1893 just outside of Boston, Cota had worked his way up the military ladder in the typical manner: attending the right schools, excelling in academics, impressing all the right people, and making connections. He dropped out of public school at the age of fifteen to work for two years and save up enough money to attend Worcester Academy, a prestigious high school that turned out a pantheon of Wall Street types, professional athletes, and Brahmin businessmen. The only famed military man coming out of the boarding school was George B. Boomer, who went on to become a Civil War general. Still, Cota managed to get an appointment to West Point. It was at the U.S. Military Academy in New York that he became acquainted with a circle of young men who would twenty-five years later loom in the echelon of U.S. military leaders and dictate the direction of the war. Among them were Gen. Dwight D. Eisenhower; Joe Lawton Collins, commander of the Seventh Corps; and Omar N. Bradley.[18]

Cota was of fighting age in World War I, but he spent the time at Governors Island in New York, an ocean away from the frontline, training soldiers. Between World War I and World War II, Cota attended, and later taught at, various U.S. military schools, among other assignments. Over those years he was promoted from captain to lieutenant to major to colonel; also in the interim he got married and had two children, a daughter and a son.

His moment to shine came in World War II. In 1942 he participated in the invasion of North Africa as part of an amphibious operation. In 1943 he was promoted to brigadier general and charged with the training of U.S. troops in preparation for the invasion of Normandy. The Cota name and amphibious operations became synonymous. His biographers write glowingly about the good fortune of being mentored by the British war hero and naval officer Lord Mountbatten. Cota's heroic effort on D-Day is forever etched in the history books.

But now, staggered at the Siegfried Line, Cota and his battered Twenty-Eighth Infantry Division were about to be pulled from the

The Autumn of Its Reign

frontline and sent a distance away to get itself together. Under the reconstitution plan, he was about to be asked to do something to which he was, and always had been, philosophically opposed.

And that, in a way, was the irony of Cota's life as a division commander, and the reason, at least in part, for his lackluster performance at Uttfeld. He was at his best in the thick of a fight and not in a chair far from the action. He was a general of adrenaline. In theory Cota had earned an appointment higher than any he had ever been given in his thirty-one-year career in the military; they let him run the show on the battlefield while his superiors stood back and watched in amazement. Now his bosses were going to tell him to step away from the front, situate himself in the rear of his army, and take orders from them in the upcoming battle in the Hürtgen Forest. Uttfeld was only a prelude.

# 7

## Replacement Depot No. 15

Over the river a golden ray of sun came through the hosts
of leaden rain clouds.

—*The Red Badge of Courage*

Octobe is a relatively warm month in Belgium. Temperatures hover in the high fifties and low sixties during the day. The trees, which start to lose their foliage in early September, are all but bare, their yellow arboreal debris collected in windswept piles on the ground. An unmistakable dreariness tinges the air, caused in large part by the incessantly pelting rain, which turns the brown dirt into mud. Everyone said that that year—1944—saw the rainiest October in recent Belgian memory.

For Sydney Weaver, huddled in his plastic poncho alongside his comrades in the Twenth-Eighth Infantry Division, the warm climes of the Salinas Valley must have seemed like a distant dream—ten thousand miles away in California, where he had spent the late spring and early summer training as an infantryman. Even more unreal was the two-week furlough he'd received at the end of camp to return to his modest three-room house on the edge of Lake Okoboji. On an August afternoon in rustic Iowa, there is no place like home, for those who grew up there. The ninety-degree heat skims the surface of the water and wafts over a hundred thousand sleeping toads and leopard frogs like a lullaby. Such was the silence of the lake, soothing and melodious, to an Iowa country boy. Sydney spent his time at home no differently than he had any other year: he helped his father with his boat livery business, played with his two young daughters, and passed the humid evenings with his extended Weaver family of siblings, uncles, and aunts, telling stories, playing cards, and watching the children run around under a sky full of stars.

The routine was so familiar that when Peggy Weaver, who was then five years old, thinks back to that time in her childhood, the memories don't flow. It must be that she thought her father was never going away again. There isn't an emotional marker in Peggy's consciousness to help her recall the second parting with her dad that year. Sydney must have done a good job pretending that everything was back to normal, unlike the time five months before when he couldn't mask the pain of leaving his family to report to boot camp. Peggy had picked up on his sadness, and she has little trouble remembering the pang of being abandoned, as her dad hugged and kissed his daughters before walking out the door. Back then he was headed to a place just two time zones away. Now he was bound for a land on the other side of midnight.[1]

He said goodbye to each of his relatives, one by one. "I hope to be back soon," he repeated, almost as a refrain. That, at least, was his prayer. Everyone, including his dad, Curtis, begged him to write, and vowed to do the same. Allied victory was all but assured, they said—perhaps to comfort themselves more than anything—and wished Sydney a safe tour.

On August 10 of that year, Sydney boarded a train in Des Moines that took him east, to Baltimore. When he disembarked at the Maryland station days later, he was not alone. A sea of olive-green uniforms—men like him trying to look soldier-like in the sweltering sun—flooded the streets and sidewalks. From there a caravan of army trucks ferried them the twenty miles to Fort George G. Meade, one of a series of military stations where the servicemen were prepared to be sent abroad.

As military camps go, Fort Meade was several notches higher on the comfort pole than boot camp. The army knew it needed to keep the spirits of its men high. Many were homesick; many others were afraid. Their lives were about to change in a way they had never known before. For about two weeks, Weaver and his army cohorts were treated to movies, concerts, and more downtime than they had ever enjoyed in uniform. One of the movies they saw was *A Wing and A Prayer* with Don Ameche and Dana Andrews. They were given passes to go into Baltimore. For live entertainment there was a USO club on the base. Food was plentiful at the expansive mess hall: all-you-can-eat hot meals three times a day. The doors of the haberdashery swung back and forth endlessly. With fall just around the corner, the troops were provided warm winter clothing: a wool shirt, a high-neck sweater, thick field trousers, a gabardine wool coat, a few pairs of woolen socks, rugged outdoor boots, a rain poncho, a new helmet, and a rifle.[2] After two weeks at Meade, Weaver climbed aboard a train bound for Camp Kilmer, just outside of East Brunswick, New Jersey. The camp, which operated its own launching berth, was conveniently perched on the Raritan Bay. It was the largest overseas processing camp during World War II and the final destination in the United States for hundreds of thousands of GIs before they sailed across the Atlantic to join the war in Europe.

In the latter half of 1944, there was an urgency to get men from U.S. camps to replace the wounded and the dead on the battlefields of France, Belgium, and Germany. On some days as many as eight to ten ships would slip their moors in New Jersey, New York, and Boston and sail to destinations in England, Scotland, and Wales. With names like the *Queen Mary*, the *Wakefield*, the *Argentina*, the *Hermitage*, the *Queen Elizabeth*, the *Mauretania*, the *Mormacmoon*, the *Mount Vernon*, and the *Aquitania*, the vessels raced across the Atlantic, each carrying ten to fifteen thousand GIs on board.[3] As the troop ships neared their destinations, they would be met by a flotilla of Royal Navy antiaircraft cruisers, to protect against Luftwaffe attacks, that accompanied them into ports in Gourock, Scotland; Liverpool, England; and Cardiff, Wales. They then crossed the English Channel and disembarked on French soil—many for the first time—in landing crafts en route to their yet-to-be-disclosed battle stations.

Their first stop: the town of Le Havre, right on the edge of the channel alongside Normandy Beach. It was designated as Replacement Depot No. 15. From there the GIs were trucked in lorries to Le Mans or Paris—two more army centers further inland. There, replacements sat for days, sometimes more than a week, awaiting the news for which they had traveled across the ocean: the divisions to which they would be assigned.

As they waited, the soldiers had time to write home. Battling seasickness, the persistent rain, and the general discomfort of traveling with thousands of men, just feeling good was of prominent concern for a lot of them. That apparently was on Sydney Weaver's mind when he penned this postcard home—then called Victory Mail, or V-mail.

My darling wife and daughters,

How are you? I am getting along all right, have been feeling pretty good today. We got through early tonight, cleaned our guns and shaved and washed my feet. Would have like to have gone swimming but didn't have time.

We are still in France just where did you expect us to be. . . .

I had a few spare minutes this morning and read your letter, the one in the blue envelope. I am glad you didn't go to the show that night as that sure is a nice letter. Darling, I love you and want to see my girls. I will be seeing you one of these days, I hope. . . .

Good Night my Sweetheart.

With All my Love,
Sydney E. Weaver[4]

Sydney soon received his assignment. His destination: the low mountains near the Ardennes Forest in southeastern Belgium. Other replacements who drew similar lots in the fall of 1944 included Jack Farrell of Arlington, Massachusetts; Robert Wiginton of Hamilton, Alabama; Otto Peterson of Boy River, Minnesota; Waverly Lane of Virginia Beach, Virginia; Carl Dewitt Sanders of Hawkinsville, Georgia; and Joseph Merlock of Dorothy, New Jersey. All were picked for the Twenty-Eighth Infantry Division of the First U.S. Army, which had just engaged in a bruising battle at the Siegfried Line.

The new environment for these men was not exactly the most welcoming of places. It would be safe to say that their accommodations were far more primitive than any outdoor campsite today. In an October 1944 letter to his wife, Grace, in Atlanta, 1st Lt. Julian

Farrior provides a glimpse of how and where he and his comrades in the 28th Division lived at the time:[5]

My Darling Grace,

I'm writing by candlelight in my dugout, so if this letter appears a bit weather beaten you'll know the reason why.

This particular dugout is fairly comfortable—that is as far as dugouts go—at least no water has run in as yet and there has been plenty of rain. Here we use the buddy system, so the C.O, Lt. Huston and I dug this hole together. You see we always work and sleep in pairs, so one man can protect the other—one sleeps while the other stands guard. The shifts are rotated during the night. We travel in pairs during daylight too, so one man can keep the other covered.

I will try to describe this dugout to you. The actual excavation is 4 feet wide, six and a half feet long and three feet deep. All around the edges of the hole the sides are built up another foot and a half with big spruce logs. Spruce logs form the roof too and all this is covered over by a mound of dirt. Next on top come the shelter leaves and then comes the camouflage. The floor is covered with chopped up spruce boughs. The walls inside are partially covered with poster-board boxes. The place is practically airtight so we're able to have a candle burning at night. Lt. Huston has a gasoline stove and it has heated the place up nicely. This is an enclosed dugout—Most of the time we aren't nearly so comfortable.

I love you
Julian[6]

And there was another problem—one more systemic than accommodations, although there was nothing that could be done to help the situation. It was just who they were, which were IRs, or individual replacements. There was a penalty that came with that status. IRs were the bane of generals. General Cota, for one, didn't like them. The common view was that they were inexperienced and undertrained soldiers expected to step into the same jobs of the experienced and well-trained fighters they were replacing. Without extensive training that would be virtually impossible. Some of the men who were killed or wounded had been with the division for at least a year or two, and they became casualties not because they weren't good at what they did but because they were unlucky. IRs tended to drag down an entire division's performance, for which a general is ultimately held accountable. Hence the disdain suffered by many of them.

When General Cota and the Twenty-Eighth Infantry Division is discussed in a graduate course at the Command and General Staff College at Fort Leavenworth in Kansas, the consensus among students— all of whom are military officers— is that Cota's big handicap going to battle against the Germans in the Hürtgen Forest was the large number of IRs he was carrying in his army.[7] The Twenty-Eighth had suffered more than 1,500 casualties at Uttfeld, the battle on the Siegfried Line from which it had just withdrawn, a number so large that the division had to be removed from the line.

It wasn't just the general that didn't like IRs. Veterans in the division didn't, either. In his *Army Journal* article, Bradbeer notes that "a vast majority of replacements arrived with little infantry training," and that many of the veterans in the division were "leary of the new men." Thus, to them, the replacements were "unknown quantities who might put them at risk."[8]

It was around this time that another IR—the poster boy of individual replacements, as it were—walked into the Twenty-Eighth Infantry's Belgian bivouac: Pvt. Eddie Slovik. Slovik had deserted the group about two months before, in August. He had been assigned to the division as a replacement, but, as his transport truck reached the Twenty-Eighth in the French town of Elbeuf, it came under heavy shelling by the Germans. Slovik and his truckmates had to scramble out of the burning truck and dig themselves into foxholes for the night. The next morning the others in his group joined up with the army unit. Slovik, however, decided to seek out a unit farther away from the intense fire drawn by the Twenty-Eighth. He found the Canadian Thirteenth Provost Corps, a military police unit back in the advancing column. The first thing Slovik did was to explain to the Canadians his fear of combat and ask if he could work somewhere safe. Apparently, the commanders of the Thirteenth Corps didn't have a problem with that; they accommodated his wishes and detailed him to their kitchen. Slovik and another American deserter—Pvt. John Tankey from Detroit—stayed with the Canadians until they felt it was time to leave. Both felt guilty about deserting.

Slovik's success negotiating a detail with the Canadians emboldened him to try a similar argument with the Twenty-Eighth from which he was AWOL. He and Private Tankey, who had also been assigned to the division, walked up to their regimental superiors, confessed what they had done two months before, and begged for assignments that were a safe distance from the frontline. The commanders listened and agreed not to court-martial the two. Then they assigned them both to rifle platoons. Riflemen are usually the first to enter the thick of the fighting. The casualty rate among them is the worst of any other army group.

Private Tankey accepted the assignment, albeit reluctantly. But Slovik remembered how he had become paralyzed with fear only eight weeks before in a foxhole as the Germans shelled the area. He thought he could never go through that kind of agony again and decided to desert the division a second time. He didn't want to be sneaky about it, however, so he wrote something on a slip of paper and handed it to a cook in the unit. The cook glanced at it and called for the unit commanders. The note, read in part, in all caps: "I'LL RUN AWAY AGAIN IF I HAVE TO GO OUT THERE."[9] Cota and his commanders had been keeping an eye on Slovik all this time. As he walked away from the encampment, they arrested him and charged him with desertion.

Just as Slovik was pleading his case with the commanders of the Twenty-Eighth, Sydney was steeling himself for what lay ahead. Combined with his feelings of longing to be home in Iowa were strains of a soldier that his family had never witnessed before, until he wrote this letter:

Dear Molly and girls,

Monday morning, looks like rain. I suppose you have your washing done by now. I washed out some socks last night. They aren't dry yet.

I have several sticks of gum, wish I could send them home to Peggy. Can you write letters, get little sweetheart. I bet it won't be too long before I get a letter from you.

We get a paper here called the Stars and Stripes and one called the Yank, from what they say, it will be several months after the war before anyone to be discharged from the army can get home so don't plan on seeing me in a day or two.

I love you girls and hope we can be together again before too long. Take the best of care of my girls, darling, and of yourself.

With All of My Love,
Sydney E. Weaver[10]

Cota was not so much against IRs in general; he was opposed to the U.S. Army's system of training them. In his opinion, IRs required weeks to get in shape. They needed to become both mentally tough and acquainted with the modus operandi of their respective fighting units. Also, their leaders needed to get to know the "traits and skills" of the new additions. Were they brave or timid, clear-thinking under stress or prone to panic, reliable or irresponsible? In the rush to recruit the millions needed to staff an army, the United States often ignored its twenty-twenty vision requirement, and field commanders were quite aware of it. Good eyesight in close combat was critical. Was their vision blurry, or would they make good "spotters"? Did they have the physical stamina to go without sleep or food for days? Were they fast on their feet? Could they read a map? How long did it take them to comprehend instructions? Could they memorize a battle plan? Could they shoot accurately? It took time for commanders to make accurate assessments on 1,500 new replacements.[11]

Cota also argued that the training be done at the recruitment depots and training centers, and not on or near the frontline, where the divisions had to focus on the enemy. He was also an advocate of replacing large units as a whole and not individual soldiers. His recommendations, however, were largely ignored. The army continued to use depots as transfer stations between basic training and the frontline. As a result, the responsibility of training replacements fell on the battalions and companies, and the training under such a system rarely worked.[12]

A big part of training was the development of camaraderie. Espirit de corps didn't happen overnight; the bond had to marinate. Unit records for October, however, show that the division had little time to get the replacements prepared. For one thing, it was saddled with soldiering tasks for much of the month of October. Furthermore, heavy rains and bad weather disrupted the training sessions.

Benajah H. Brunner, 1st lieutenant for the 112th Infantry, entered this into the unit's diary:[13]

Sunday, October 1. We were responsible for a lot of patrolling between our position and the rear of the 109th Infantry. Protestant and Catholic church services were held.

Monday, October 2. In same position near Steffeshausen. All during the day assault training was stressed. The new men were instructed in general tactics.

Tuesday, October 3. In same position near Stefeshausen. The weather was rainey (CQ) and men and vehicles bogged down in the mud. Stefeshausen is in Belgium near the Germany border. From there some of the units moved on foot about 20 miles north to Wirtzfeld, another Belgium town close to the border. The order of battalions was third, second and first and went into a defensive position approximately 2 miles east of Krinkelt, Belgium. Many mines were encountered in this area and the engineers were busy removing them.

Monday, October 9. In the same position as the previous day. The weather was rainey (CQ) and everything was muddy.

Saturday, October 14. The rains continued as they had for weeks and the roads were practically impassable.

It wasn't until Monday, October 16, that the men got a chance to train again. They went to a range and practiced firing bazookas, machine guns, rifle grenades and other arms; they "also looked over a model platoon defensive position." That morning "the men were given an opportunity to visit the Red Cross for donuts and coffee,

Replacement Depot No. 15

see a movie and a USO show. In the afternoon a parade was held in honor of the men who received awards. General Cota, commander of the 28th Inf. Div. was our honored guest."

The rains continued over the next few days. The men built a log cabin to help store their ammunition and other combat essentials out of the downpour. On the 18th, forty-eight-hour passes were given out to a lucky few to truck all the way back to Paris for some rest and relaxation. 1st Lt. Julian Farrior was among those on the receiving end. As he wrote to his wife, Grace:

> The battalion executive officer called me over the phone in my fox-hole in the front line and said Julian I know you won't believe what I am going to tell you but you have been selected with one more officer from the regiment to go to Paris at government expense and spend 48 hours there.... The quietness of Paris in all its gaiety was somewhat nerve-racking because I am so used to the noise of battle. It was wonderful however to get two days rest and to sleep in a real bed for a change.

Since he was "completely covered with mud from head to foot," he was given a new uniform and a combat steel helmet to look presentable, he wrote. He and his group were put up in the Ambassador Hotel, which had been taken over by the Red Cross. The following day they took in a number of tourist sights, including the Eiffel Tower, the Arc de Triomphe, and the Grand Palace, and were treated to a performance by a Russian orchestra. As they walked the streets of Paris, many noticed the "Keystone" insignia on the men's uniform and remembered the glorious day in August when the Twenty-Eighth Infantry Division marched through the city. The men dined on roast beef and gulped down champagne. Julian was lavished with gifts— nine quarts of Cognac and Bordeaux wine—that he brought back to Belgium for his frontline cohorts.[14]

The Parisian revelry was to help the men forget the war, however briefly. But no amount of gaiety would erase the awareness of what lay just around the corner for the Twenty-Eighth. General Cota was fully conscious of it. The confidence and admiration that he once enjoyed among the top echelon of the U.S. Army had dissipated in the wake of Uttfeld. The casualty list from that fight was actually a lot worse than the 1,500 reported; it didn't include the captured, the missing and the sick. The Fifth Corps, an army unit that fought alongside the Twenty-Eighth Infantry, was keeping a separate tally for the division. It reported casualties of 3,342, almost all of it occurring during the month of September.[15] A number of officers lost their jobs in the wake of Uttfeld. Regimental leader Daniel Strickler relieved its commander, Lt. Col. Benjamin Trapani. Brig. Gen. George Davis, assistant division commander for the Twenty-Eighth, replaced company commander Capt. Andy Homanich, who broke down under the strain of battle. And Col. William Blanton was discharged of his post as regimental commander of the 109th.[16]

Now the performance of General Cota himself was closely being monitored by three superiors: 5th Corps commander General Gerow, 1st Army Gen. Courtney Hodges, and Gen. Omar Bradley. He too faced the prospect of getting fired if he didn't perform.[17] As he prepared his men for battle that October, Cota had many concerns— primarily, the safety of his men and a critical lack of preparedness. But his objections were overruled. The generals were all under pressure of various sorts. They disagreed on the best way to advance to Berlin, where Hitler was holed up in an underground bunker. The British, under the command of FM Bernard Law Montgomery, advocated a narrowly focused assault concentrated at a single point of attack. The idea behind the strategy was to overpower the enemy by outnumbering them. The theory was tried in September with Operation Market Garden and failed. The Americans, on the other hand, headed by Gen. Dwight D. Eisenhower, preferred a wide-swath deployment, spread out over hundreds of miles, to thin out the German ranks. Now Eisenhower's strategy was being put to the test. In *A General's Life* Bradley confesses that "Ike made it clear that if we had not achieved success by the first of the year (1945), my Ninth Army would be given to Monty (Field Marshal Montgomery) for a renewed effort in the north."

Generals also competed among themselves. 4th Cdr. George Patton was in an ugly rivalry with 1st Cdr. Courtney H. Hodges. Along the wide swath that Eisenhower had mapped out, Patton was assigned a southern route into the heart of Germany, while Hodges's men operated the line slightly north of Patton's troops. Whoever broke through first would get the glory. In a letter home to his wife, Patton wrote, "We are in a horse race with Courtney, if he beats me across the Rhine, I shall be ashamed."[18]

Amid this urgency, Cota was asking for time so that he could survey the terrain and assess the enemy's strength. But Hodges and his commanders couldn't delay any longer. They picked a battle plan designed by Brig. Gen. George Davis, a one-star general and assistant to Cota, a two-star general. Their choice was an affront to Cota's experience and acumen as a theater of operations tactician.

In *Normandy to Victory: The War Diary of General Courtney H. Hodges and the First Army*, Major Sylvan writes in his November 1 entry:

> General (Hodges) left at three o'clock for a visit to the 28th Division, which is to spearhead the attack. He found the Division in fine fettle, rarin' to go, and optimistic over their chances of giving the Boche a fine drubbing. The General said their plan was excellent; they are feinting to the north in hopes of fooling the Boche into the belief that this is the main effort, and then whacking him with everything in the direction of the town of Schmidt. General Davis was chiefly responsible for the plan, and the General said that he had never looked in better shape. Weather reports for tomorrow are still uncertain.[19]

Few, if any, among the rank and file of the Twenty-Eighth Infantry Division were aware of the strife among the generals. Everyone, though, had a sense that the U.S. Army was about to launch a major offensive against German defenses, and that the Twenty-Eighth would be the one doing the fighting. That night many of the infantrymen wrote letters home. Some even penned a second letter.

# 8

## Tucked into the Alluvial Folds

Under foot there were a few ghastly forms motionless.
They lay twisted in fantastic contortions. Arms were bent
and heads were turned in incredible ways. It seemed that
the dead must have fallen from some great height to
get into such positions.

—*The Red Badge of Courage*

The Germans called it Hürtgenwald. The Americans called it
the Hürtgen Forest. Before 1944 almost none of the more
than one hundred thousand GIs who stepped into its pine-
needle-strewn shadows had ever heard the name in German or in
English. But those who entered the place during World War II and
survived the experience thereafter called it other things.

Gen. James Gavin, commander of the 82nd U.S. Airborne Division, stood on its frozen surface at twilight one evening and described
the forest as "an eerie scene, like something from the lower levels
of Dante's *Inferno*." With the ground around him littered with the
corpses of American soldiers, he likened the forest to a monster, "an
ice-coated Moloch," an insatiable war god hungry for human sacrifice.[1] The U.S. Army, quoting those who were there, compared the
place to the dark forest of the cannibalistic witch in the Brothers
Grimm's tale of Hansel and Gretel: upon "entering the forest you
want to drop things behind to mark your path."[2] There, the Americans faced not one foe but two—the German Army and the forest

itself, which turned GIs into casualties without a German ever firing a weapon.

The forest is tucked into the alluvial folds of the Ardennes-Eifel Mountain Range, which rise 1,500 feet to 2,700 feet in northwestern Europe, spanning the countries of France, Belgium, Luxembourg, and Germany. In the southern part of the range—on the French, Belgian, and Luxembourg side—the mountains are known as the Ardennes; on the German side they are called the Eifel. The range was created by the clashing of continental landmasses more than three hundred million years ago. Turbulent weather systems, seeded over the Atlantic Ocean millions of years later, created torrential downpours that battered the mountains. The waters collected in rivers that rushed through the valleys, carving out the crevices, plateaus, and ridges that make up the region today.[3] After the formations solidified and the volcanoes below spewed their lava, what emerged was a shooting gallery nicely arranged in layers—a superb work of natural design. Each ridge overlooked the other, like a vista point on a scenic route, giving a clear advantage, with lines of unobstructed sight, to the defender over his foe.[4]

As forests go, the Hürtgen Forest, which sits on the Eifel side near the borders of Luxembourg, Belgium, and Germany, isn't that big: twenty miles long and ten miles wide. It could fit in Rhode Island, the smallest state in America, at least five times. In effect, the heavens had created a cozy little battlefield for the German Army. As Hitler secretly prepared for war in the 1930s, the Germans began a tree-building program in the forest. Nourished by heavy rains and the Eifel's loamy soil, the trees took root and grew quickly so that by the time the Americans arrived in 1944, the arrangement of the timberland couldn't have been more perfect. The young Spruce and Douglas fir had grown to heights of thirty-five-plus feet, filling out the spaces alongside older stock that towered over one hundred feet.[5] Combined, they created a canopy thick enough to block out the sunlight and render a night-like blackness, even during the day, for the German Army to hide up on the ridges overlooking the valleys. Almost every hill, path, and firebreak in the forest was either within range of German artillery and machine gun fire from camouflaged pillboxes, or implanted with mines. The forest had become a triangulated matrix.[6]

"So severe and deadly accurate was the German fire that any man we left in an area for a day unfailingly was dead or a combat exhaustion case by night," recounted James A. Condon, acting commander of E Company, 112th Infantry, in a postbattle interview.[7] Alexander "Sparky" Kisse, a private first class with the 112th Infantry of the 28th Division, who fought in the Hürtgen Forest, recalled in an interview how a sergeant with whom he shared a foxhole once tried to survey the enemy's position: they were holed up in "a valley that was like a cow pasture," he said. "[The sergeant] had a pair of binoculars and he was looking out the foxhole" with just his head and neck exposed. The Germans were deployed in the woods about one thousand yards away. "He's there looking around and this sniper must have seen the flash of the light and, ping! this bullet hits this stone just about three inches from his cheek. And a piece of the stone flew up and cut his cheek. The sergeant sat down back in the foxhole and the only thing he said to me was that sonnabitch is good."[8]

The Hürtgen Forest also possessed the perfect formula of humidity, precipitation, cold, and bacteria to make you deathly ill. When urine, feces, and fluids from decaying dead bodies mixed in the pouring rain, it turned into a toxic brew. Among those most vulnerable were sufferers of a little-known disease called "trench foot," not to be mistaken for frostbite. The latter occurs in temperatures below freezing; the former is categorized as a disease that develops in above-freezing temperatures from thirty-two to sixty degrees, where bacteria can thrive. When a soldier stands in a trench or foxhole in wet socks for hours, blood circulation becomes greatly impaired, leading in turn to a breakdown of capillaries and surrounding tissue in the foot. The biodeterioration produces open sores that then become life-threatening when exposed to bacteria. The first symptoms of trench foot—a small tingling or itching sensation—may seem harmless. But, as the disease progresses, which is within hours, the foot starts to swell, sometimes to twice its size, causing excruciating pain.[9] Many soldiers were forced to take off their shoes, exposing their open sores to the contaminated rainwater and mud; climbing out of foxholes in

Tucked into the Alluvial Folds

clear view of the enemy to seek treatment could be suicidal. At the same time, untreated trench foot can lead to sepsis, overwhelming the body with infection and sending the sufferer into shock. Fighting from foxholes with enemy sharpshooters and artillery squads looking down on you is a virtual catch-22: avoiding enemy fire by staying in foxholes made you susceptible to trench foot, and seeking treatment for trench foot placed you in enemy fire.

This is what the men of the Twenty-Eighth Infantry Division—approximately ten thousand in number—faced as their generals prepared for battle. They had been waiting for a week. On Wednesday, October 25, the infantrymen had piled into trucks on the town's edge in Wirtzfeld, Belgium. The thick morning mist mixed with the smell of gasoline, the stillness interrupted by the barking orders of sergeants and the squish of combat boots in the soupy mud. With everyone on board, the trucks had driven north, about twenty miles, to the German town of Roetgen, just across the Belgian border. From there the convoy pushed forward another four miles in a northeasterly direction to Rott, where the division commander, Major General Cota, had set up headquarters in a fieldstone inn.[10]

General Cota carried an air of confidence, humming tunes with a cigar dangling from the side of his mouth. That's the Cota the men of the Twenty-Eighth Division saw at Rott, with the same swagger the men of the Twenty-Ninth Division saw on Normandy Beach. At Rott, however, Cota's outward appearance was a facade. Inside he was worried about his men. A few days before, a decision was made twenty miles away by three generals, without him. Hunched over a large map of Germany spread out over a conference table in Verviers, Belgium, Gens. Courtney Hodges, Joe Collins, and Leonard Gerow discussed a plan of attack that involved Cota's army.[11] It called for Cota's division to take on the Germans in the Hürtgen Forest, while Gen. Joe Collins's unit, the Seventh Corps, would slip by to the left of the forest and advance to the two rivers ahead, the Rohr and the Rhine. The Rohr was ten miles away and the Rhine about twenty miles beyond that. The waterways marked the industrial belt of the Fatherland; controlling the rivers could cripple the manufacture and transportation of German war necessities.

Joe Collins received that assignment because—well, many among the top military brass knew that he was Hodges's "fair-haired boy." He received special treatment.[12] Why? The First Army general depended heavily on Collins to make him look good. For a top general, Hodges was not very smart.[13] He dropped out of West Point after one year because of poor test scores. His lackluster academic performance haunted him for the rest of his military career and provided ammunition for his critics, who say he lacked the brains to think creatively. "Yet there he was, an Army commander. Obviously, he knew the right people," notes Dr. Daniel P. Bolger, an author and a historian and retired lieutenant general of the U.S. Army, in the army's prestigious *Military Review*, in 1991.[14] Gen. Collins, on the other hand, was a West Point graduate, a smart and can-do general who wanted to be immortalized in military history as the one who undid Hitler. Hodges was aware of Collins's personal ambition and intelligence. As a result, "he and his VII Corps starred in every key First Army operation," Bolger writes.[15] Thus, according to the plan hatched by the three generals, the Twenty-Eighth Infantry Division was to do the dirty work so Collins's Seventh Corps wouldn't have to worry about the Germans in the Hürtgen Forest and could advance more rapidly into German territory.[16]

On Sunday, October, 29, the Twenty-Eighth moved forward another seven miles to Germeter, a village on the edge of the forest. The scenery along the road to Germeter looked like a tornado had just hit the place; the convoy passed splintered trees, emergency rations strewn around, damaged vehicles, battered road signs, destroyed bunkers, and hundreds of craters in the ground. But the shell casings scattered about gave away the cause of the debris. The Germans didn't give up Germeter easily.[17] Two weeks before, they had taken on the Ninth Infantry Division of the U.S. Army. It gave Germeter up to the Americans, but battered the division so badly that it had to be relieved by the Twenty-Eighth. As the two divisions passed each other, there was no mistaking which was which: the Twenty-Eighth was clean-shaven and decked out in clean uniforms, while the Ninth looked like ghosts, with thousand-yard stares "as if they had fought in Hell."[18]

As October came to a close and with winter just around the corner, time was of the essence. November 5 had been set as the launch date for Collins and his men to make their advance, which made it imperative for Cota's division to run interference for the Seventh Corps by November 2 or 3 at the latest.[19] But the Twenty-Eighth Division was far from prepared to enter the forest. The shipment of the nine thousand pairs of arctic overshoes it needed to protect against trench foot hadn't yet arrived, and the division hadn't done adequate reconnaissance of the area. For one, Cota didn't even know whether there were roads between the village of Germeter, the launch point of the attack, and Schmidt the objective of the assault. On the day the division arrived in Germeter, he asked his combat engineers to construct a road through the forest for his tanks, trucks, and vehicles. This meant that the infantrymen were going to have to take Schmidt "without vehicles until adequate roads become available." Attacking without tanks, as the Twenty-Eighth had discovered in their previous battle at Uttfeld, was as risky as it gets in close combat.[20]

Cota exuded confidence as he stood before General Hodges prior to battle. But, weeks later, General Cota said in an interview that he remembered thinking at the time that the Twenty-Eighth had only "a gambler's chance of success."[21] Judging from their letters home, none of the infantrymen were made aware of the army's unpreparedness and the dangerous nature of the mission. Pvt. Sydney Weaver was blissfully enjoying that Sunday with a bunch of buddies; it was a rare sunny day. In the luck of the draw where the choices were tents, foxholes, and bunkers, Private Weaver fared well—his company was provided indoor shelter. He was feeling good. At some point near the end of day he sat down to write home. The letter is full of tender longing, quite different in tone from a previous letter he had written, which warned that the war wasn't about to end and asked that his family stay brave. There is no sense of foreboding to the letter—it was his longest yet. It was also his last.

October 31, 1944

My Dearest Darling,

Another Sunday to spend in camp. All days of the week are a good deal the same. I sure be glad to get home where the days of the week mean something.

I went hunting this morning about daylight, saw a big deer but didn't dare shoot him because he was on nearly level ground and I didn't know what I might hit if I missed him. I think duck hunting is more my type of hunting. I missed breakfast but had a good dinner for once and feel pretty good now. . . .

[Two days before, the division was treated to the movie *Casanova Brown*, starring Gary Cooper whose character, as the story goes, divorces his wife, (played by Teresa Wright,) to marry a second, played by (Anita Louise). As the wedding is about to start, Cooper finds out that Wright is about to have his baby and put her up for adoption. Overcome with fatherly love, Cooper rushes from the wedding to intercept the adoption. It is possible that the movie made an impression on Sydney. In the following paragraphs, his two daughters were definitely on his mind.]

There is something I want to ask Peggy. Peggy do you remember the candy I and you used to make? Well I can't make any candy over here because I don't have any brown sugar so maybe you could make some and send it to me. We have everything we need but are hungry a lot of the time, no chance to get anything to lunch on. We eat three times a day too. Once in a while we are around the artillery or tanks, they are the best, the tanks and get some extra rations from them.

The Sergeant said he was going to ask for some pancake flour, but we can't always have a fire, most of the time not, so it is hard to tell if we could make them. Of course some jam or jelly would have to come with the flour, or syrup in a tin.

We seem to have trouble in getting stationary but so far I had plenty, guess it is because I don't hardly write to anyone but you. The next time you send me a package you might send a few airmail envelopes, don't ever send much of anything, it is better to send them oftener and not so big a box.

Tucked into the Alluvial Folds

I love you girls and hope Marjorie don't think Uncle Cecil is her dad. I sure would like to get hold of her right now.

Did you girls go to Sunday school this morning? We didn't have church services here at least I didn't know about it, could have been while I was hunting.

I hope we stay here a while because we have a nice place, it is quite large and we fixed up an old half steel barrel for a stove and can have a fire if it don't smoke too much. The only trouble is all the smoke don't go up the chimney and sometimes I think we will have to put on our gas masks, we get it fixed pretty good though. . . .

Remember I love you,
Sydney E. Weaver[22]

In his memoir *Frozen Rainbows: The World War II Adventures of a Combat Medical Doctor*, Lt. Marion Bedford Davis, a physician with the Twenty-Eighth Infantry, writes: "None of us were told the purpose of our suicidal attacks against superior forces with great tactical advantage. It was left for us not to 'question why but to do and die.'"[23]

At the Hürtgen Forest, 1st Army Gen. Courtney Hodges was up against FM Otto Moritz Walter Model, one of Hitler's top lieutenants, widely acclaimed as among the best German defense strategists. Model had proved his battle smarts a little over a month before, when he defeated both the British and the Americans simultaneously at two separate bridges in Holland, Arnhem and Nijmegen, stopping Operation Market Garden in its tracks. In 1944 Model was fifty-two years old and Hodges fifty-six. Both men had made their mark twenty-five years earlier: Hodges for his heroic effort in leading an attack across the Marne River in France during World War I, and Model for his expert knowledge of how the Prussian Army rebuilt itself in World War I and the high esteem he enjoyed in German military schools.

Model was the man in charge of defending the forest; all the divisional commanders in the German Army took instruction from him. On the American side Hodges was Model's counterpart. Model had two advantages: the high ground and home court advantage. The Germans were familiar with the lay of the land. Hodges also had two advantages: air superiority and lots of bodies. The U.S. Air Force was more advanced than Germany's Luftwaffe. American bombers and fighter planes, such as their P-38s and P-51s, were nimble and quick; they could pound their targets from on high and fly low and strafe, clearing the deck for the infantry to come in and clean up. A dozen other divisions were at the ready to thrust forward simultaneously with the Twenty-Eighth Infantry Division's attack on the Hürtgen Forest. The U.S. Army had enough manpower to stretch the decimated German Army into a thin line of defense across a 150-mile-long front.[24]

Hodges's two advantages, however, were contingent on good weather. The U.S. generals had set October 31 as the target date for the autumn offensive, but the launch had to be postponed because of rain and overcast skies, which made it difficult, if not impossible, for U.S. pilots to spot the enemy on the ground.[25] On the night of November 1, three regiments of the 28th Infantry Division—the 109th, the 110th, and the 112th—were bivouacked in the rugged terrain stretched over two and a half miles on the fringes of the Hürtgen Forest. The night air was chilly and dank from the rain and heavy mist that had cloaked the region. Some men lay under tents partially protected by boulders and trees from enemy rockets; others hunkered down in foxholes. A few, luckier ones got to sleep in captured pillboxes, some of which could house as many as thirty occupants. A few men squeezed into bombed-out buildings and barns.

As they tried that night to get some shut-eye, they were also waiting to hear the words "The officers liquor ration would be in at 1100."[26] That was the code phrase to let the division know that there would be a major offensive the next morning. Everyone was to subtract two from eleven to determine the H hour, which is military-speak for "starting time." Just before midnight, the code phrase crackled over the portable radios of captains and lieutenants. Pvt. Anthony Grasso was dozing off in a drenched foxhole, thousands of miles away from his native Needham, Massachusetts, when his SCR-300 backpack radio startled him. He wasn't exactly sure what the words meant. The alert was not meant for him, but for 1st Lt. Frank DuBose with the 112th Regiment of the 28th Infantry Division, who was propped up against a bedroll nearby.

Tucked into the Alluvial Folds

The job was relatively new to Anthony. He had previously been with an armored unit in the 112th Regiment before he got the nod from DuBose in October during a reconstitution of the 28th Division. "The lieutenant just came up to me one day when we were in Belgium and said, 'You're my radio man,'" Anthony recalls. "That was it. I wasn't told if the guy I was replacing was killed, or wounded or got transferred. Nothing. The army never told you nothing. They just said 'Do it' and you did it.'"

Anthony had been quite content handling artillery chores for the 112th. He often got to stay in the rear, as his unit fought its way from Percy, Gathemo, Breteuil, and Conches, before reaching Versailles and participating in the Paris parade. From there it was onto Compiegne near the French-Belgian border, and then down to friendly Arlon, Luxembourg and Belgium. As in Paris, the townsfolk of Arlon screamed with delight when the 28th passed through. Up until then Anthony was relatively safe. As an artilleryman Anthony's job required him to load and fire mortar bombs at the enemy far beyond the range of the rifles and machine guns of the infantry. Since the shelling was done from a distance, Anthony never really saw anyone get killed. This made it easier on his conscience, although he had to believe that he was responsible for at least a few casualties. The bombs were devastating when they landed.

Another perquisite of the job was that he never had to fix bayonets, a type of combat that Anthony abhorred. Still, with each passing day on the battlefield, Anthony couldn't help but feel the sting of his mortality. Back at boot camp, he'd never thought about dying, but, after the bombs started dropping around him and the bullets whizzed by, fear took hold, no matter how hard he tried to stay brave. Anthony starting thinking: "I'm not going to make it out of here alive." Just a year before, in high school, he had to read *The Red Badge of Courage* for a history assignment on the Civil War. He realized he was going through what Henry Fleming had experienced: "As he, leading, went across a little field he found himself in a region of shells. They hurtled over his head with long wild screams. As he listened he imagined them to have rows of cruel teeth that grinned at him. . . . He experienced a thrill of amazement when he came within view of a battery in action. The men there seemed to be in conventional moods, altogether unaware of the impending annihilation."[27]

Crane got it right. Fear does turn to numbness, if you let it. Anthony's thought patterns gradually evolved from "I'm going to die" to "Better prepare for it. I'm just going to die." He had become resigned to death, not by choice but by necessity. By making his peace with death, Anthony was no longer always anxious. He, as a nineteen-year-old, had come to understand an irony of life that would have perhaps taken a lifetime to grasp in a time of peace: sufferance, acceptance of the inevitable. A sense of calm had washed over him like the Hürtgen Forest rain, with which he was becoming all too familiar. Anthony thought, "It is going to be okay."

The code phrase was repeated over the radio: "The officers' liquor rations would be in at Eleven Hundred." The crackle of the metal box added an urgency to the words. Anthony looked at his lieutenant to see if he understood the code. DuBose did. He, too, was listening. No words were exchanged between the men. They lowered their heads onto the scratchy woolen army issue, closed their eyes, and waited for the dim light of dawn. Grasso and DuBose didn't converse much. In many ways they were worlds apart. If this had been the Civil War, they would have been enemies. DuBose was from Kershaw County, South Carolina, attended Clemson University, and graduated with a degree in vocational agriculture; Grasso was from the North and didn't even have a high school diploma. Grasso spoke with a Boston accent; DuBose sounded just like a southerner. DuBose was twenty-three and a lieutenant; Grasso was nineteen and a private. DuBose was tall and slender, with curly brown hair; Grasso was short and stocky, with black hair. DuBose was married; Grasso had never even gone on a date. But DuBose never treated Grasso as an underling. He was very respectful and appreciative of him carrying the heavy radio pack on his back. Grasso didn't mind; he had broad shoulders. He was just grateful that he had in DuBose an officer and a gentleman. DuBose was a good man to work for, Grasso thought that night. The next morning he would have to follow the lieutenant wherever he would lead. Although he didn't know where that would be, Grasso had a sense that the following day would be the most dan-

Tucked into the Alluvial Folds

gerous of all the assignments he had ever been given as a member of the Bloody Bucket. DuBose was part of the regiment's reconnaissance team. He would be ahead of the pack, scouting enemy positions and relaying the information back to the regiment. For Grasso the night of November 1 was a moment of reckoning. He had come to terms with his mortality.[28]

For Sgt. Jack Farrell, this was what he had signed up for two years before on that seemingly distant November morning in Boston at the red brick U.S. Army recruitment office across the street from the U.S. Marines enlistment center. He had been shipped overseas and assigned to the Twenty-Eighth Division as a replacement for a little over a month. For him, like for many others encamped that night, the looming U.S. offensive would be the first major encounter with an enemy in their young lives. Unlike many of his army colleagues, Jack had spent a long time in five different training camps in the United States. Whereas the custom was to put an infantryman through seventeen weeks of training before shipping him overseas, Jack had received nearly ninety weeks. In the process he was promoted five times—two levels of private, one specialist, one corporal—and was commissioned a sergeant before being assigned to the frontline in the Hürtgen Forest. That meant that at age twenty-two he was telling men five to twelve years his senior what to do. On this night, the eve of the battle, Sgt. Farrell headed a squad of eight men. In the group were:

Pvt. Otto Peterson of Boy River, Minnesota was the youngest of the group, having convinced his mother to sign papers that allowed him to join the army at age seventeen. Otto was anxious to join for two reasons. First, an army recruiter had convinced him that the United States badly needed young men like him if it was going to win the war. Second, Otto wanted to follow in the footsteps of an older brother, Dale, whom he tried to emulate in almost every aspect of life. Dale was at the time serving in the Pacific.

Pfc. Robert Wiginton, thirty-two. For ten years following his high school graduation, he had waited patiently for a break. It was the height of the Great Depression. And then, like pennies from heaven, three fell his way: a job as a banker after toiling for a decade in customer assistance at a hardware store; a marriage to a beautiful woman; and the purchase of a house, the day before his draft notice arrived in his mailbox. The house was one of the things on his mind when he wrote his sister, Helen, and two other family members for the last time. In a letter dated October 28, 1944, Robert raved about home-ownership. "I know you will be happy when you can have a home of your own," he wrote. "It makes lots of difference when one owns their home. You take much more interest in it and you feel like what you do is worthwhile."

Pfc. Waverly Lane had been working as an airplane mechanic at the Naval Air Station in South Norfolk, Virginia, when Uncle Sam came calling. Even though the Lanes had already given three of their boys, Waverly's older brothers, to the war, the U.S. Army drafted a fourth Lane brother shortly after his twenty-first birthday.

Pfc. Carl Dewitt Sanders, thirty-four. U.S. enlistment had reached nearly 9.3 million in 1943, but the army needed more bodies. In the fall of that year, a big brown envelope arrived at Carl's home in Hawkinsville, Georgia. The navy and army had each called up two of Carl's younger brothers. As the last of the Sanders's children to remain at home, the responsibility of caring for their ailing dad, Thomas, fell on Dewitt—the name that everyone called him by. Dewitt had little choice but to report for duty. Thomas died a couple of months later on New Year's Day, 1944.

Pfc. Carl Harbison, twenty-nine. Carl's draft notice came as a surprise. He was married with three small children. He was also caring for two infirm parents. Every day he commuted fifteen miles from Xenia, Ohio, to his job as a machinist at General Motors Frigidaire Division in Dayton. But the government had began tapping into its married-with-children Selective Service pool. Three days after Christmas, 1943, Carl reported to boot camp.

Pvt. Leonard Greenway, twenty. He also had an older brother in the army. He too felt the call to enlist. The middle son of Dutch and Irish immigrants, Leonard and his family had established residence in Philadelphia.

Cpl. Edward Jones Jr., twenty-six. Jones worked in the local farms and quarries near the Vermont-New York stateline. He was also a hunter and fisherman, and single. Jones was part of a young crowd that guessed correctly that the United States would soon be drawn into the global conflict. Along with fifty other young men, Jones walked into the local U.S. Army office in Rutland, Vermont, one day in March 1941 to enlist. Nine months later Pearl Harbor was bombed.

The squad was part of Company A of the 1st Battalion of the 112th Regiment of the 28th Infantry Division. Also in Company A were Pvt. Joseph Merlock of Dorothy, New Jersey; Pvt. Michael Loncar of Weirton, West Virginia; Pvt. Mark Wilson of Hampton, Tennessee; and Pvt. Sydney Weaver of Spirit Lake, Iowa. Sydney's hope of sleeping in a house with a furnace in the room for a few nights was quickly dashed. In his October 31 letter home, he expressed worry about having to don a gas mask while he slept, to keep from breathing the smoke from the fire, because of chimney issues. Instead he had to curl up under a blanket and poncho in a foxhole or two-man pup tent to stay dry under a yellow-gashed fir forest. It rained steadily all night. All three battalions of the 112th Regiment had to rough it out in the woods the night of November 1. To its left as it faced the forest was the 109th Regiment, and to its right the 110th Regiment. Ten thousand infantrymen in all were camped out behind a two-mile stretch of country road that connected three forest villages: Hürtgen in the north, Germeter in the middle, and Simonskall in the south.

The road—called Bahnof 399 today—is a quiet two-lane, tree-lined country highway. On November 2, 1944, it was the bomb-cratered launching point for the Battle of All Souls Day. On the Christian calendar it is designated as a holy day: a time for the religious faithful around the world to commemorate their dead. Unbeknownst to many of the young men on both sides of the frontline on that morning, their names would soon be registered in that necrology.

# 9

## Flashes of Fire Danced like Distant Lightning

> The cold passed reluctantly from the earth, and the retiring
> fogs revealed an army stretched out on the hills, resting.
> As the landscape changed from brown to green, the army
> awakened, and began to tremble with eagerness.
>
> —*The Red Badge of Courage*

MILITARY ORGANIZATIONAL STRUCTURE IN WORLD WAR II

1st Army (Gen. Courtney Hodges)

5th Corps (Lt. Gen. Leonard Gerow)

28th Infantry Division (Maj. Gen. Norman Cota)

    109th Regiment (Col. Daniel Strickler, approx. 3,000 troops)

    110th Regiment (Col. Ted Seely, approx. 3,000 troops)

    112th Regiment (Col. Carl Peterson, approx. 3,000 troops)

Each regiment is comprised of 3 battalions: 1st, 2nd, 3rd (1,000 troops per battalion)

Each battalion is comprised of 3 companies: A, B, C, D, etc. (250 troops per company)

    1st Battalion included Companies A, B, C, D (A, B, and C were rifle companies; D was a heavy weapons company)

    2nd Battalion included Companies E, F, G, H (E, F, and G were rifle companies; H was a heavy weapons company)

3rd Battalion included Companies I, K, L, M (I, K, and L were rifle companies; M was a heavy weapons company)

Each company is comprised of 3 platoons (80–100 troops per platoon)

Each Platoon is comprised of 2+ squads (40–50 troops per squad)

The army doesn't have a J Company. Reasons vary, from superstition (there was a time when J companies suffered more casualties than others) to the possibility of mistaking I and J, since the letters look similar.

The November offensive was to involve four armies—First, Third, Eighth, and Ninth—representing a dozen divisions.[1] The sheer numbers alone would have been a terrifying sight: more than one hundred thousand fully armed soldiers, a dizzying armada of tanks, a seemingly unending wall of cannons, and tens of thousands of warplanes filling the skies. But, across the entire western front, spanning more than 150 miles, the First Army's Twenty-Eighth Infantry Division was the only Allied unit to show up on the morning of November 2—about ten thousand soldiers with a backup brigade of tanks and cannons.

Why didn't the rest show up? It was not a good day for war. The air was chilly and dank. Soldiers were shivering, their will to fight greatly impaired. Visibility was poor, which made it dangerous to fly and increased the risk not only of planes crashing but also of bombs being dropped on one's own army. As it turned out, all of the other generals postponed their battle plans for days, including Gen. George S. Patton, who seemed to be the most impatient of the lot; he was in a race to reach the Rhine before anyone else. Still, army records show that Patton held back until November 8 before launching an attack, while the other armies followed a week later.[2]

Sunrise was at 7:28 a.m. on November 2, though no one could see the sky. The thick, low-hanging cloud covering that lingered after a wearisome night of rain blocked out the sun. Artillerymen, thousands of yards behind the frontline, were busy hauling heavy ammunition and piling them on the liquid mud next to cannons. Tilted at thirty-to forty-five-degree angles toward the sky, the batteries were lined up alongside one another. On a different day at a different time, the colors would have made for a perfect abstract painting, gray and brown dominating the dingy black of cannon muzzles and the forest interior. Elsewhere in the subterranean land of dugouts, trenches, and foxholes, the Twenty-Eighth was getting ready for battle. GIs were chowing down on hot breakfasts, gulping coffee made of artificial beans, stretching their arms and legs, which were aching from their cramped sleeping quarters, tightening their bootlaces and checking the safety locks, bolt handles. and magazine chambers of their firearms. For some, the question must have crossed their minds: Were the bacon and eggs on their metal plates that morning the equivalent of a condemned man's last meal? To distract themselves, some engaged in card games, idle banter, and prayer. It was a good way to avoid dwelling on the emotion of the moment, which was an uneasy blend of fear and apprehension. The young men realized they were preparing for a level of stress they had never experienced before. At least for some of them—particularly the recent replacements— homework, final exams, and scoldings from angry parents were the worst hardships they had suffered.

At 8:00 a.m. sharp thunder roared. It didn't come from the sky; instead the noise emanated from the U.S. Army—blasts of forty- and ninety-five-pound cylinders propelled at near sound barrier-breaking speeds out of cannons. The Americans were shelling German defense positions in the forest. The deafening sounds and nail-polish-like smell of burning cordite, from the 105 mm and 155 mm rounds filled the moist mountain air. White phosphorus smoke ascended slowly, as if rising out of chimney tops, toward the drifting clouds. Farther away, where forest and sky penciled a thin gray line across the horizon, flashes of fire danced like distant lightning as shells exploded. After an hour of relentless pounding, totaling 11,313 rounds, the guns fell silent.[3]

The infantrymen of both armies now prepared for battle. The 28th Division lined up in trenches along a mostly straight road with two forty-five-degree bends about a mile apart. The thoroughfare connected three villages: Hürtgen on the north, Germeter in the middle,

Flashes of Fire

Fig. 8. The jump-off point of the attack by the Twenty-Eighth Infantry Division on Vossenack on November 2, 1944. National Archives and Records Administration/U.S. Army.

and Lamersdorf on the south. The 109th Regiment of the U.S. Army positioned itself on the north side, facing the Hürtgen village. The 112th lined up in the middle, huddled behind the barns and houses in Germeter. To the right of the 112th, looking toward the German defense line, the 110th Regiment faced a row of well-camouflaged pillboxes near the village of Simonskall.

At 9:00 a.m. the 109th Regiment emerged from their muddy trenches on the northern edge of the salient and scurried forward, glancing both at their feet for enemy mines and straight ahead for machine gun nests masked by the woods. After traveling approximately three hundred yards, they moved squarely into the rifle range of the German Army.[4] For much of the way from there on, the regiment crawled on its belly, shivering helplessly in the near-freezing cold. Just two months before, they had moved in triumphant fashion from Paris to the French border at a clip of twenty-seven miles a day. The Hürtgen Forest was not the French countryside. It would take the 109th three days to move the equivalent of ten football fields, or a mere thousand yards.

On the southern end of the battlefront—the division's right flank—thousands more GIs, belonging to the 110th Regiment, waited in their foxholes. Unbeknownst to them, at the ready was a more formidable force: a German defense unwilling to give up as much as a yard. The regiment was mowed down "singly, in groups and by the platoons" as soon as their crouching figures emerged from their hiding holes; by day's end they had gained no ground.[5] Riflemen have one of the most dangerous jobs in the army; often they must get close enough to see the enemy before taking their shots. In comparison, the position of an artilleryman is, arguably, a safer assignment. They get to launch their mortar and artillery shells from thousands of yards behind enemy lines. In that sense 1st Lt. Frank DuBose and Pvt. Anthony Grasso were lucky; they were artillerymen assigned to the Cannon Company of the 112th. But, in a sense, their jobs were more dangerous than a rifleman's. Riflemen are typically ordered to attack after the cannons bombard a target area. As part of the Cannon company's reconnaissance team, DuBose and Grasso had to get to the target area long before the riflemen. The assignment

Flashes of Fire

required the two to sneak up close to German defensive lines, discern their positions, triangulate their coordinates with the aid of a compass, and radio them back by telephone to the command posts and bomb-launching teams more than a mile behind them. Grasso would strap the communication apparatus to his shoulder; the rectangular thirty-nine-pound Motorola pack covered his entire back down to his waist. An antenna stuck out from the radio transceiver two feet above his head, and a telephone was attached to the battery pack with a cord. Grasso would turn his back to DuBose whenever the lieutenant indicated he wanted to transmit a message to the cannon cockers. When he spoke, the transmission of his voice triggered static electricity and created a scratchy noise that made both men nervous. Sometimes they wondered if the Germans could hear them. It was also incumbent on DuBose and Grasso to remain out of the binocular vision of snipers, who were hidden in treetops and perched on other lookout points. The field-gray uniforms of the German Army blended nicely into the checkerboard fields of the Hürtgenwald. Thus, it was difficult to see them from afar. But both men were aware that the Germans were equipped with state-of-the art lens technology designed by the hundred-year-old Carl Zeiss German manufacturing company. So, the closer they got, the greater the danger of looming into the scope of the enemy's lenses.

The task of these two men on the morning of November 2 was even more difficult than usual, and it required them to take a few risks. The division hadn't done much prebattle reconnaissance, partly due to bad weather and also time limitations.[6] As a result DuBose and Grasso were in a hurry to ascertain enemy positions for their cannon unit. Under the battle plan for the day, a group of men from the 112th Regiment was to start its attack at noon from a dangerous point in the battlefield. That group—Company B of the 1st Battalion— would have to race across a wide open field of yellow grass toward a copse of pine and fir trees about four hundred yards away. If German soldiers were entrenched in there, the Americans could be slaughtered. The 109th Regiment had already experienced something similar, shortly after it commenced its attack at 9:00 a.m.: it unwittingly ran right into a German defense line, partly because of little prior reconnaissance. Grasso and DuBose were charged with the responsibility of preventing elements of the 112th from similar fates; they needed to find out whether there were German soldiers in the cluster of trees up ahead. To do so, however, required them to run right out into the open field from where they could get a closer look. With little hesitation, DuBose ran, and Grasso followed. At a certain point, the lieutenant thought he saw some Germans, so he stopped and reached for the telephone on Grasso's back. Grasso turned his back to DuBose, and, just at that moment, an artillery shell landed near the two men. The blast catapulted Grasso about thirty feet in the air, as if he was an action figured tossed by an angry child. The sound was deafening. All went blank. When Grasso hit the ground it looked and sounded to him as though he were peering up from underwater in a swimming pool. Time came to a stop: the faces of the people above him were blurry and ghostlike, their voices muffled. A medic applied some sulphur powder to a wound on top of Grasso's head, which was bleeding badly; a piece of shrapnel had lodged itself in his scalp. Grasso felt the warm blood run down his ear and the side of his neck as he lay on the ground. The best that the medic could do was to hope that the sulphur would prevent the wound from becoming infected. Grasso's body throbbed from falling thirty feet. The pain was so intense that he slipped into unconsciousness.

The bomb had also hit the lieutenant. He too was hurled off his feet and had fallen some distance away. The medic ran to tend to DuBose next.[7] It was mid-morning by this time. The 112th Cannon Company was to provide supporting fires from positions in the woods some two thousand yards west of Germeter. The commanders of the 112th Regiment, ensconced in a captured German pillbox a few hundred yards behind Germeter and Cannon Company more than a thousand yards further back, lost communications with the two men and would not know whether the cluster of trees in the middle of the open field was hiding a squadron of German fighters until noon that day, when a good many of the men of Company B of the 112th Regiment were mowed down as they ran through the yellow field toward the trees.

Charles B. MacDonald, who was charged by the U.S. Army to provide some of the first accounts of scenes from the battle, wrote, "The 112th Cannon Company was to provide supporting fires from positions in the woods some 2,000 yards west of Germeter. . . . No preparatory artillery barrage preceded the men of Company B as they passed through the Richelskaul defenses shortly after noon in a column of platoons. . . . As the first platoon advanced towards the trail, it was fired upon from woods in the vicinity of the trail and pinned to the ground by intense fire from small arms and entrenched automatic weapons."[8] In another report Maj. Richard S. Dana, who was with the 112th Regiment, explained that "this attack failed because the 1st Battalion ran into strong German positions heavily defended with automatic weapons. The battalion was chewed up somewhat and the third battalion was substituted that night to carry out the same mission the next day."[9]

Meanwhile, the 110th Regiment—which launched its attack at noon—was struggling in its embattled trenches about a half a mile to the south. It, too, had a poor notion of where the enemy was. Its progress at the end of the day: zero yards.

THE AMERICANS ENJOYED AIR SUPERIORITY OVER THE GERmans, but on November 2 that advantage was nullified by bad weather. About twenty-five miles west of the Hürtgen Forest, in Verviers, Belgium, a squadron of fighter planes and bombers were lined up on the tarmac as Army Air Corps pilots in their thick leather bomber jackets and mechanics in their grease-stained overalls stood at the ready all morning, waiting for the clouds to lift. The aircraft stretched across an open cornfield: the 365th, 366th, 368th, 370th, and 474th Fighter Groups, as well as the 422nd Night Fighting Unit. It was a daunting assemblage: 180 planes in total, with varying capabilities. The P-47s were equipped with machine guns onboard and could carry 2,700 pounds of bombs. The P-38s, made by Lockheed, were known for their deadly accuracy, because both their cannon and machine guns were mounted in the nose section, making it much easier for a pilot-gunner to take aim; it could also drop canisters of napalm. The P-61s could fly in the dark with the aid of radar, a relatively new technology at the time, and they required a three-man crew: pilot, gunner, and radar operator. All were grounded because of the weather. In the afternoon, after some of the mist had burned off, the U.S. air command sent just a few of their planes—12 P-38s—on a mission to bomb Bergstein, a ridge in the Hürtgen Forest and a site where some heavy German artillery launchers had been spotted. The mission was accomplished, but visibility was so low that the U.S. planes also mistakenly bombed a U.S. artillery position nearby, causing two dozen casualties. Under clearer skies the pilot may have noticed that he was flying over Allied-occupied land instead of enemy territory.[10]

All in all, November 2 wasn't a good day for the 28th Infantry Division in the Hürtgen Forest. The exception was the 2nd Battalion of the 112th Regiment: its mission that day was to take Vossenack, a town that sat about a half a mile up a gradual slope from Germeter and the point of departure for the battalion. The distance was relatively short, but the battle commanders expected some heavy resistance from the Germans because it stood as the gateway to a town that the Americans wanted. That town was Schmidt. A strategically located road ran through it, and, by controlling the town, and the road along with it, the Allies would be able to deliver ammunition, medicine, food, and other supplies to its troops as they pushed further into Germany. At an elevation of about 1,400 feet, Schmidt sat two hills away from Germeter, and Vossenack was the portal to Schmidt.

The Germans were no match for the Americans on this particular day. Vossenack was in the Hürtgen Forest, but it sat on a wide-open plateau with not a single tree. The only place for German defenders to hide were in houses, and the houses were clearly visible from a half mile away. They lay neatly on each side of the town's only main road, more or less in the same layout of the old Wild West frontier dwellings. There were about 150 Germans defending the town, and the Americans were coming at it with a force of about 1,000 men, led by approximately ten tanks. Still, Vossenack wasn't easy to take.[11] Two U.S. Sherman tanks ran over its own mines placed near the town's entry points by U.S. troops from the Ninth Infantry Division as they were being driven out of Vossenack by the Germans a week before. Both tanks were disabled.

Fig. 9. Completion of the attack by the Twenty-Eighth Infantry Division on Vossenack on November 2, 1944. National Archives and Records Administration/U.S. Army.

The battalion also had to deal with snipers, for whom picking off GIs that morning as they marched into Vossenack in large numbers must have been like target practice. One particular sniper was perched in a house that afforded him "good fields of fire," wrote 1st Lt. Eldeen Kaufman, a member of the 112th Regiment, who was part of the attack; he was able to stop a whole platoon in its tracks with just a burst of fire from his automatic weapon—anyone who moved he killed or wounded seriously. He had already caused four casualties. Luckily two tanks rolled by, and Kaufman managed to run behind one of them, using it as a shield. He then instructed the tank operator to fire a couple of rounds at the building the sniper was in, which enabled the lieutenant and a few of his men to enter the building, where they found nine Germans inside. The Americans killed two German officers and took the rest prisoners. It isn't known whether the sniper lived or died.[12]

As it entered the town, the Second Battalion systematically proceeded from one end of the main street down to the other, checking the rooms and cellars of each house along the way—a column on each side, accompanied by tanks in the middle. The sight was overwhelming. As they passed each house, German soldiers emerged from their hiding places, their uniforms unbuttoned at the collar and their hands over their heads.

In Sankt Josef Kirche the battle ensued, with German soldiers firing from the choir loft as the Americans entered the church (bullet holes are still visible today). Toward the middle of town, the Americans hit the jackpot; they had stumbled upon the command post of the German defense at Vossenack. It didn't take very long for Oberleutnant Venemmer, battalion commander of the Wehrmacht, to emerge from the building to give himself up. The Americans had captured the man who knew exactly where his army was hiding in town. All 1st Lt. Eldeen Kauffman of the 112th Regiment had to do was stick a .45 revolver in Venemmer's stomach, and the German showed the Americans on a map where his men were. As 1st Lt. James Condon, who was part of the invading unit on that day, would say in an interview about a month after the battle, Venemmer also warned his U.S. captors that "one of his other compa-

Flashes of Fire

nies had the mission of retaking the town, and that we could expect a counter-attack."[13]

By midafternoon on the first day of the Battle of All Souls Day, Vossenack was in American hands. The 2nd Battalion did suffer a few casualties, most of which involved stepping on mines and booby traps. But, unlike its two sister battalions, it had achieved its objective. After a full day of fighting, as the sun slipped behind the Eifel Mountains and temperatures fell to near-freezing, the 2nd Battalion crew carved two-man foxholes in the wet dirt on the eastern perimeter of the town and settled in for the night. Little did the men know that the decision to place the foxholes there was ill conceived; the officer who issued the order was either uninformed or had picked it without much forethought. It isn't known whether the decision came from the regimental or divisional level, but, wherever it came from, the battalion would suffer greatly over the next ninety hours because of it. The company that would take the biggest brunt of the placement of GIs to defend Vossenack was the 2nd Battalion's Company G, the group to which 1st Lt. Julian Farrior belonged. He had learned how to write home while curled up in foxholes over the months of combat. In fact, his letter writing had become almost a daily routine. But on this night Julian didn't write home. He and dozens of men in his unit were directly under the gaze of the Germans, who were perched on a ridge in the village of Bergstein, overlooking their foxholes from less than a mile away. In the pitch-black Eifel night, a lantern, the flick of a lighter, or even the burning end of a cigarette would be an invitation for an artillery barrage. The Germans were ready with an arsenal of their own.[14]

On this first day of battle, troops F and G had only suffered minor casualties, but their luck soon turned.

# 10

## I Felt Like a Little Napoleon

It was of no use to batter themselves against the granite.
And from this consciousness that they had attempted to
conquer an unconquerable thing there seemed to arise a
feeling that they had been betrayed.

—*The Red Badge of Courage*

Earlier in the day, FM Walter Model had gathered a group of German officers to walk through a mock battle against the Americans in the Hürtgen Forest. The group included leaders of the 89th Infantry Division and the 116th Panzer Division, which were already positioned in the forest. Leaders of a third division—the 275th Volksgrenadier—were also participants. Partway through the war game, a messenger stepped into the room to inform the group that the 28th U.S. Infantry Division had commenced an attack on the German Army in the Hürtgen Forest. The scenario in their diorama had moved from the realm of the hypothetical to the real. Model didn't seem alarmed by the news; after all, he had just recently repelled the 9th U.S. Infantry Division after a two-week engagement in October. He knew the United States would be back again, launching another assault. Maintaining his composure, Model ordered his commanders to stay and finish the game. In effect, the war game had turned into a game plan against the 28th. After the generals had devised it, Model made a slight alteration to the German deployment: instead of having the 275th relieve the 89th, he ordered the former to join

the latter in the Hürtgen Forest. Model's generals and commanders, who had been sequestered in Shlenderhan, a nearby medieval-
era castle, were just a half-hour jeep ride away. Since there was no
activity elsewhere on the Siegfried Line, the field marshal could
spare the additional troops to help shore up the Hürtgen defense
line. One of the war-game participants, Maj. Gen. Rudolf Von Gersdorff, explained in a postwar interview that the forest was important to the Germans for three reasons. First, an essential road—for
the transportation of troops and supplies—ran through it. Second,
it held some of the highest points in the area, including the villages
of Vossenack, Schmidt, Hurtgen, and Bergstein, and whoever occu-
pies the high ground in battle holds an advantage over its opponent.
And, third, by protecting the forest the Germans also kept the Americans away from two of its major dams, the Schwammenaul and the
Urfttalsperre, which supplied water to numerous cities and towns
in the area, including the large industrial German city of Cologne.[1]
There was yet a fourth reason: the Germany Army was planning
to use the forest as an assembly area for some of its troops prior to
the upcoming Battle of the Bulge. As a result they were prepared to
defend the forest, however bitter an engagement that would require.
For Hitler the Bulge was a do-or-die fight; on it would depend the
fate of the Third Reich. The Hürtgen Forest, which was just thirty
miles up the road, loomed large in what would ultimately prove to
be the German Army's final conflict.

NOVEMBER 3, 1944: DAY TWO OF THE ALL SOULS DAY BAT-
tle. The weather was no different than day one. The temperature was
near freezing. A cold steady drizzle that at times looked like snow-
flakes reminded the troops of winter's approach. Their uniforms felt
heavier than the day before, as mud and moisture soaked into the
wool of their overcoats, following a full day of combat. "There wasn't
any part of me that wasn't cold, wet or damp," recalled Albert W.
Burghardt, a sergeant who fought in that battle. "The damp part was
having the hell scared out of me."[2] The wetness could have been from
your own blood, but without visually checking it was hard to tell.

   Due to intense German resistance the day prior, U.S. battle commanders searched for a safer route for their units to advance, especially the 1st and 3rd Battalions of the 112th Regiment. Both were stymied that first day in their objectives, which were to take the towns of Kommerscheidt and Schmidt. Kommerscheidt sat on the southern side of a steep gully from Vossenack; a shallow river called the Kall meandered along the mud and rock at the bottom of the canyon. About a thousand yards farther south from Kommerscheidt, up a slight incline, lay Schmidt. Instead of making the units brave an open field—which had turned out to be disastrous for the Americans the day before—battle planners found a more discreet path around the exposed area. Under the revised route, the 1st and 3rd Battalions would pass through or near the towns of Germeter and Vossenack, both of which were in friendly hands.

The plan worked. Day two was relatively easier than day one. For much of it members of the 1st and 3rd Battalions followed a fleet of armored vehicles from the 707th Tank Battalion. With the tanks firing at German hideouts along the three-mile trek, the Americans had little to worry about. After putting up feeble resistance, German defenders scrambled for safety. Some surrendered. Two of them— one tall and one short—even gave a few U.S. servicemen a good chuckle. "They looked like Mutt and Jeff," one of the men in Company C of the 1st Battalion was reported as saying.[3]

When the two battalions filed past Vossenack and started their descent down a steep slope, the tanks stayed behind, leaving the infantrymen on their own. At first they received light artillery, followed by heavier shelling, which forced them to seek shelter behind boulders in the wooded ravine. Still, the units made good progress. The Third Battalion, which led the way, moved through the town of Kommerscheidt with almost no resistance and reached the neighboring town of Schmidt shortly after noon. Its arrival caught a number of German soldiers by surprise; some were finishing their noon meal and others were riding bicycles, apparently oblivious to the movement of hundreds of American troops through the valley. After the Germans surrendered to the Americans, the Third Battalion hastily attempted to set up a perimeter around Schmidt before darkness fell. The men were hungry, exhausted, and suffering from

Like a Little Napoleon

lack of sleep after two days of combat. The First Battalion, meanwhile, moved into the town of Kommerscheidt toward evening and dug foxholes and set up a defensive position.

The two top leaders of the 28th Infantry Division—Maj. Gen. Norman Cota in his command post ten miles away in the German town of Rott; and Brig. Gen. George Davis in Germeter—reflected on the performances of their three regiments on day two and congratulated each other. Outside of the town of Hürtgen, about one and a half miles north of Vossenack, the 109th was engaged in heavy but ineffective fighting against an enemy: the town was not along the route to the division's main objective, but in a battle two weeks earlier the U.S. 9th Infantry Division was attacked from the side by Germans coming from that direction. About one and a half miles west of Vossenack, in the town of Raffelsbrand, the 110th was locked in a futile battle for a second day against strongly held German positions. However, the division's third regiment—the 112th—brought a smile to both military leaders.[4] By nightfall on November 3, the three towns of Vossenack, Kommerscheidt, and Schmidt were securely in their hands. Mission accomplished; another victory by the Bloody Bucket.[5] As word spread that the 28th Infantry Division had achieved in just two days what its predecessor couldn't in two weeks, Cota would later say that he began to feel like "a little Napoleon"; his telephone buzzed with congratulatory messages from commanders across the front. If newspaper editors back home knew the excitement that night in Rott, west of the Hürtgen Forest, a few of the more aggressive ones may have been tempted to typeset a headline: "War in Europe Nears End."

Of course, they would have been wrong. Cota was about to be rudely knocked off his pedestal, by a deadly mistake made by planners of the All Souls Day Battle, a flaw that his superiors had failed to adequately address and one that Cota perhaps tried to ignore. With its air force crippled by bad weather and its artillery compromised by a well-dug-in enemy, the Twenty-Eighth's infantrymen badly needed its tanks. Unfortunately, there was only one road into Schmidt, and that road became impassable when the tanks were most needed.

That night, as they prepared to defend the towns of Schmidt and

Kommerscheidt against the Germans—who were rushing reinforcements to the forest following Model's meeting with his generals in Castle Schlenderhan—U.S. tanks were nowhere in sight. Capt. Jack Walker, one of the officers of the Third Battalion guarding Schmidt that night, was warned by his commander that as many as four thousand to five thousand Germans could attack the town that night.[6] The road, called the Kall Trail, was steep and narrow, with a cliff on one side and a jagged wall of rock on the other; it connected the three towns of Vossenack, Kommerscheidt, and Schmidt, meandering over rugged terrain for more than two miles. To get to Schmidt from Vossenack, tanks would have to inch down a slippery gorge on a path of loose dirt to a wooden bridge at the bottom of a valley that straddled a twelve-foot-wide river. On the other side of the ravine, they would have to climb up a hill along a set of switchbacks to Kommerscheidt. The rest of the journey from Kommerscheidt to Schmidt was not an issue; the road was wider and the incline more gradual. The challenge lay in negotiating the downhill from Vossenack to the bridge at bottom of the valley. The U.S. Sherman M-4 tanks weighed thirty-three tons apiece, slightly exceeding the thirty-ton maximum of the stone arch bridge. But the bigger problem was the width of the path: nine feet, the same as the tanks. That left no room for soil erosion on the shoulder of the road that pushed up against the edge of the precipice.

There was an additional problem. At one point down the slope from Vossenack to the river, a large boulder protruded sharply into the path, narrowing the passable area to seven feet. The trail was designed for horse-drawn carts, not Sherman tanks.[7] But the Americans were racing against the clock. It was almost a certainty that the Germans were sending a fleet of their dreaded Mach IVs and Mach Vs to retake Schmidt via routes much more suitable for tank travel. In almost every struggle between tank and human, even when the human is armed with a rifle, the human loses.

The tank company commander decided to test the Kall Trail before endangering the entire platoon of thirteen Shermans. About a quarter of the way down the commander, Capt. Bruce Hostrup began to feel nervous. His tank was slipping; the edge of the trail had started

Like a Little Napoleon

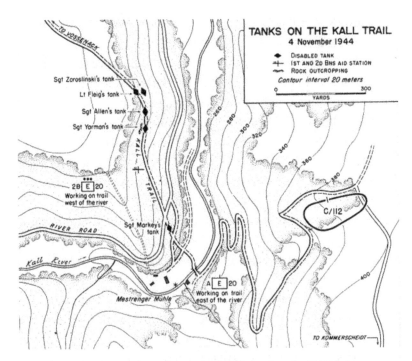

Fig. 10. Positions of the U.S. tanks immobilized on the Kall Trail on November 4, 1944. National Archives and Records Administration/U.S. Army.

to crumble under the weight of the armored vehicle. He backed up and informed his company that the army needed to send in his engineering crew to widen the road, which they would only be able to do by cutting through the granite rock outcrop on the inside of the road. It was 7:00 p.m.; the engineers would have to work through the night in total darkness. The moon, in its waning gibbous phase, would have been 89 percent visible that evening, were it not for the covering of thick dark clouds that hid it completely. And, to cut the rock, all the army engineers had were picks and shovels.[8]

While the engineers worked on widening the road, a supply train of M29 Weasels made its way to the infantrymen in Schmidt. The Weasels—wagons the size of compact cars that ran on tank-like tracks—were small enough to negotiate the Kall Trail. Starting at midnight it carried food, ammunition, and sixty anti-tank mines.[9] The men at Schmidt were cold, tired, and hungry; they had been on their feet since 7:30 a.m. When the Weasels arrived, they devoured their rations. But when it came time to bury the anti-tank mines in the ground, they found themselves too exhausted for the task. At 2:00 a.m., November 4, they decided to just leave them above ground and retire either to foxholes or the warm fireplaces inside the few remaining buildings left standing in town.

Back on the Kall Trail, dawn arrived, and the engineers sent word that they had completed the work of readying the road for tank use. The 707th Tank Battalion cranked its engines and began its slow descent down the slope. About six hundred yards from the bottom, the lead tank hit a mine. Working in the dark, the army engineers had failed to see it when they swept the road for explosives, and the tank lost its tracks, holding up three others behind it. In a hurry to get to Schmidt, the tank commanders decided to take a chance, securing the remaining tanks with a winch as they precariously dangled over the edge and tracked their way around the disabled tank. The winching worked, and the tanks were on their way to the rescue.

KOMMERSCHEIDT, THE NIGHT AND EARLY MORNING OF November 3–4. While the 3rd Battalion at Schmidt tried to get some rest, a thousand yards away the 1st Battalion worked through the night, setting up a perimeter defense. The task was a tall one. The U.S. Army generals knew the Germans were going to try to retake the town from them; that was the German Army's modus operandi. The tactic is called "counterattacking," similar to "counterpunching" in boxing, a ploy that made Muhammad Ali, Sugar Ray Robinson, and Gene Tunney the heavyweight champs they ultimately became. The idea in both boxing and armed warfare is the same: counter immediately after an attack or a punch, exploiting whatever weakness the enemy may show. "That's what the Germans always did. It was part of their battle strategy," Prof. Thomas G. Bradbeer likes to point out when studying the All Souls Day Battle at the U.S. Army Command and General Staff College in Fort Leavenworth, Kansas. "When you're rotating your soldiers and getting them warmed up (inside from out in the cold) following an attack, the Germans liked to catch them by surprise and kick the Americans out."[10] The military officers in Prof. Bradbeer's class also discuss a second weak-

Like a Little Napoleon

ness: Cota had wanted to overwhelm all three towns—Vossenack, Kommerscheidt, and Schmidt—by using almost all of his entire division in the attack, which would have been the equivalent of a knockout punch in boxing. When an opponent is knocked out, he isn't capable of counterattacking. Thus, instead of spreading his army thin—by having three battalions of the 109th Regiment attack the town of Hürtgen to the north, and three battalions of the 110th Regiment to the south—Cota wanted to have seven battalions go through Vossenack, Kommerscheidt, and Schmidt.[11] This was the object lesson the general had learned just a month before, when his 28th Division failed to take the town of Enfield and had to be withdrawn from the frontline and reconstituted in its aftermath. The scattered attack plan was also tried by the 9th Infantry Division just two weeks before, and it didn't work. "Cota says this is a bad plan, I don't want to do it," Bradbeer says. "Maj. Gen. Leonard Gerow and Gen. Courtney Hodges—Cota's two military superiors—say, 'Shut up and take orders. This is what you're doing to do. This is the plan.'"[12] Cota does as he's told, despite serious misgivings. "He knows it's foreboding; it's not well thought out."[13]

Like neighboring Vossenack and Schmidt, Kommerscheidt was a farming town built on top of one of the Hürtgen Forest's numerous hills. Hundreds of acres of trees had been cleared to create an open space of cultivable land, where local residents grew a variety of crops and produce—corn, wheat, barley, tomatoes, apples, and potatoes—in the rotating seasonal cycles of the highlands of western Germany. In the nexus of the growing fields of Kommerscheidt sat a community of about fifty homes. At an elevation of about 1,450 feet, the town commanded a panoramic view of plateaus, ravines, lakes, and hamlets nestled in the evergreen forest. Some 500 feet below, the Kall River snaked through the valley. On this night, however, the peaceful scenery and rustic air meant little to the Americans. They had just moved in with rifles and machine guns to occupy the town. Foxholes took precedence over fir trees, as the men hurriedly dug holes in the ground to protect themselves against the shelling that had already begun. Like Vossenack and Schmidt, Kommerscheidt was in plain sight of the enemy, who sat in the dark on ridges not very far away, equipped with Germany's signature 88-mm guns, which were so versatile they doubled as both anti-aircraft and anti-tank artillery. According to one soldier's calculation, the head-throbbing booms went off "at least a total of 20 minutes out of every hour."[14]

While the Americans in Kommerscheidt had to take cover from the 88s, they were also saddled with the task of preparing for a counterattack on the ground by the Wehrmacht's tank and infantry units. The 1st Battalion had to work quickly through the night; it had in essence been asked to build a fortress around Kommerscheidt with no tanks, little ammunition, and a good number of its soldiers missing. Company B had not accompanied Companies A and C into Kommerscheidt; it had walked right into a German machine gun nest the day before. Also, one of its platoon leaders hadn't returned from a forty-eight-hour leave in Paris, and his absence required an emergency personnel change that night. "They put me in charge of the 3rd platoon," said S/Sgt. Stephen Kertes in a postbattle interview. "I put the third squad under Sgt. John J. Farrell, astride the road."[15]

In Sergeant Farrell's squad were nine men: Pvt. Waverly Lane, Pvt. Carl H. Harbison, Cpl. Edward Jones, Pvt. Leonard Greenway, Pvt. Carl Sanders, Pvt. Robert Wiginton, Pvt. Otto Paterson, and one other sergeant (whose name is missing in the write-up of the interview on December 7, 1944). It is difficult to imagine what went through the twenty-two-year-old Boston College junior's head at the moment; this was most likely his first battlefield management assignment, and he must have felt a mixture of excitement and apprehension. His squad would be the first line of defense if the German counterattack were to come from the town of Schmidt, which was a probable scenario. It was known that the Germans had an armada of Panzer IV and Panzer V tanks. And word was spreading that it was preparing a blitzkrieg of four thousand to five thousand men. Sergeant Farrell and his squad would stand no chance. The American lines were so thin that a gap of as much as five hundred yards existed between the third and second platoons. For artillery, it had Company D—or, at least, a part of the company—which holed up with a few bazookas and mortar shells in the cellar of a bombed-out

Like a Little Napoleon

building back in town, while the rest of the company was engaged elsewhere about two miles away.

The U.S. Army isn't given to sugarcoating the nature of war. One of the first things soldiers are told after their cross-Atlantic voyage is that, in battle, it is better to be lucky than skilled. Farrell and company drew the short end of the stick: they were assigned to guard the only road from Schmidt into Kommerscheidt. If the German tank commanders were looking for solid ground for their heavy Mach Vs (which weighed sixty tons, almost twice as heavy as a U.S. Sherman), they would inevitably rumble down on the hard surface of a road.

Farrell's group wasn't the only unlucky one. Other members of Company A, including Pvts. Sydney Weaver, Michael Loncar, Mark Wilson, and Joseph Merlock, were nearby as well, guarding the same part of town from inside foxholes armed with basic M1 rifles. At least some of the men in the 1st Battalion must have been thinking: "Let's hope the 3rd Battalion can fend off the Germans."

"It was pretty nearly daylight by the time we were dug in," S/Sgt. Stephen Kertes said in his postbattle interview.[16]

# Like Caskets Tossed from the Deck

There was a lull in the noises of insects as if they
had bowed their beaks and were making a devotional
pause. Then, upon this stillness there suddenly broke a
tremendous clangor of sounds. The trees hushed and stood
motionless. Everything seems to be listening to the crackle
and clatter of and ear-shaking thunder. The chorus
pealed over the still earth.

— *The Red Badge of Courage*

**S**aturday, November 4, 1944. Just as the men of the First Battalion began to doze off in their foxholes after a full night of shoveling dirt on the headlands of Kommerscheidt, they were awakened by the sounds of German artillery. Shortly before 7:30 a.m., it started coming down on Schmidt, just up the road from where their helmeted heads peeked over the rims of their dugouts. The shelling startled its sleepy sister, the Third Battalion, the sharp whistle of flying metal piercing the stillness of the rustic morning. Starting from the south end of town, the bombardment steadily moved north like a hammer punching nails in a coffin. Panic set in among the Americans. With explosions going off all around him, a U.S. infantryman raced to a battalion's command post with news of a sighting of sixty German soldiers about a thousand yards away. Through a pair of field binoculars, the infantryman saw that they seemed to be readying themselves for an attack.[1] This was followed by another sighting of more Germans coming over a hill from a different angle. The Americans fired a few shots in their direction, and the Germans replied with the rapid fire of machine guns. It now appeared that the Americans were surrounded on three sides—front, left, and right. The riflemen of the Third Battalion looked anxiously to their sergeants and lieutenants for instructions. What were they to do now? All they received in response were blank stares. The battalion had tried calling for artillery support, but the radios weren't working. The vaunted Allied Air Alliance was of no help, as the skies were unsuitable for flying. Isolated on a hill, the Third Battalion had only one last line of defense: the mines they had hurriedly strewn on the ground in the wee hours of the morning.[2] While clearly visible, there was a chance they would be out of the periphery of the German optical periscopes. At around 9:00 a.m., five Panthers emerged from the woods; soon after, five more loomed into sight. The Americans watched, fingers crossed, to see whether the fleet of ten tanks clanking down the hill would hit any of the sixty anti-tank mines. But the maze proved to be more of a slalom course than a minefield. Despite their unwieldy size, the Mach IVs and Mach Vs deftly snaked around the explosives, not running over a single one.

In contrast, the story of the American tanks wasn't as pretty. As many as thirteen Shermans were on hand to rush to the defense of the Third Battalion in Schmidt. The afternoon before, to the accolades of the military brass, it claimed the division's prize: the crossroads town of Schmidt. Yet the armored cavalry was nowhere in sight to protect its spoil. In all probability the reason for its absence made a few German commanders chuckle over their breakfast. The Shermans had skidded down a path no tank should have traversed. Gen. Cota had failed to familiarize himself with the forest; he mistakenly thought that it was too dense for tank travel and that the Kall Trail—with some engineering—would be the only passable roadway. He was wrong on both counts, and he would have known that if only he had consulted with the commanders of the Ninth Infantry Division, who had just spent two weeks in the Hürtgen, albeit in a futile campaign. After hours of slip-sliding, five Sherman tanks assisting the Twenty-Eighth Division were left stranded at various points on

Fig. 11. The German counterattack on U.S. forces at Schmidt on November 4, 1944.
National Archives and Records Administration/U.S. Army.

the trail, blocking each other's way. One hung dangerously over the side of a mountain; only three, after being winched around a hairpin turn, managed to reach the town of Kommerscheidt. None, though, made it to Schmidt, leaving an entire U.S. battalion at the mercy of a twenty-Panther-led German Army (see fig. 10).

With such an overwhelming force, it didn't take long for the Germans to penetrate the U.S. battalion's defenses. By 9:00 a.m. it had cut off about a hundred men from the rest of their group, taking some as prisoners and killing others. From the scouting it did the night before, the Germans knew that the Americans had dug themselves in foxholes in a 360-circle defense around Schmidt. Armed with that knowledge, the tanks squeezed the perimeter on three sides, firing their M2HB machine guns and 75-mm and 88-mm guns into the foxholes, working methodically hole by hole. The sound alone of a blast was the equivalent of a blow to the head, wrote M. Bedford Davis, a Twenty-Eighth Infantry Division physician who tended to the wounded and dying at that battle, in his memoir. "The resulting concussion created momentary fogging in our heads and a headache," he described.[3] Unhinged, all three companies—I, K, and L—took to their heels. In their frenzy many didn't even bother to grab their weapons. They ran in all directions: some headed straight for the stone walls of bombed-out houses, while others leapt over hedges and fences or tumbled down hills. More than two hundred soldiers bolted in the wrong direction, right into the arms of the enemy.[4]

Pvt. Gerald Wipfli, a baby-faced twenty-three-year-old Wisconsin native with a disarming smile, was assigned to Company I, which was in the best position to flee. The other two companies—L and K—were positioned more squarely in the Germans' path, while Company I mostly faced an open field that sloped gently downhill toward Kommerscheidt, a town that was, at least for the time being, in U.S. hands. No Germans stood in their way. If there was anyone capable of making the dash, it was Private Wipfli. At 5 foot 7 inches and weighing 135 pounds, he was born to run. His platoon guide, S/Sgt. Lewis John Brady, handpicked him as a designated platoon runner. His duties consisted of relaying messages between the platoon and company headquarters, and the two qualifications for the job were speed and stamina. Tom Brady learned of Private Wipf-li's fleet feet from conversations about the war with his father, Staff Sergeant Brady. The assignments required covering distances of up to four miles each way. They also required smarts. "My dad used to say . . . (Wipfli) also had to be sharp enough to take verbal instruction then accurately relay them at the other end," Tom Brady said.[5]

A large number of soldiers from Company I fled, some after the company commander issued an order to withdraw, while others didn't even wait; they just took off. But there is no indication that Wipfi joined his panicked company-mates. When seventy-two of them regrouped in Kommerscheidt two hours later, he was not among them. Had he run, he may have survived. His name was listed among thirty-three other Company I members reported missing in Schmidt on November 4.[6]

By 11:00 a.m. the battalion's scramble for cover had turned into a full-scale stampede, and the Germans had reclaimed the north and south sections of town. By noon Schmidt in its entirety was theirs again, bringing to an end an American occupation that lasted less than a day. "They're throwing everything they've got at us" was a common refrain among GIs in flight, terror etched on their faces.[7] None of the higher-ups on the American side knew what was going on. Radio communications were sketchy. A single wire line—an SCR 300 radio—connecting the regimental leadership with units on the frontline worked fitfully. Word of a complete battalion breakdown in progress at Schmidt had reached neither the regimental nor divisional command posts. Gen. Cota was still basking in the afterglow of Napoleonic glory at his command post in Rott. Several miles closer to the front in Germeter, Lt. Col. Carl Peterson was getting anxious. He dispatched his chief executive officer to get a firsthand assessment, but he didn't get far. Word reached Peterson later that his regiment CEO was captured by the Germans on his way to Kommerscheidt, so Peterson headed to the scene himself. The assistant division commander Brig. Gen. Gerald Davis joined him a little later.[8]

Compared to Schmidt, the situation at Kommerscheidt looked a little brighter. Three U.S. tanks reached the town, and the officers of the Third Battalion managed to collar some of its fleeing men.

Like Caskets Tossed from the Deck

In total about two hundred men agreed to stay and join a reconstituted ragtag defense; they took their positions alongside the First Battalion.[9] For the first time in days the heavens cooperated, and the skies brightened enough for U.S. planes to spot enemy tanks on the ground. A regimental colonel and divisional general were on their way to the thick of the fight, to micromanage the defense of Kommerscheidt and oversee the deployment of a four-pronged attack of air, armor, infantry, and artillery against the enemy.

Having retaken Schmidt with relative ease, a confident German army was coming for Kommerscheidt. A phalanx of two hundred infantrymen from the 1056th German Regiment, led by eight Mach IVs, advanced on the town.[10] The scenario that was about to unfold was almost identical to one earlier that day in Schmidt: a fleet of German tanks and accompanying infantry coming at a lightly armed group of American soldiers crouched in foxholes with only the dirt around them as shields. There was only one difference at Kommerscheidt: between the riflemen and their German attackers were three feisty U.S. Sherman tanks eager to intervene.

One Sherman, driven by platoon leader Ray Fleig, rolled into action, firing at two Mach IVs and knocking out both of them. A second Sherman took care of another German Mach IV. Wasting little time, Fleig went after a fourth German tank. At first he used the wrong type of ammunition, but he quickly crawled over the turret for the right kind and managed a direct hit on the German tank, breaking off its gun tube. Three more rounds put the Mach IV out of commission, and the Germans scrambled from the flames as the tank burned. Just then a squadron of American P-47 fighter planes emerged from the billowy clouds and circled the battlefield. One dove daringly close to the ground, strafing and dropping two bombs on the vehicle. Together with a bazooka team, they set the fifth German fighting machine ablaze. The Germans then pulled back, their attempt to reclaim Kommerscheidt thwarted, at least for the day, by a courageous combination of forces by the Americans.[11]

For General Cota, November 4 was not a good day. The people to whom he was answerable weren't happy. At 1st Army headquarters in Roetgen, General Hodges fretted the loss of ground to the

Germans. "Things did not go very well," wrote Maj. William C. Sylvan, who kept a war diary for Hodges.[12] "The 3rd Battalion of the 112th counterattacked at ten o'clock, withdrew almost a mile to the vicinity of Kommerscheidt. . . . Our progress towards Schmidt was at nightfall only 300 yards."

The problems of the day were many, but their common root lay in the inundated Kall Trail, which had turned into a tank graveyard. That evening, following his meeting with the three generals, Cota delivered an ultimatum to his engineers: he wanted the tanks repaired or tossed over the ridge by daylight. To the tank battalion the request was the equivalent of a frontier soldier being asked to shoot his limping horse.[13] The tank mechanics went to work in an attempt to save them, but, after a furious effort, the engineers reconciled themselves with the inevitable: the tanks had to go. Like caskets tossed from the deck of a naval vessel into the deep, the tanks were shoved over the brink into the gorge.

Sunday, November 5, dawned gray and misty. It was the appointed day for the forward movement of the fair-headed Gen. Joe Collins's Seventh Corps toward the Rhine. It was also the underlying reason for all of the blood shed by General Cota's Twenty-Eighth Infantry Division. Gen. Joe Collins decided that the weather was still not good enough for his men to take on the enemy; there would be no launch of a Seventh Corps advance that day. No written records exist of how Cota felt when he learned of General Collins's decision to postpone his advance. What we do know is that the generals weren't done with Cota. General Gerow drove to his command quarters to have a talk, and he returned later in the day with General Hodges and General Collins to deliver further admonishment. Apparently there was a chasm between perspectives of the battle at the top level (among the generals) and on the ground (among the infantry): the one pressed aggressively to retake a wrested town while the other shivered in trenches, hoping to see another dawn.

Cota's men, meanwhile, continued to keep vigil in their watery trenches. A blast of cold air from the north descended just after dawn, deepening the chill among the masses huddled across the battlefield. Due to transportation difficulties, many of the Ameri-

Like Caskets Tossed from the Deck

cans were without overcoats and blankets; to stay warm they exerted themselves by digging deeper into their foxholes. From all appearances the German Army remained keen on taking back the town of Kommerscheidt, now defended by a patchwork assembly of men from the First and Third Batallions of the Twenty-Eighth Infantry Division that had grouped into a "covered wagon" deployment. Thanks to a reopened Kall Trail, five more Sherman tanks and nine tank destroyers wended their way through the gorge to the side of the Americans in Kommerscheidt. That day the U.S. infantry was able to force their Panzer attackers to retreat to their redoubt nine hundred yards up the hill in Schmidt. From there and from a nearby ridge, the Germans pounded the Americans with a seemingly ceaseless artillery stream.

An order early in the day by Cota to drive the Germans out of Schmidt was duly ignored, which reflected a disturbing disconnect between reality on the frontline and plans made with a map inside of the warm houses of the battle masters. From his beset command post in Kommerscheidt, Lieutenant Colonel Peterson sent a message back to Cota via a lieutenant after nightfall: his men were shell-shocked, the battalions disorganized, the tank destroyers lacking in aggression, and the armory not as strong as he would like. He would seek to defend Kommerscheidt, he said, but expectations of of retaking Schmidt were more measured.[14] At about 11:00 p.m. the messenger headed by jeep to Cota's quarters ten miles away. Harold Denny, a *New York Times* reporter, wrote this eyewitness account of the U.S.-German engagement that day in more glowing language:

> With American forces in Germany, Nov. 5—German troops have been ordered to hold on to the village of Schmidt, at the entrance to the Cologne plain, at all costs. Accordingly they fought again today with stubbornness and ferocity at most points on this cramped and bloody field.
>
> Tonight they still hold the burning ruins of this town, which is valuable now only for its situation and the roads that run eastward from it. The Germans also hold the high ground just south of the town and they also have direct-firing artillery on a ridge running from

Brandenburg to Bergstein and cutting into our troops from the rear. In no battle since St. Lo have our men been in a nastier position. . . .

But our forces made steady though limited progress all day and the fighting was decidedly in our favor. The best weather in weeks for air operations let our aircraft get into the battle all day long in strong force and with costly effect on the enemy's troops and tanks in the front line and his supplies and communications supporting his front here. Our pilots flew more than 100 sorties today over Schmidt and its vicinity and probably 150 more over areas not far behind the line.

From an observation post on high ground overlooking the battlefield, it was possible to see the devastating attack and our artillery. Schmidt, in the valley ahead, was hardly visible for the smoke of its burning houses and the thick white dust that lingered over each air-blast and shell burst. What one could see at Schmidt was only broken walls and naked chimneys and, in the foreground, the hulks of two burned-out German tanks.

Off to the left a few miles in another valley were other tall chimneys, about all that is left of towns and other hamlets. They scarred a landscape that is one of the most beautiful in the world and was at its best today in the bright sunlight.[15]

LATER THAT NIGHT THE MEN OF THE TWENTY-EIGHTH leaned on their rifles and shut their eyes with hopes of getting a few fitful moments of sleep. Awaiting them in the morning was another bruising day of war. Throughout the night they heard German tanks clanking high on a southeastern hill; following close behind were infantrymen silhouetted against the sky. "They were possibly picking up their dead and wounded," recalled S/Sgt. Stephen Kertes in a postbattle interview a month later. Then the litter crew of medics and morticians did something out of the ordinary. Perhaps it was because of the quiet of the night, which often blunts the edges of a war's brutality, or because of the tenderness in a man's heart when picking up a fallen friend, or maybe the Germans heard the ticking clock of victory over their foes in the foxholes. They sidled down the hill until "they got to within talking distance of our own positions and asked for the surrender of our men," Kertes recounted.[16]

Like Caskets Tossed from the Deck

The proposal was returned with a volley of small-arms fire into the sky, signaling an unambiguous "No." It was a defiant statement by a group of American infantrymen who were now positioned as the only shield between a determined German Army and a stranded U.S. regiment.

It was no longer a question on whose shoulders the battle rested. It was the infantry, the men in the foxholes, who bore the weight. Air support was virtually nonexistent. Tank support was sparse and timid, as Lieutenant Colonel Peterson noted in his message the evening before to General Cota, when he said he couldn't "fight tanks with an infantry."[17] For the Germans to come "within talking distance"—as close as twenty or thirty yards—must have been intimidating for the Americans; the proximity was an indication of how little the Germans were afraid of them. It may also have been a case of a chess player toying with his opponent just before checkmate.

MONDAY, NOVEMBER 6, 1944. THE GERMANS RETURNED the next day in overwhelming numbers. More than a dozen tanks accompanied by hundreds of infantrymen loomed over the partially lit morning skyline. The Germans liked predawn attacks because they were harder to spot by American pilots, who indisputably ruled the skies. Predawn movements were also not as easily detected by excellent U.S. field observers, who directed artillery and mortar battalions on German armory with alarming accuracy. That morning the Germans were unstoppable.

At first light the Panzers rumbled down the hill from Schmidt, firing their 88-mm long-nose guns at buildings and foxholes. Company A of the First Battalion took the brunt of the initial blitz. "Five German tanks had surrounded me," said Pfc. Carl Harbison, a thirty-year-old private with the third squad in Company A. "Five times they shot directly at my foxhole almost burying me. All I had was my rifle and it had been knocked to pieces. I was ready to give up when I turned around in my foxhole to find a German standing there pointing a gun right at me. I still can't understand why he didn't shoot."[18]

Seven others in his squad had been shot down in their tracks:

Fig. 12. The German counterattack on U.S. forces at Kommerscheidt on November 6, 1944. National Archives and Records Administration/U.S. Army.

Thirty-two-year-old Pvt. Richard Wiginton of Hamilton, Alabama;

Twenty-one-year-old Pvt. Leonard Greenway of Philadelphia;

Thirty-four-year-old Pvt. Carl Dewitt Sanders of Hawkinsville, Georgia;

Twenty-seven-year-old Cpl. Edward Jones of West Pawlett, Vermont;

Eighteen-year-old Otto Peterson of Boy River, Minnesota;

Thirty-five-year-old Sgt. Lemuel Herbert of Scranton, Pennsylvania; and

Twenty-two-year-old Sgt. John J. Farrell of Arlington, Massachusetts.[19]

Like many GIs killed in foxholes, Sgt. Farrell died from wounds to the face. Also dug in nearby—within yards of one another—were other members of Company A, among them

thirty-two-year-old Pvt. Sydney Weaver of Spirit Lake, Iowa;

twenty-three-year-old Pvt. Mark Wilson of Hampton, Tennessee;

twenty-three-year-old Pvt. Joseph Merlock of Dorothy, New Jersey; and

twenty-seven-year-old Pvt. Michael Loncar of Weirton, West Virginia.[20]

The Germans didn't kill everyone in Farrell's squad. In addition to Private 1st Class Harbison, they also took twenty-two-year-old Pfc. Waverly Lane prisoner.[21] According to men who have fought in war, the best chance of survival in foxholes during an attack is not by shooting at the enemy but running or getting as low as possible in the pit. S/Sgt. Sydney Kertes, who was also with Company A, scrambled for cover. As the Panzers clambered down the hill into Kommerscheidt, Kertes was fortunate enough to be holed up in one of the buildings, a bit further back from the foxholes rimming the town; he had time to run. "I was knocked down three times (from the force of the blasts) trying to get out," he said in a postbattle interview. "One tank moved up and down, firing point-blank into one of our squad areas." The other German tanks shelled buildings and set fire to them with tracers.[22] As the men fled to escape the flames, many were gunned down.

For the division the morning of Monday, November 6, marked the beginning of the end. That morning the U.S. fleet of tanks that had so gallantly come to the rescue of the infantry two days before failed to deliver an encore. A steady drumfire of German artillery beat down on the American war machinery and on the swashbuckling spirit of their operators. Just like that, nine Shermans were reduced to six and nine Wolverine tank destroyers to three. The can-do bravado of a couple of days before was all but gone. As the Panzers came into town on the morning of the sixth, "our tanks weren't up there to hold them," lamented S/Sgt. Eugene Holden in a postbattle interview. Where were they? Back behind the crest of a hill. Every so often they would make an appearance, fire, cover up, and duck back down. The tank crewmen said they were low on gas, but the fact was that the American Shermans were overmatched by the German Tigers by almost three to one. "This kept them from firing as much as we would have liked," said Sergeant Holden.[23] Later that afternoon regimental commander Lieutenant Colonel Peterson called off an effort dubbed "Task Force Ripple" to try to take back the town of Schmidt. TFR didn't have enough arms and supplies, and it lost two of its commanders—one killed, the other wounded—before even getting started. Its successor, Task Force Davis, which was cobbled together a day and a half later, was also aborted.[24]

With Schmidt retaken and Kommerscheidt about to be reclaimed, Vossenack represented the only remaining trophy for the Twenty-Eighth Division. But there also the enemy was banging at the gates; for four days the Germans lobbed exploding fire from the other side of the ridge with clockwork rhythm. A persistent freezing rain turned foxholes into feet-numbing wells. Virtually frozen in place, the men were reduced to eating and defecating while crouching in a cacaphony of artillery and mortar shelling. Rather than risk death, they tossed their excrement over the top along with tissue and handkerchiefs. It was preferable to a sniper's bullet or shrapnel in their backs.

As night fell and the men clung to their lives, two forces tugged

Like Caskets Tossed from the Deck

on the 28th Infantry, coming to a clash in the cellar of a bombed-out room where two U.S. commanders argued angrily, their voices echoing dangerously in a valley full of enemy ears. On the one side, the deputy division commander, Brigadier General Davis, pressed hard to effect the will of his bosses, which was a high-water order to retake Schmidt and hold Vossenack and Kommerscheidt. Equally vehement on the opposite side: the commanding officer of the 112th Regiment, Lt. Col. Carl Peterson, argued that the wills of his soldiers had reached their breaking point.

The next day the lieutenant colonel was inexplicably summoned to the division's headquarters in Rott. It took him nearly twenty-four hours to travel the ten-odd miles there and nothing short of a miracle to answer the summons of the general in his removed hideout. To get there Peterson had to speed through enemy lines, abandon his jeep while escaping a heavily armed German attack, hide in the leaves, ford an icy river, and stumble, barely conscious, into a swamp. Along the way Peterson was wounded twice by mortar rounds, once while crossing the Kall river; he was hit multiple times in the legs and lower abdomen, and his sciatic nerve was severed. But Peterson's night wasn't as bad as it was for his assistant, Pvt. Gustave Seiler, who was raked by machine-gun fire while striding alongside his regimental commander, essentially acting as a human shield for the lieutenant colonel. Unable to resuscitate Seiler, a crippled Peterson crawled on his knees toward his destination, eluding detection by the enemy at several points along the way. A group of friendlies found him exhausted in a field. For the final leg of his journey, Peterson was jeeped over a bumpy road and carried on a gurney into Cota's office.

In Rott, the general was surprised to see the lieutenant colonel. He hadn't called for him. Was the commander abandoning his regiment in Kommerscheidt? What was he doing in his boss's office? Peterson said that he had received a radioed message to report to Rott. Cota was nonplussed. For the lieutenant colonel, the face-to-face meeting in the privacy of the division commander's office was a rare opportunity. He seized the moment and gave Cota an eyewitness report of the pitiful state of affairs at the frontline. Staring down at a prone Peterson, Cota fainted. Hardscrabble fighting generals don't typically swoon; the unusual reaction triggered a range of conjecture, from a sudden low-blood-sugar diabetic attack (he suffered from the disease) to disbelief at the 180-degree turn the battle had taken.

It was, all and all, a bad day for both commanders. Peterson discovered that he was no longer needed on the battlefield; he had been replaced as commander of the 112th Regiment. As for Cota, he had just received a tongue-lashing from three angry generals: Gerow, Hodges, and Eisenhower, the supreme commander, who said, with typical understatement, "Well, Dutch, it looks like you got a bloody nose." Then came the dagger: "Some personnel changes" may be in order, he warned before leaving.[25] For the infantry the week was bloody on both sides. The Germans suffered casualties of three thousand, the Americans twice as many. Adding salt to their wounds, 1st Army commander General Hodges let it be known that he wasn't happy with the performance of the Twenty-Eighth Infantry Division. Clearly, Cota was the defeated general. If five days earlier he had felt like "a little Napoleon," this was his Waterloo.

A short while later, the relief that many had been hoping for arrived. It wasn't the drone of planes from above or the grinding armor of reinforcement troops, but an order from headquarters that the Twenty-Eighth Infantry Division was cleared to withdraw from the frontline. When a retreat is ordered, an army pulls back in an organized fashion: it typically sets up traps and mines behind them to keep the enemy from pursuing them, destroys radios and telephone equipment, disables tanks and vehicles, collects its weapons, blows up ammunition it can't take, and shreds battle plans. It also engages in an ostentatious display of shelling activity to conceal the withdrawal. The process is elaborate, but it must be done in a hurry to minimize further casualties. Retreats are when an army is most vulnerable.

The 2nd Battalion, which had been exposed to unrelenting enemy fire for four straight days on the bare slopes of Vossenack, was in such danger. Its battalion chief had suffered a nervous breakdown and had to be removed from the line. As the battalion packed up its gear to depart from the ridge, its commanding officers hastily called a meet-

Like Caskets Tossed from the Deck

ing to discuss a withdrawal plan. Instructions were to be quick; German troops, which had infiltrated a part of Vossenack, were already upon them. 1st. Lt. Julian Farrior and 1st Lt. James Condon were among the cos in attendance. The meeting began at 6:30 p.m.

Farrior was in a hurry. His company, which had numbered 180 men a week before, had been whittled to 19 able bodies. But the withdrawal coordinating commander was stuck on detail that evening. He listed a number of things he wanted: that the mortar crews remain in place, that the battalion forward observers also stay, and that he meet with tank and tank destroyer officers. The emergency instructional session should have taken less than an hour, but "all this seemed to take an ungodly long amount of time and all the company commanders were waiting for the word to go," Lieutenant Condon recounted in a postbattle interview the following month. Finally, at 10:00 p.m., the meeting was adjourned. The two officers—First Lieutenant Farrior and 1st Lt. James Condon—hurried back to their respective companies, Farrior ahead of Condon. Minutes later Condon saw a bright flash and heard a loud noise.[26] The retreating battalion withdrew from Vossenack to safer U.S. controlled territory more than a mile away. Farrior was never seen again In his final letter to an older brother, who, like him, was in the U.S. Army, and with whom he had grown up and confided his innermost thoughts, Farrior wrote:

Dear Edward,

I appreciate your long letter telling all about yourself and home so very very much. . . . If you have a job that will keep you back in the States and like it I certainly wouldn't worry about the monotony of it all. Furthermore I wouldn't let the lack of advancement worry me at all. . . . The business of combat is Hell and I sincerely hope that neither you nor Alan has to face it. I am not feeling sorry for myself when I say that because I have as much guts under fire as anybody else; but let no one ever kid you—any sane man is scared under fire and one never gets used to fighting. It gets progressively harder and harder to go into battle. . . . Don't ever let anyone ever romanticize combat to you. Only those who actually have been in it will ever

**Fig. 13.** 1st Lt. Julian and Grace Farrior in 1943.
Courtesy of the Stanley Farrior Family.

have the least conception of it. It cannot be properly described or pictured. I have lived underground for three months and the ground has certainly saved my life many times. I have seen enemy artillery drive men absolutely crazy and I was awfully shaky too for the lack of sleep and also concussion from big shells. Many times I've lain flat in the bottom of my foxhole wondering if the next artillery shell was coming in on top of me. All day shells landed just short and just over my foxhole and had covered me with dirt. I was shaking like a leaf and praying that I be spared. It certainly is a helpless feeling to hear the 500 and 1000 pounders whistle through the air and not know where they were going to land. I am sorry that I have taken up so much of this letter with battle experiences but the above is just part of a day's work up here in the frontlines.

I am glad that you had a chance to visit Grace and Wade Jr. . . . I know Grace is a wonderful little mother. She sends me pictures

Like Caskets Tossed from the Deck

regularly so that I can see Wade's growth. . . . Don't get too optimistic about this war; plenty of fighting action lies ahead.

Very Sincerely, Julian.[27]

Weeks later, in the presence of five military officers, Colonel Peterson was cleared of any wrongdoing. One of the officers—COS Charles H. Valentine—verified that there was indeed a message dispatched between 9:30 and 10:00 a.m. on November 7, 1944, "ordering Colonel Peterson to report back to Headquarters to give the complete situation (of the battle front.)" This cleared Peterson of any charges of abandoning his regiment.[28]

# 12

## If I Leave Now, Would It Be Desertion

---

In the clouded haze men became panic-stricken with
the thought that the regiment had lost its path, and was
proceeding in a perilous direction.

—*The Red Badge of Courage*

---

The case of *U.S. vs. Private Eddie Slovik* (36896415) of the Twenty-Eighth Infantry Division had been scheduled for November 3–4, 1944. But, because his unit was in combat in the Hürtgen Forest and witnesses were unavailable to testify, the trial was postponed to November 11, two days after the battered Bloody Bucket division was pulled from the frontline.

The trial was held in Roetgen, a German town under American occupation about ten miles behind the frontline, near the Belgian border. A makeshift courtroom had been set up at city hall, a stone-walled building where the local town folk queued up for food vouchers. In a separate room on the second floor sat a panel of nine judges.[1] One of them, Capt. Benedict B. Kimmelman, would later describe the building as "scarred," and the surroundings as grim. "It was a cold, gray day with snow off and on," he wrote.[2] All were staff officers with the Twenty-Eighth Infantry Division. Their main responsibility was to provide back-office support services to the men in battle, but on this day they were also functioning in the capacity of tribunal arbiters.[3]

Before them at two separate tables sat the prosecutor, Capt. John

I. Green, and the defendant, Pvt. Eddie Slovik, who was accompanied by his legal representative, Capt. Edward P. Woods. The trial didn't take long; though the army had set aside two days for arguments, the hearing was concluded in a little more than an hour and a half. Slovik's charge: violating the Fifty-Eighth Article of War—the absenting of oneself from his military unit with intent to avoid hazardous duty.[4] As a legal representative in a life-and-death matter, Woods was not an ideal choice. He was twenty-six years old and not a lawyer, although, to his credit, he had successfully represented clients in a number of previous court-martial cases.[5] For the purposes of this case he would suffice. Slovik had hatched his own defense strategy beforehand; all that was required under his scheme was a breathing body in the defense counsel's chair. Slovik would plead not guilty and then sit back and allow the prosecution to make its case of desertion, unchallenged.[6]

Unlike defendants in most cases, the defendant in this trial wanted to be found guilty. The reason: a conviction would send him to the stockade for the remainder of the war. The penalty for desertion was imprisonment or death. While capital punishment loomed as a possibility, it was a gamble that the defense was willing to take. Slovik figured that the odds were in favor of him receiving imprisonment, based on the statistic that the U.S. Army had not shot a deserter since the Civil War. In Slovik's mind defying the army to sentence him to death through a court proceeding was his only viable option; the frontline was almost certain death, and it was uncomfortable in the rain and the cold. Jail, in comparison, promised three square meals, a warm bed, and safety. It would be like crawling into the protective womb of Mother America, and it would ensure a safe berth back to the United States, where his wife awaited him. But Slovik's calculated risk was flawed on one front: the All Souls Day Battle. Neither the defendant nor his counsel had anticipated that the trial would coincide with the worst beating an American army would suffer at the hand of an enemy in Europe in World War II.

The trial began at 10:00 a.m. As his witnesses, the prosecutor brought out five soldiers—all members of the Bloody Bucket—straight from the frontline, in their tattered clothes, soiled with mud and blood. The prosecution set out to establish premediation on the part of the defendant. One of the witnesses, company commander Capt. Ralph Grotte, testified how on one day in early October Slovik was careful to ask him what constituted desertion. The defendant had separated himself from his division twice within a span of eight weeks: the first time in France in August, when he and fourteen other new "replacements" from U.S. training camps were reporting for duty with the Twenty-Eighth Division, which was was engaged in a firefight with the Germans at Elbeuf in the Falaise region. The second time was in October, when he caught up with the division outside of Rocherath, Belgium, but tried walking away two days later.

In his testimony Grotte gave the military court the following account.[7] He said Slovik wanted to know whether his failure to join the division in August was considered desertion. Grotte said he told Slovik he didn't know, but he'd check with a legal expert and get back to him. Grotte told the court that he got clarification and explained to Slovik that what he did was in fact an act of desertion. Slovik then asked Grotte, "If I leave now, would it be desertion?" Grotte said that he answered Slovik in the affirmative and told him that it would prompt him to file a charge against Slovik. With that assurance, Slovik then walked away from his unit, in a deliberate act to violate the article of war.

At the hearing Captain Woods declined to cross-examine the witness.[8] In case there was any doubt about his intentions, Slovik scribbled out a confession on an army flour-order form. It read in part: "I told my commanding officer my story. I said that if I had to go out there again I'd run away. He said their [sic] was nothing he could do for me. So I ran away again and I'll run away again if I have to go out their [sic]." Slovik told 1st Lt. Wayne C. Hurd about the confession, and the prosecution called Hurd as a witness and entered Slovik's confession as evidence.[9] The defense neither cross-examined Hurd nor objected to the admission of the confession as a court exhibit.[10] For its part, the defense declined to make any opening statement, presented no witnesses of its own, made no closing argument, and informed the court that Pvt. Slovik had elected to waive his right to speak at his trial. "I will remain silent," he told the court. At 10:50 a.m. the prosecution rested. The panel called for a ten-minute recess.

The case was a no-brainer. Capt. Kimmelman recalled the backroom, closed-door discussion among his fellow judges. "Three ballots were taken in closed doors," he wrote, "the verdicts guilty on all counts."[11] The decision was unanimous. The defendant was found guilty as charged. During sentencing the judges voted, again unanimously, for Slovik to be shot to death by a firing squad.[12]

Did Private Slovik receive a fair trial? As military officers with the Twenty-Eighth Infantry Division, the panel of judges had just emerged from the bloodiest engagement against an enemy they had ever experienced. Furthermore, they personally knew many of the men who had gone to their deaths fighting a battle they had almost no chance of winning. Roetgen also happened to be the headquarters of 1st Army Gen. Courtney H. Hodges, who made it clear that he was not at all happy with the division's performance on the battlefield. On the panel of judges, Col. Guy M. Williams was the presiding officer. In an interview he later explained, "There was his confession: he had run away from his duties as a rifleman . . . and he would run away again. Given the circumstances of a division locked in bloody battle and taking heavy casualties, I didn't think I had a right to let him get away with it. That's how I felt; apparently the others felt the same way."[13]

There was still a thread of hope for leniency. Because Slovik's was a capital punishment case, Maj. Gen. Norman Cota as commander of the Twenty-Eighth had to sign off on the tribunal's decision. Without a signature, Slovik would not die. Cota signed. Explaining why he did so, the general said, "I don't know how I could have gone to the line and looked a good soldier in the face."[14] The sentence also needed approval from an even higher authority: Theater commander Gen. Dwight D. Eisenhower. He, too, gave his consent.

As a result, Slovik was ordered to be shot by members of his own infantry division because it was his divisional colleagues that the defendant had betrayed.

IF THE EXECUTION OF PRIVATE SLOVIK WAS INTENDED TO serve as a deterrent to would-be deserters, the army didn't do a good job of making that known. For nearly a decade after Private Slovik was shot, virtually no one knew how he died—not even his widow, Antoinette, who, from her home in Pontiac, Michigan, repeatedly pleaded with the government for information about her husband.[15]

Private Slovik wasn't the only American to go AWOL. In addition to the Detroit native, there were about 2,863 other deserters who had gone before various military tribunals from January 1942 to June 1948 and were found guilty of a similar crime, 49 of whom received the death penalty.[16] They, too, were condemned to death, but none faced a firing squad. By the time their cases queued up for sentencing dates, the war had ended. There was also a large contingent of GI deserters—more than 40,000 in number—who had been suspected of violating the Fifty-Eighth Article of War. Many of their cases may also have been tried by army general court-martial, but they were fortunate enough not to have been caught. Of those who were caught and tried, some were lucky to have their sentences commuted to imprisonment, thanks to mitigating circumstances. Remorse, time put in on the battlefield, and service with their units for any length of time were all taken into consideration by the judges.

But the desertion problem extended way beyond the forty thousand. In fact, it was much more systemic throughout the armed forces. Behind closed doors, generals, colonels, majors, and lieutenants pondered the problem. The army kept its concerns under lid because it feared offending the American people. As the war was winding down, hundreds of thousands of families were receiving letters and telegrams that their sons and husbands had been killed or wounded. The time was clearly inappropriate. What vexed the military leadership was this: the fact that a large number of American men were cowards. Astonishingly, their numbers were in the millions. Based on an analysis of the records, the army had concluded that approximately four million physically fit American men couldn't be relied on by the country's armed forces in a time of war. These individuals were psychologically unfit to fight. On a battlefield they were the types who would not hesitate to flee, abandoning their comrades on the frontline and endangering their lives.

The study was commissioned by Gen. George C. Marshall Jr., who served as the U.S. Army's chief of staff under two presidents, Franklin D. Roosevelt and Harry S. Truman. Marshall had convened an investigative committee of psychiatrists to look into the matter. The researchers were given access to several data sources kept by the military on soldiers, including a file on the 1.75 million men of draft age who were rejected for military service during World War II by their psychiatric evaluators for "reasons other than physical." For the most part, these men had nothing wrong with them other than a lack of will to fight. Another was a microstudy of a U.S. unit of 3,000 servicemen, one-third of whom had either run away or committed acts of cowardice that got them removed from the frontline or from active duty. Many of these men inflicted wounds on themselves in an attempt to be taken to a medical facility. In the language of the day, they were classified as "cowards" and "psychoneurotics," One category of psychoneurotics was bluntly labeled as "mama's boys." Conscripting mama's boys into military service, it was thought, would endanger the safety of their fighting comrades at critical times in battle when survival was contingent on numbers. A small subset in the study group—about 12 percent—were deemed to be "constitutional psychopaths," which included men who had difficulty dealing with authority; the army called them "the hooky players and the drunkards." Another group of runaways—about 3 percent—were determined to be "mentally sick." The committee concluded that, because of these psychological issues inherent in the American male population of the time, approximately one-quarter of the country's potential draftees—numbering about 4 million—would be deemed to be too timid or psychologically unfit for battle in the event of another major global conflict.[17]

The findings of the investigating committee were included in a book titled *All But Me and Thee: Psychiatry at the Foxhole Level*, written by Brig. Gen. Elliot D. Cooke, one of the principals involved with the study. These men were made sick not as a result of combat but by virtue of "just by being in the army," the study concluded.[18] Military planners at the time suggested to policy makers that the nation implement a program called Universal Military Training (UMT), under which men eighteen years and older would be required to train with a branch of the armed forces. Left unsaid was the fact that UMT would provide the military an opportunity to indoctrinate a broad spectrum of young men, programming them with a will to fight.

Despite heavy lobbying, discussions didn't make it far up the decision-making ladder. Most recently an iteration of UMT was introduced by the 107th Congress as a bill—HR 3598—in 2001. It would have required the induction of men registered with the Selective Service to receive basic military training and education for a period of up to a year at any time between their eighteenth and twenty-second birthdays. Women could participate on a voluntary basis. The bill never went beyond the subcommittee level, even though the United States was at war with Al-Qaeda at the time.

Despite resistance to the notion of mandatory combat training from Washington, DC, the imbuing of young men with a spirit of bravery continues to remain a critical discussion point at military academies. At the U.S. Army's Command and General Staff College at Fort Leavenworth in Kansas, "we talk about it all the time," says Prof. Thomas Bradbeer, the MG Fox Conner Chair of Leadership Studies with the college's Department of Command and Leadership.[19] "Everybody's afraid. Everybody's scared. None of us want to die." Asked what he thought about Stephen Crane's *The Red Badge of Courage* as a primer for soldiering, Bradbeer gushed with praise for Crane's insight. He was not only familiar with the book, having studied it carefully; he had also seen the movie several times. In the short story, he said, Crane was able to encapsulate the elusive essence of fortitude and valor: "That's why the *Red Badge of Courage* is a classic. I think everyone should read it. It is the story of the American soldier. In it, the protagonist Henry Fleming goes through a transformation. He goes from 'I can't do this' and runs away and hides to where he convinces himself, 'I've got to go back to the battlefield, this is not right,' and he does and he becomes a hero."[20] While the book may provide a road map to bravery, Bradbeer cautions, one does not become brave just by reading literature. Bravery is not a learned hymn or an anthem to country or fellow man, nor is it a state, a status, or acquired knowledge. It isn't the inuring of oneself to hardship, pain, and death, either. In a sense, it is the antithesis of all of the above. "The biggest thing about bravery is you don't think about it," Bradbeer says. It is transcendence over rational thought, a fleeting quintessential moment of pure action. Just as a man lifts a truck off of someone trapped under it, a soldier will fall on a grenade to save the men in his unit. It is an act of not thinking.[21]

Therein lay the value to the U.S. Army of soldiers like Anthony Grasso and Julian Farrior and Sydney Weaver and Jack Farrell and Mark Wilson and Michael Loncar and Joseph Merlock and Robert Wiginton and their other cohorts in khaki who had just given their lives in towns whose names they couldn't pronounce and in a forest they had never heard of before.

ANTHONY GRASSO BECAME BRAVE WITHOUT EVEN KNOW-ing it. As the Germans shelled the Americans on the morning of November 2, 1944, and black-smoked bombs exploded all around him, he ran right alongside his reconnaissance officer, 1st Lt. Frank DuBose. Without any thought, he followed him wherever he went. The smell of sulphur and phosphorus pervaded the air, its pungency constricting his throat and nasal passages. But Grasso paid little heed to his discomfort. He was consumed with only one mission: get the coordinates of the enemy and relay the numbers back to his artillery unit so the lives of his fellow Americans could be spared by neutralizing the guns in their way. He had thought about death a million times since landing on the shores of Normandy three months before, in July, and he had become convinced after a number of close calls—eventually too many to count—that his luck would one day run out. That rainy gray morning in a clearing in the forest could have been the day. And when the moment arrived, he knew it: he would never return home. All sensation of invincibility left his nineteen-year-old body, energy draining from his muscles like the blood that gushed from the shrapnel wound to his head. He saw wings of lightning, he heard a rumble as the ground beneath him trembled.

Two weeks quietly passed. When Grasso woke up, he was in

an entirely different world from the one he had left just a moment before—or so it seemed; in the netherworld of unconsciousness the clock stops ticking. When his eyes opened, his immediate thought was, "Where am I?" For Grasso, the previous two weeks was what it feels like to be dead. In a bed in a U.S. medical facility in Paris, he now was in a unique position, having returned from the dead, as it were, to speak on behalf of his departed comrades. He remembered everything that happened to him before he was blasted into the air.

Once again the unseen, mysterious, and wondrous had helped him elude death. DuBose's body and a forty-pound s c r 300 radio transmission equipment strapped to Grasso's back saved his life. His radio lieutenant, Frank DuBose, wasn't as lucky. He did not make it. All of the thoughts that ran through Grasso's head had rushed through DuBose's, too, right up until the invisible line where bravery intersected with dying was crossed. "Neither of us did much thinking," Grasso said. "We just did. There was no time to think, artillery was falling all over the place. Then, in one second, it was all over." The last words Grasso heard from DuBose was: "I need to call in, give me the phone."[22] In DuBose's footsteps followed Weaver, Farrell, Wilson, Loncar, Merlock, Wiginton, Peterson, Greenway, Farrior, Herbert, and many others. The army loved men like them, the type that, in the words of Stephen Crane, "accepted the pelting of the bullets with bowed and weary heads." As the trees of the Hürtgen began to softly sing a requiem to those who had fallen so bravely in a land that wasn't even theirs, the U.S. Army, in reciprocal fashion, became beholden to them, to make sure that, for as long as it takes, none are left behind.

It has been a long time—a total of seventy-five years and counting—and there are still between 150 and 200 men unaccounted for. A vast number of them are Keystoners who belonged to the Twenty-Eighth Division. These men have simply vanished, their disappearance creating a mystery. They didn't die in the middle of a jungle or the bottom of an ocean; they perished in and around three towns—Vossenack, Kommerscheidt, and Schmidt, where the terrain isn't as hostile and except for a small section that slopes down to the Kall River. Yet the search for these missing soldiers has been among the most exhaustive—and frustrating—MIA projects for the U.S. Army. It has turned an entire staff of historians at the Defense POW/MIA Accounting Agency (DPAA), which is tasked with the responsibility of recovering MIAS, into a group of hyphenated professionals. They have become historian-detectives.

# 13

## From the Lower Levels of Dante's *Inferno*

Presently there was a stillness, pregnant with meaning.
The blue lines shifted and changed a trifle and stared
expectantly at the silent woods and fields before them.

—*The Red Badge of Courage*

To Americans in World War II, the Germans were the bad guys. But there were moments when the two sides behaved as brothers, fighting arm in arm in a humanitarian war against a common enemy: death itself.

Both sides gave the distinct appearance at times of battle fatigue. They had tired of shooting at each other and were hoping that some giant whistle in the sky would call the battle to a draw and that a big someone, mightier than dictators and generals, would order everyone to pack up their mildewed bedding and go home. As a little boy listening to his grandfather's stories about the battle in the Hürtgen Forest, William Snider recalls being struck by something he was told. His grandfather—Lt. Col. Carl Peterson, commander of the 112th Regiment—talked on several occasions about an uncommon agreement that was struck on the quiet among German and American soldiers during that engagement: an understanding that if a gun was pointed toward the sky, that meant the man holding it had no desire to shoot the other man. This became an unspoken signal of peace and a code among the war-weary that, unless they received direct orders to fight, they were quite content to keep the bloodletting to a minimum.[1]

Such stories circulated in plentiful abundance in the wake of that battle. Marion Bedford Davis, a combat medical officer with the Twenty-Eighth Infantry Division, recalled how one morning he saw a German soldier sitting on top of a pillbox, eating breakfast, his rifle to the side, leaning against a rock. It wasn't unusual for an American to spot a German in an off-guard moment, when fighting at close range. What the physician thought unusual, however, was that there was an American GI sitting next to the German and sharing his food. No translators required—just a smile, a nod, a knowing eye. After breakfast the German indicated to Doctor Davis that he wanted to surrender. The two Americans escorted the German to their military superiors to be taken into U.S. custody.[2]

Such glimpses of goodness were perhaps most apparent to the medical staff of both armies. Midway through the seven-day battle, after the Germans reclaimed some of the territory that they had lost to the GIs, a group of U.S. medics suddenly found themselves tending to their wounded on the wrong side of the battlefield, surrounded by Germans. The logical thing to do at that point was to raise the white flag and move the minihospital to GI territory, but the location in which the Americans had set up their mobile medical facility was quite suitable for triage work: in a dugout well protected from the shelling falling around it, near a river and a sturdy stone bridge strong enough to bear the weight of military weasel ambulances and trauma transports. The Germans not only allowed the Americans to continue treating their wounded there; they assigned a team of German guards to protect them and supplied them with bandages, tourniquets, the antibacterial agent sulfonamide, and even the assistance of their own medics.[3] The Twenty-Eighth Infantry Division was never able to take back the territory, but, as long as the aid station remained under German control, U.S. medics and litter bearers came and went without much more hassle than being checked for weapons.

One evening the Americans needed to remove some of its more seriously wounded patients to a bigger facility, but continual shelling by Germans artillerymen made the transport dangerous. Maj. Albert Berndt, the U.S. surgeon for the 112th Regiment of the 28th Division, waved a white flag and walked up a heavily patrolled German-occupied trail to ask the artillery commander for a two-hour cease-fire while they evacuated their wounded in ambulances. Permission was granted, and the Germans honored the cease-fire for the entire two hours, even though the medical caravan had finished its business some time before. The transport was an elaborate production: to move forty-four wounded soldiers, the U.S. medics had to drive seventeen ambulances and weasels down a soggy logging trail partway into a valley and then carry the men in stretchers from the aid station to the waiting vehicles. The Germans gave the litter bearers a hand.[4]

Three weeks after the 28th Infantry withdrew from the Hürtgen Forest, Maj. Richard Dana with the 112th Regiment reported this act of German kindness for the record in an interview with Capt. William J. Fox. For some, in risking their lives to perform a good deed, they may have actually procured for themselves a berth to safety. Two German medics saw a wounded American officer on the ground shortly after an attack by a group of German patrols and stopped to treat him. As they tended to his wounds, the injured officer, Capt. Hunter Montgomery, talked the medics into surrendering. In accordance with U.S. protocol under the Geneva Convention of 1929, the German soldiers were escorted to a U.S. base, fed, medically treated, and shipped to a prison camp in the United States.[5] During World War II nearly four hundred thousand Germans and fifty thousand Italians were taken prisoner by the U.S. Armed Forces and housed in quarters on some six hundred U.S. military bases or training camps in forty-six states. Many German and Italian POWs renounced allegiance to Hitler and Mussolini and even assisted the United States during the war as aides and translators. They ate the same meals as the U.S. soldiers and enjoyed many of the same amenities, including medical and dental care and after-hours entertainment.[6]

It took three more months and multiple offensives by several U.S. divisions before the Americans loosened the German grip on the Hürtgen Forest. In February 1945, when German defenders finally began backing out of the forest, they performed another act of kindness. During lulls in the fighting, they took the time to bury some American dead. The interment was done hastily in shallow graves, but with German protocol, to show respect: the deceased's rifle was stuck in the ground, bayonet first, to mark the grave. For identification purposes they hung the soldier's dog tags over the butt of the weapon. A helmet, either the GI's or one of their own, covered the top of the rifle, holding the identification plate of the deceased in place.[7]

This is the scene that the U.S. grave registration crews witnessed as they trucked in behind the last two U.S. military divisions to engage the Germans in the forest: the Seventy-Eighth Infantry and the 82nd U.S. Airborne. It was the job of these units to find and transport fallen GIs to American cemeteries. Unlike the time in early November when the Twenty-Eighth had to hurry out of the forest without collecting its dead, this time the caretaker crews could work at a more leisurely pace without the fear of enemy bombardment. The German Army was now only a ghost of the force that had confronted the Twenty-Eighth in early November. They put up some resistance as the Americans stormed the towns of Kommerscheidt and Schmidt, but the defeat of Hitler's forces at the Battle of the Bulge had broken the back of the Wehrmacht. They were now a ragtag amalgam of disheartened, frightened men fighting on their heels. Soon they would be seeking cover in the ruined towns, hills, and countryside of the Deutschland interior.

Despite the much more conducive environment for mortuary work, the grave registration units faced a daunting clean-up task. Gen. James M. Gavin, the high-spirited, colorful commander of the 82nd Airborne, provided an eyewitness account of the five-month-long bloody campaign against the Germans. He was mortified by what he saw one February afternoon as he retraced the path taken by the Twenty-Eighth: walking down the torn-up logging road, he observed "all along the sides of the trail there were many, many dead bodies, cadavers that had just emerged from the winter snow. Their gangrenous, broken, and torn bodies were rigid and grotesque, some of them with arms skyward, seemingly in supplication. They were wearing the red keystone of the 28th Infantry Division, 'The Bloody Bucket.'"[8]

Further down along the banks of the Kall River were dozens of litter cases, their contorted bodies long dead. The aid station, where the men once sought emergency care, was abandoned. Men still lying in the stretchers on which they expired—some perhaps left there to die by an army in panic—lined the sides of the medical station. A little further up, the general saw the stiff figures of three or four American soldiers who had been killed in the act of laying mines. From their positions Gavin could tell that they were trying to conceal them in the ground. On the other side of the mines lay an equal number of dead German soldiers. It appeared that death had come suddenly; everything seemed frozen in time. Across the valley near the top, where the trail opened up into a vast farmland leading to the town of Kommerscheidt, the ground was strewn with many more bodies, all American. Next to their carcasses lay a scattered collection of jeeps, firearms, and anti-tank guns. As the sun set over the hill and darkness stretched across the canyon, it was "an eerie scene like something from the lower levels of Dante's Inferno," the general would write. "To add to the horrors, a plaintive human voice could be heard calling from the woods some distance away."[9] A young soldier, taking in the sight, turned pale and looked like he was about to vomit. Gavin said he tried to calm the youth with an assurance "that we never abandoned our dead, that we always cared for them and buried them." Over the next few days, the Americans seized the towns of Kommerscheidt and Schmidt, meeting a modicum of resistance and artillery fire but nothing like the one encountered in the fall by the Twenty-Eighth Infantry Division.[10]

The Hürtgen Forest was no longer a battle arena; it was now a wasteland of the dead. GIs who were buried by the Germans had to be disinterred. Those corpses, along with the ones above ground, had to be ID'd, wrapped, put on a truck, and driven to a newly built cemetery about twenty-five miles west in Belgium, in the province of Liege. The fifty-seven-acre burial facility, which had opened in the fall of 1944, was only meant to store the bodies of American soldiers on a temporary basis, but it filled up so quickly that moving the remains to another location would have been an insurmountable task. Subsequently, it became the resting place for 7,792 deceased members of the U.S. Armed Forces. Today it is known as the Henri-Chapelle American Cemetery and Memorial. Many of those buried there were killed while fighting in the Hürtgen Forest.[11]

The work of transporting the dead began in early February 1945. When members of the Seventy-Eighth Infantry Division were told one day that they were going to help pick up the bodies of their fallen comrades from the Twenty-Eighth, Ted Temper, a staff sergeant with the Seventy-Eighth, eagerly jumped on the truck to volunteer his services. He did so because he had a strong suspicion that his older brother, 1st Lt. Ernest Temper, who fought with the Twenty-Eighth, was among the dead. At the time he was listed as missing in action. Ted wanted to say goodbye to Ernest, but shortly after he boarded the truck, an officer ordered him to get off. "I want to go see my brother," Temper protested. A group of men who had been coordinating the body removal operation that day insisted that Temper not come along. The truck drove off without him. According to his son Ted Temper Jr., the sergeant was never given a reason why he couldn't accompany the group.[12]

Until then the family knew nothing about Ernest's fate. Was he alive or dead, wounded or detained in a prison somewhere behind German lines? It wouldn't be for another month that information began to trickle in. This is the story that eventually emerged.

On November 5, First Lieutenant Temper's company was engaging an enemy well entrenched in pillboxes and defilades. The regiment had been on the losing end of a battle for a third straight day in Raffelsbrand, a village about a mile south from Vossenack. Ernest's Company, K, which had been in reserve for the first two days, was ordered to join the fighting. The regiment had lost a lot of men to shelling and camouflaged German machine gun nests at the edge of the woods. Company K was advancing close to enemy lines in clear view of German artillery lookouts. A signal was given, as well as Company K's coordinates. Ernest Temper, along with other members in his unit, were hit by heavy mortar and artillery fire. The cause of death would be listed as an injury caused by "shrapnel to the head." It is possible that Ernest Temper's Seventy-Eighth Infantry cohorts didn't want Ted Temper to see the damage to his brother's body. As the Seventy-Eighth combed through the cratered corn fields of Raffelsbrand, they came upon a frozen figure with a gaping head wound. On an identification platelet around the soldier's neck was printed the name Ernest L. Temper, serial number 021293494. They slid the lieutenant's body onto an army-green mattress cover and hoisted it onto a truck, where two other servicemen took hold of the cover and gently laid Temper's body alongside his other dead comrades. From there the truck drove west out of the forest on a paved road toward the German Belgian border. The bodies were neatly stacked off to the side by the chapel, where they awaited burial at Henri-Chapelle.

Ernest was put in a machine-dug grave, five feet deep and two feet wide. Next to Ernest were two other members of the Twenty-Eighth Infantry Division who also died in the same battle: William C. Davis, serial no. 34338261 on the right and Frank H. Caylor, serial no. 34734080 on the left. Theirs were graves 91, 92, and 93 in row 5, plot PPP. Piles of fresh dirt lay nearby. The time was a few minutes after 11:00 a.m., February 15, 1945. More burials were scheduled for later in the day.[13]

No one other than the caretaker crews witnessed Ernest's body being lowered into the ground—not even his brother Ted, who was just a fifteen-minute truck ride away. The Temper family back in Huron, Ohio, didn't know about this part of Ernest's story. The cemetery plot number and its location was typed onto a yellow piece of paper in New York and mailed to the Temper's Ohio address a month later. Inviting family members to Henri-Chapelle would have been a logistical nightmare. Casualties for the Twenty-Eighth Infantry Division alone—including the wounded, killed, captured, and missing—numbered 6184. Among its three regiments, the toll was heaviest for the 112th: 2093 in total casualties, 232 captured, 167 killed, 431 missing, 719 wounded in combat, and 541 incapacitated as a result of trench foot and other ailments.[14]

The Allies pressed eastward toward Berlin, making the crossing at Remagen, which had previously spelled their ruin during its ill-attempted Operation Market Garden initiative in the fall of 1944. The U.S. Ninth Army rolled on past the Rhine. News of the death of President Roosevelt on April 12, 1945, shocked America and Europe, but the American forces sallied ahead, momentum clearly on their side. By late April, in Berlin, Adolf Hitler knew the end was near. The oil he so badly needed and thought he could get from Africa and Russia had slipped into Allied hands. Those same armed forces that took back those lands were in Berlin, just a few blocks away from his underground bunker. Hitler was surrounded: by the Russians to the east and the combined Allied forces to the west. On April 30, 1945, realizing the end of the Third Reich was near, the Fuhrer decided to take his life. To make sure he would be dead by the time his captors battered down the door of his underground bunker, he swallowed a cyanide capsule and then shot himself in the head. On May 7, 1945, at the behest of Adm. Karl Donitz, Hitler's successor, all of Germany laid down its arms. The news of the Reich's unconditional surrender was broadcast by radio. The celebration began to spread as darkness was pushed back, a time zone at a time, by a rising sun in the entire western hemisphere. On May 8, 1945, Victory in Europe (V-E) Day was declared. For the seventy million people in Germany who had somehow survived six years of bombing and infernal fires, *Stunde Null*, or the Zero Hour, was at hand.

The citizenry of townships in the Hürtgen Forest got a jump-start on their fellow countrymen. By mid-February, when the Americans began burying their dead, they sensed the start of a return to normalcy. Beginning in April, the civilian populations of Vossenack, Kommerscheidt, and Schmidt, among other forest municipalities, made the trek home from where in Germany they had sought temporary refuge. For many the rebuilding of their lives required a new mindset and an allegiance. Herr Ludwig Fischer, the former mayor of the combined townships of Kommerscheidt-Schmidt, said the town had to get used to transitioning from German Army auxiliaries to consorting with an enemy turned friend.

There was a time during the early 1940s when the war was no more than a conversation piece. "It hardly affected us," Fisher recalls. "Occasionally we would talk about the war." Then, after the English began attacking German cities with planes, the townsfolk turned informants, reporting on the positions of British paratroopers. "The young men in town would go out during the nightly English bombing raids and report to authorities if enemy airmen were bailing out or being captured," Fischer says.

In 1943 all of the forest's young men were drafted by the German Army. Fisher, who was eight years old at the time, remembered being mesmerized by searchlights—four or five at a time—crisscrossing in the sky whenever a plane was detected. He would then hear the antiaircraft guns going off to complement the celestial display. Everyone was told that they were in Combat Zone Three, in case any reporting to authorities had to be done. When things quieted down at night, the sky, it seemed, became noisier, with the sounds of sputtering planes and the drone of heavy bombers. The people of the Hürtgen Forest never felt that they were the targets of a bombing raid. When bombs occasionally fell, the people thought the drops were accidental or done to lighten the load of a plane in distress. One of the first signs of danger came one hot day in summer when Allied planes dropped flaming paper plates. In school the children were told that this was an effort to light the forest on fire and burn the towns down. "All the children went into the woods around Schmidt," Fischer recalls. "The teachers were there. They had a bucket and long wooden tongs to place what was called a 'fire plate' into the bucket. The 'fire plates' never created a forest fire."

In the summer of 1943 the residents of the forest were made to gather primrose flowers and broadleaf plants so the German Army could make them into medicine. "It was the citizenship to support the War effort," Fischer says. School lectures increasingly took on a war focus, and life grew more difficult for local residents. It became more dangerous for children taking care of cattle and sheep in the open farm areas. The adults scaled back the days of tending flock. Word spread around town that the Americans would soon start shelling the villagers with artillery. "So neighbors worked together to build underground bunkers and shelters and pack emergency bags in preparation for attacks," Fischer says. The local school postponed the reopening of school that fall. Everyone was instructed to leave the forest.[15] The German army began digging in for a vicious fight.

Moving from the Hürtgen Forest into the industrial zone made people like Fischer more fearful of Allied bombing, which became a

Lower Levels of Dante's *Inferno*

daily affair in the big cities. "Our family and relatives suffered through the terrifying wait of the air raid alarms in our cellar every night with neighbors and strangers," recalls Fischer, who was then ten years old. The bombs shook the concrete buildings from their foundations. Walls would collapse, covering everything with layers of dust. After the planes had gone, the people would run outside and take deep breaths of fresh air. At the conclusion of each bombing run, Allied prisoners would be made to scour the ruins looking for corpses, which they would then carry off and bury in a cemetery or in makeshift graveyards. It was good preparation for their return to the Hürtgen Forest in the spring of 1945; that was exactly the way their once-tidy homes looked.

Upon their return to the forest, the residents found their towns destroyed. Not a single home remained standing. Barns were leveled. All landmarks were gone. Rooftops had collapsed, the thick stone walls that had held them up through centuries reduced to sand and dust. The carcasses of cows, pigs, sheep, and chickens could be seen in the thawing mud. More than fifty armored vehicles—tanks and tank destroyers, cannon carriers and jeeps, respectively marked by their signature German Iron Cross and U.S. Winged Star symbols—blocked the roadways like sleeping beasts. The plateau fields had turned into aircraft landing strips. A sickening stench pervaded the sweet mountain air. It came from the rotting corpses of the German and American army men that dotted the landscape. Like mannequins in a museum, some were seated in the same upright positions in which they died.[16]

After the residents returned to their hometowns in April 1945, a first order of business was the mass burial of soldiers. Everyone pitched in, but some took on more responsibility than others. Bernhard Frings knew where many of the bodies were in Schmidt. A brave man, Frings didn't leave Schmidt in the fall of 1944 when the local civilian population was ordered by the German army to evacuate; he remained behind to take care of the cattle, hiding by day and sneaking out at night to tend to the animals. After the Germans left the forest in February and the fighting ended, Frings began burying the Americans who were killed in Schmidt and Kommerscheidt.

When the residents returned, they pitched in. In all, Frings buried approximately fifty GIs. His leadership qualities in postwar affairs quickly became apparent, and he took over as Bürgermeister of the municipalities of Schmidt and Kommerscheidt in 1945 and 1946.[17]

In Kommerscheidt, the Lennartzs, a father-son team, was among the harder-working gravediggers. In a statement to the U.S. officials dated October 28, 1947, Rudolf Lennartz wrote, "In April 1945, I returned to Kommerscheidt from evacuation. Together with my father, I buried almost all deceased soldiers which were lying in this village and its vicinity in shell holes or trenches." Lennartz at the time was a strong young man, nineteen years old.[18] Also helping out in Kommerscheidt was another young man, Christian Falter. The burial sites were fresh in the memory of the local residents when later that year the U.S. Army sent teams into the Hürtgen Forest to find its fallen. Speaking to the townsfolk, the U.S. teams soon identified the key figures in the mass burials at the various towns and asked for their assistance. Frings, Lennartz, Falter, and others led the the American Graves Registration Command (AGRC) teams to the burial sites for disinterment. Some of the fallen Americans had identification plates around their necks; their families were notified by letter from the adjutant general's office, alerting them that the army was changing the MIA status of their deceased relative to KIA.

That month Margaret Peterson in Boy River, Minnesota, received news about her son, who, at seventeen, volunteered to serve in the U.S. Army a year before he became eligible for the draft. She had gotten a notice from the army back in November that he was MIA. Now his body had been discovered. "Dear Mrs. Peterson," read the letter, dated April 13, 1945, from a Maj. Gen. C. H. Danielson. "The War Department has informed me that your son, Private Otto W. Peterson, has given his life in the performance of his duty." The letter contained no details about how and where her son had died. That information remained "classified material."

As the remains of other members of the Bloody Bucket were unearthed in the spring of 1945, the families of twenty-one-year-old Leonard Greenway in Philadelphia; thirty-two-year-old Robert Wiginton in Hamilton, Alabama; and thirty-four-year-old Carl

Lower Levels of Dante's *Inferno*

Dewitt Sanders in Hawkinsville, Georgia, received status changes from MIA to KIA at around the same time. For some families the news was devastating. Norma, Robert Wiginton's new bride, disappeared from Hamilton, Alabama, leaving behind the home that she and her husband had purchased the day before Robert received his draft notice. The Wigintons never heard from her again.

Meanwhile, families who didn't receive word from the War Department grew impatient with the government and began writing letters to their representatives in the House and Senate, to pressure the army for information about their loved ones. Their efforts to get congressional heat on the military was, by and large, unsuccessful. A vast majority of MIA families continued to exist in limbo.

The U.S. Army maintained teams on the scene at the Hürtgen Forest to search for the missing. For added incentive the army offered cash rewards to the Germans for their help in identifying American burial locations.[19] The army even hired translators. Yet, in spite of the apparent good intentions of both the U.S. Army and native Germans, the body recovery effort stagnated in a frustrating impasse. Tasked at the end of the war with the responsibility of finding bodies and conducting mortuary affairs was a brand-new arm of the U.S. Army: the American Graves Registration Command (AGRC). One of its first undertakings was the recovery of the fallen left behind in the Hürtgen Forest. The AGRC embarked on recovery efforts in 1945 and 1946 and conducted grave location investigations in 1947, 1948, and 1949. Each time a new investigation was undertaken, the search teams kept returning to the same group of Germans—the daring Bernhard Frings, who remained in Schmidt during the entire Hürtgen Forest battle; Josef Lauscher, the Bürgermeister of Schmidt; and two local farmers, Rudolf Lennartz and Christian Falter, both of whom were active participants in the burial of American soldiers in the spring of 1945. Their responses were almost identical each time: there are no more American soldiers buried here. How do we know? Because we found all of them and buried them.

On September 22, 1948, Bernhard Frings provided this statement to U.S. investigators:

During the time fighting took place in this area I frequently went to the village during the night in order to take care of the cattle that was still living. Thereby I often found American and German soldiers which had been killed. After the final occupation of the village by the Americans I buried all these deceased, later on then I led American searching teams to the grave of the American soldiers which disinterred and removed the diseased. In my opinion they amounted to about 50 American soldiers. . . . All American soldiers who were buried by me have been removed.

It was the same sentiment he had expressed in a statement to a different AGRC team on October, 28 1947. The investigators included in their reports statements such as those provided by Frings and filed them with the U.S. Army, which in turn wrote letters to the families of the MIA, apologizing that it had no new information about their son, father, or uncle. One well-connected Dallas family, however, didn't give up. It helped that their son was as heroic as any young man who had put on an army uniform in World War II.

# 14

## Am I Wounded Badly?

> He lay and basked in the occasional stares of his comrades.
> Their faces were varied in degrees of blackness from the
> burned powder. Some were utterly smudged. They were
> reeking of perspiration and their breaths came
> hard and wheezing.
>
> —*The Red Badge of Courage*

Turney Leonard was a tall and handsome Texan who proudly wore a gold ring on his finger. It was adorned with a large star that symbolized the seal of the State of Texas, and a wreath of olive and live oak leaves that represented the prized virtues of a righteous life: achievement, a desire for peace, and the strength to fight for justice and goodness. Leonard didn't have a typical childhood; he had been brought up by a grandfather who taught him to love nature in its magnificent beauty and bounty, and a hardworking single mother who raised a family of six.[1] In its glittering grandeur, the ring stood as a metaphor for the man he had become. It also happened to be his class ring at Texas A&M University, of which he was a 1942 graduate. With his upbringing and his college days still fresh in his mind, Leonard was afraid he was about to lose a cherished treasure.[2]

His left arm had been shredded from his bicep to his wrist by searing shrapnel from a round fired by a German Tiger tank. His hand, along with part of his arm, could fall off at any time, and the ring dangled precariously at the end of the blood-soaked limb. As a platoon commander with the 893rd Tank Destroyer Battalion, the twenty-three-year-old Leonard was injured while directing the fire of his gunners at enemy positions.[3] He now needed medical assistance to save his arm. It isn't clear whether he made it to an aid station; what is known from documented accounts is that at some point after his injury Leonard found himself trying to escape from a second enemy tank blast. He could have been hit with shrapnel from that explosion as well, but he ducked into a hole in the ground—a trench about six feet deep, six feet wide, and about ten feet long. In it he huddled with four other American military officers. Stretched out on the ground near the feet of the five men was a sixth: an artillery captain, who was dying.[4]

"Am I wounded badly?" Leonard asked the 112th Regiment Commander Lt. Col. Carl Peterson, who was squeezed in alongside him in the sheltering ditch. From the looks of it, Leonard, too, was dying, and Peterson was careful about what he said. In addition to his mangled arm, there was either shrapnel or a bullet lodged in the young lieutenant's face, his curly brown hair matted with blood and sweat. As he sat with his back against a wall of earth, Leonard grew afraid. He asked Peterson to pray for him. Then he made a second request: Could the colonel write a letter to his mother for him? Peterson said that he would, but—in an apparent attempt to get Leonard to fight to stay alive—he added that he "might just as well attend to it when he arrived at the hospital."[5]

With the captain lying on the ground and Leonard's sagging frame propped against the wall, "both getting ready to pass," Peterson wrote in a letter to a superior, "I was scared stiff."[6] German tanks were advancing toward them, firing point blank above where they were crouching. This was the state of the American army on November 7, 1944; that embattled, cramped hole in the ground of an old orchard was functioning, essentially, as its command post, minutes away from being overrun by approaching German tanks. Sensing imminent danger, Peterson ordered the other officers in the trench to crawl out of an opening and head for the woods. Three of them managed to do so and regrouped about fifty feet away to look behind

Am I Wounded Badly?

them. Leonard had remained. Seconds later the tanks rolled over the trench with Leonard and the captain (Robert C. Driscoll) still in it. Shortly thereafter Lieutenant Colonel Peterson was injured himself as he needled his way through throngs of German soldiers en route to General Cota's office ten miles away in Rott, near the Belgian border.[7]

Two days later, overwhelmed by an indomitable Germany Army, the decimated Twenty-Eighth Infantry Division pulled out of the battle and retreated to Belgium. After Leonard failed to answer roll call, he was reported missing in action. His mother, Lily V. Leonard, got the notice in a telegram from the army at her Dallas home on November 27, 1944. For the next five years, she pursued every avenue available and contacted every person in high office to find out what happened to her son. At an October 1945 ceremony in Dallas honoring his bravery, she said, "I haven't grieved for him a bit. I just don't believe there's a German alive that could catch him."[8] Mrs. Leonard wrote letters to the army and to the Quartermaster Graves Registration Service. She solicited the help of U.S. senator Tom Connally (D-Texas) and U.S. representative Olin Teague (D-Texas), who himself was a decorated World War II veteran; he had served with the Seventy-Ninth Division as a first lieutenant. And she got her brother, Tyree Bell Jr., a Texas A&M graduate himself (class of 1913), to join the fight to find Turney Leonard.

Mrs. Leonard's efforts appeared to be a waste of time. Like so many other parents looking for their missing sons, the Texas mom kept receiving polite, "sorry-no-new-information" letters from the government. In the fall of 1947 a search team directed by U.S. Cpl. Robert Gibeau discovered the graves of fourteen GIs in Kommerscheidt. In their searches for the remains of U.S. soldiers, U.S. teams, for the most part, had stayed away from German graves. But, on this particular recovery mission, they dug up a burial place where German helmets marked each grave. The soldiers buried there turned out to be Americans. Turney Leonard's remains, though, were not among them.[9] The find was a fluke. Other German graves, including nineteen in the Mestrenger Muehle area of Kommerscheidt, proved not to contain Americans. Meanwhile, other recovery missions produced negative results. Frustrated, the leaders of U.S. graves investigations began coming up with various theories why they weren't finding the remains of U.S. soldiers, including Leonard's. Americans may be buried in German cemeteries by mistake. They were burned in forest fires. They were eaten by bears or carnivorous animals.

Then came a breakthrough. Maj. Gen. Edward F. Witsell of the Adjutant General Office of the U.S. Army himself got involved. On March 16, 1949, he wrote to several members of the 112th Regiment of the 28th Infantry Division, asking if any of them had seen 1st Lt. Turney Leonard at the November battle. In Bradford, Pennsylvania,. Lt. Colonel Carl Peterson was among those who received the query. He quickly replied in a letter dated March 31, 1949, that he remembered very vividly being in the trench with Leonard on November 7, 1944, and he provided a detailed narrative of those final moments before the German tanks rolled over what was then the Americans' command post. Peterson also provided the geographic coordinates to pinpoint the location of the trench.

Seven months later, on October 27, 1949, Qtr. Mr. Co. Maj. R. E. Deppe went to Kommerscheidt to interview German villagers in the area, including a resident named Hubert Dohman, who provided the following statement, that same day. In part it reads:

> In September, 1944, my late sister and I were residing in Kommerscheidt. Adjacent to the house, a large orchard with old apple trees was located. With the approach of the front, we dug ourselves a standing trench, measuring appr. 3/1/2 meters in length, appr. 2 meters in depth and appr. 2 meters in width, right in the aforementioned apple orchard, for our own protection. We covered the trench with wooden planks and then with earth. The entrance was located at the eastern end and led down in a right angle. The entire local populace was evacuated in October 1944. . . .
>
> When we returned from our evacuation in June 1945, we observed that our standing trench had been made use of by the Americans and had caved in subsequently since, apparently, a tank had driven on it which fact was also substantiated by marks left in the hedge located

Am I Wounded Badly?

between the stone road and the standing trench, the green shrub having been pressed down by the tank tracks.

Right close to the standing trench, a shell crater was located. Since the trench had caved in, we were not able to ascertain whether bodies were still located therein. To establish this fact, it would be necessary to dig up the entire trench which has not been done this far.

The standing trench was located at an appr. distance of 3 meters from the stone road.

Signed Hubert Dohmen

Kommerscheidt, 27 Oct 49.[10]

On October 31 and November 1, an AGRC recovery crew dug up the trench. In it they found First Lieutenant Leonard in the same seated position described by Colonel Peterson in his letter to Major General Witsell. Lying on the ground near Leonard was Captain Driscoll. Upon examination of Leonard's skeleton, medical examiners found major damage to the bones in his left arms and parts of his skull. Leonard's mother was notified by the army of the discovery later that month.[11] As for Turney Leonard's Aggie ring, it was donated to Texas A&M by a German family in January 2001. Shortly after the end of World War II, the United States hired a fifteen-year-old Kommerschiedt resident to help find the remains of American soldiers. Somewhere in the ruins of the village, the young Alfred Hutmacher found a gold ring. He picked it up, took it home, and put it in a box, where it remained for more than a half a century.

One day when reminiscing about the postwar period with his son-in-law, Volker Lossner, Hutmacher took the forgotten souvenir out of its dusty box. Amazed, Lossner examined the ring closely and noticed a name inscribed on the inside. A German soldier himself, he quickly sensed its value as a relic. The two Germans contacted Texas A&M and returned the ring in a specially arranged ceremony on November 11, 2000. "I have come a long way to honor a brave son of this country and graduate of this university," Lossner said at the presentation.[12] The ring is now prominently displayed in a showcase at the university's College Station campus in the Sam Houston Corps of Cadets Center.

IN 1950, FOR THE SIXTH YEAR IN A ROW, THE AMERICAN Graves Registration Command embarked on another search in the Hürtgen Forest. Search teams found the remains of two more soldiers, a U.S. Army combat boot with part of a foot in it, an M1 rifle, a prayer book, and a helmet liner. Even though there were still more than 160 missing U.S. soldiers, the AGRC announced that it was going to declare the missing "non-recoverable." In a report dated November 20, 1950, Hellmuth E. Willner, one of the agency's chief investigators, cited a number of reasons for discontinuing the recovery effort. The areas had been cultivated and rehabilitated to a point that "they no longer bear the appearance of a former battleground," he said. And, despite what he characterized as "the thoroughness of the investigation, only two remains were recovered." Willner stated that the search crews had repeatedly searched "virtually every town and village in the subject area and their surrounding forest districts," and that "it was further learned that the forest area is literally infested with wild bears and carnivorous animals that will devour or dissect and scatter a human remains." Consequently, the agency recommended that the search be put on hold for "four or possibly five years" until further demining efforts made it safe to look in those areas.[13]

At the end of its report, the AGRC's Board of Review declared the remains of 162 GIs "non-recoverable" and listed their names. Some of those on the list included:

S/Sgt. John J. Farrell Jr.,

Sgt. Lemuel H. Herbert,

Sgt. Edward T. Jones Jr.,

Pfc. Michael Loncar,

Pvt. Joseph C. Merlock,

Pfc. Mark Wilson,

Pfc. Paul Peternell,

Pvt. Shirley Bailey,

Pfc. William F. Delaney,

Pfc. Marvin Dickson,

Am I Wounded Badly?

Pvt. Kenneth D. Farris,

S/Sgt. Leo J. Husak,

Pfc. John H. Walker,

Sgt. Melvin C. Anderson,

Pvt. Floyd A. Fulmer,

Sgt. Eugene G. McBride,

Pfc. Lewis E. Price,

Pvt. Floyd A. Fulmer,

Pvt. Harry W. Wilder,

Pfc. Oscar E. Sappington,

Pfc. Leslie E. Shankles,

Sgt. James K. Park,

Tech. Sgt. Robert J. Fitzgerrell,

Pfc. Robert Cahow,

2nd Lt. Ernest E. Martin,

Pvt. James Turner,

Pfc. James C. Konyud,

Pfc. Julian H. Rogers,

Pvt. Henry E. Marquez,

Pvt. Gerald Wipfli, and

Pvt. Sydney E. Weaver.

Of these thirty-one soldiers, twenty-seven have been found. But how were they missed? Most of them had been reported lost on November 8–9, 1944.

THE REMAINS OF 1ST LT. TURNEY WHITE LEONARD— shipped from Bremerhaven, Germany in a flag-draped casket— were put on a railroad car in Jersey City at 2:00 p.m. on Monday, May 29, 1950. The train was in transit on May 30, which was when the nation celebrated Memorial Day that year. Accompanied by an escort officer of similar rank, 1st Lt. Charles D. Ellison, Leonard's body arrived in Dallas the next morning at 7:30. He was eulogized at Crozier Technical High School, one of the many schools he had attended. Burial services were held later that week.[14] After five years the Leonard family could finally begin the grieving process. Tens of thousands of other families with relatives still missing from World War II, however, continued to exist in a dream state, between hope and despair.

In Spirit Lake, Iowa, Peggy Weaver was never the same again after finding out that her father was missing. As a five-year-old she poured through pictures of concentration camps, scrutinizing the faces of all prisoners of war. She stared at images of dead bodies in ditches, on battlefields, in burned-down barns and buildings, behind rocks and church steeples, in jeeps and tanks and trucks and Red Cross tents, looking for her father. If the scenes were shown today on television, they would most likely be preceded with disclaimers, warning of their graphic nature. Her mother, Molly, seemed to be okay with it, though; she understood why Peggy was doing what she was doing. In fact, she was sitting next to her daughter doing exactly the same thing. "They were horrible pictures. They were just awful and I became very traumatized as a child," Peggy says.

Her father—Pvt. Sydney Weaver—fought in the same battle as Turney Leonard. Her family, too, received a telegram from the army around the same time as Lily Leonard in Dallas. They bore the same message: the soldiers were missing in action. The large Weaver family was gathered together in the lakeside home of Peggy's grandparents when, she remembers, the Western Union man arrived at the door to deliver the envelope. Peggy continued playing hopscotch in the kitchen with her cousin. "Aren't you sad?" her cousin asked.

"Why should I be?" Peggy replied. "He's only missing. They'll find him."

But that was the beginning of a turn in her life that she would not be able to straighten out. Since that day in November 1944, she has waited for the army to find her dad. Two years later, when the town gathered at First Congressional Church for a memorial service for Pvt. Weaver, she didn't want her mother to accept the folded U.S.

Am I Wounded Badly?

flag presented to her, because in the then-six-year-old girl's mind, accepting the flag would have given the government an excuse to stop looking for her father. It was, she thought, a straight flag-for-father exchange. Young Peggy was right—but off by about four years. In November 1950, a review board for the AGRC declared Pvt. Sydney Weaver's body "unrecoverable" and stopped looking for him.

As Peggy grew up, she found herself in a state of perpetual waiting. The quiet worry of staying up late at night, waiting for someone—a daughter, a son, a wife or a husband—to return home, became the new normal in Peggy's life. The feeling of waiting for a missing loved one is the same; the only difference is that the person you're waiting for is probably dead. She carried the pain with her wherever she went, and every so often it showed itself in unexpected places. Peggy went to Drake University, the University of Washington, and the University of San Francisco on a GI Bill—a congressionally approved government stipend to help defray the cost of higher education for members who've served time in the military.

Back in the early 1960s, when not many women attended graduate school, she would often be the only woman standing in line with other men to register for the subsidy. Many of them were a little older than she was and had fought in the Korean War. "They would kind of tease me and say, what was I there for," she recalls. "And I would say, my father was missing in Germany." She hated having to answer the question. "It sounded so bogus. How could you be missing in Germany after all this time? But I still couldn't get my head around the concept of him being dead," she says. So, every semester, the question would inevitably come up: "What are you doing in this line?" and she would continue to reply, "My father is still missing from World War II." The alternative thought was just as discomforting. If her father had to die so she could go to college, then "I felt it was blood money. I couldn't afford to go to school without the money but on the other hand he had to die so I could go to school. I just hated the whole thing, standing in line, answering the questions, being a war orphan receiving GI money and the only woman standing there with a group of men who fought in the Korean War. It was really hard for me."[15]

Fig. 14. Theater arts student Peggy Weaver preparing to go on stage at Drake University. Courtesy of the Weaver/Robinette Family.

Peggy got her undergraduate degree in drama from Drake University and studied theatrical design as a graduate student. Then she switched careers, got a teacher's credential, became a teacher, and raised a family of two. She adopted the last name of her late husband, Robinette. Talking about her father has been painful for Peggy, who is now seventy-nine years old. There have been times when I've called her at her home in the San Francisco Bay Area and she wouldn't answer the phone. I tried sending emails, but they, too, went unanswered. As a journalist, I am quite used to being ignored. People don't like to answer tough questions, especially when they have something to hide; sometimes they are ashamed of things they did or are embarrassed to talk about them. Upon occasion, I've also encountered people who are afraid that they may not sound articulate or intelligent in an on-the-record interview. Peggy is none of the above. She is one of the most articulate, thoughtful, intelligent, and forthcoming interview subjects I've had the pleasure of getting to know. But I continue to have difficulty reaching her. When we speak again, she apologizes for ignoring me. "Send me emails. I'll answer them. I promise. I won't ignore you," she says.

I'm not the only one to be kept at bay. A Dutch couple—Ed and Anita Tiebax—from the Netherlands have also been on the receiving end of Peggy's silence. In gratitude for the sacrifice of the millions of Americans who freed Europe from a tyrannical power, the Tiebaxes "adopted" four GIs who gave their lives in World War II. Like many other Europeans, they try to offer assistance in any way they reasonably can to help their adopted GI families achieve closure. They tend to the graves of GIs buried in Belgian, French, and Dutch cemeteries, and, for families of MIAs such as Sydney Weaver, they volunteer their services as information-gatherers and liaisons to government officials and library archivists in Europe.

In a recent email to me, the Tiebaxes expressed concern about Peggy's reticence. Ed wrote:

Peggy Robinette, Sydney Weaver's daughter contacted us in 2017 after we searched and contacted the library.

We were so happy that we had found family and were able to provide the daughters of Sydney with information.

Peggy wrote us a few times and she was happy too, she even offered to send us letters of her father that he send home in the war.

But unfortunately she has broken contact with us and we do not get an answer anymore.

We have already asked a few times what is going on, we even asked an American woman for help, she called the other daughter and she also asked if Peggy wanted to call back but unfortunately, we do not hear anything.

So strange and we do not know why.[16]

In a recent phone conversation with Peggy, I mentioned the Tiebaxes' concern. She apologized once again, and tried, sincerely, to explain her behavior. She said:

I don't know how to explain it but it's very disturbing, and I know sometimes I can deal with it for a while and then I have to put it aside because it keeps me awake at night and I start imagining things and I start getting angry all over again and then I start thinking about his death, my dad's death, and what he could possibly have been and gone on to become in life and that's what makes me get so I can't sleep and I wake up in the middle of the night just staying awake, just lying there staying awake because of it. I know I can handle this for a while and then I have to set it away for a while. Do you understand that? I wake up in the middle of the night. And it's there in my thoughts. It's there when I dream. Very real. It never went away. Every time I think it's gone away. It hasn't. It's just there, never gone away. It's never going to go away. I'm afraid it's never going to go away. I really don't mean any disrespect to anyone. Do you understand that?

PEGGY DIDN'T HAVE TO EXPLAIN THE "IT." MIA GRIEVERS understand. Those who don't, tend to have cookie-cutter advice for the "it" people. Grow up. Snap out of it. See a shrink. Get a life. Enough already. I don't want to hear about it. I knew what Peggy meant by "it," although I have never experienced that type of pain myself. But it's clear in these grievers' silence, and in their honesty

Am I Wounded Badly?

when they decide to break it. And it's obvious in the anger of MIA families. Peggy is angry with the U.S. Army, especially the ones who called off the search in 1950.

> They just gave up on him, like he wasn't even important. I mean they sent him out there on a suicide mission and they didn't even bother to recover his body when they could, when they had an opportunity to do so. They had the officers. They had the soldiers who were there with them, fighting right alongside. They were eyewitnesses. They had information. If they didn't have it, they could get it.
>
> They just kept saying over and over again: We don't know, We don't know. We don't know. My poor mother. She tried so hard to get any bit of information about my dad.

Peggy's mom, Molly, died in a community care center near Spirit Lake on December 27, 2010, without knowing anything more about Sydney Weaver than the scarce and slightly incorrect information she had collected for the memorial notice that ran in the local paper on March 31, 1946. The article noted that Pvt. Weaver had died on November 8, 1944, on his thirty-third birthday. In reality he died two days earlier. Molly was ninety-two years old.

IN WEIRTON, WEST VIRGINIA, LINDA BEPLER'S MOTHER, Mildred, also died knowing the little that could be known about her brother, Pfc. Michael Loncar, at the time. As in the case of Private Weaver, the information was both sketchy and slightly inaccurate. In 2003 Mildred died believing that her brother was killed in Belgium in the Battle of the Bulge and declared missing on November 8, 1944. He was indeed reported missing on that date, but the Battle of the Bulge began more than a month later, on December 16. Like so many other MIA families from that war, for Mildred Bepler the centerpiece of the information she had about her brother was a Western Union telegram informing the family that he was missing and that the army would furnish any additional details about him as soon as they became available. Despite the dearth of information in the one-paragraph notice signed by the adjutant general, for many MIA families the telegram was all they had.[17]

IN DOROTHY, NEW JERSEY, TWO GENERATIONS OF THE MER-
lock family passed without much information either. As each family member died, they handed down to a surviving next of kin the
responsibility of finding out the truth about their fallen family member. Not knowing whether her son Joseph Merlock was dead or alive,
Amelia Merlock bestowed the mantle to her daughters, Rose and
Frances. The two sisters went diligently to work. In 2001 the Merlock family got some news that made them declare in a local newspaper that the information had "brought some closure to many of
the questions the family has had for 56 years."[18] Unfortunately, the
information was incorrect. The article said that the remains of Private.
Merlock had been found and were buried at Henri-Chapelle American Cemetery and Memorial in Belgium under a marker inscribed
with his name. The two sisters went to their own graves under the
mistaken notion that the family mystery had been solved. But Millie Messina has resolved to set the record straight. The eighty-three-
year-old niece of Private Merlock has since found out that Private
Merlock is still missing from that battle of more than seventy-five
years ago, and that she must pick up where Rose and Frances left off,
trying to get anything, "even if it's just an arm, or a piece of bone" of
her uncle. And she realizes that she doesn't have much time, although
the octogenarian is still active in civic affairs and selling real estate
in Weymouth Township.

IN ROSWELL, GEORGIA, EVE CUNNINGHAM GOES ABOUT
her daily business while at the same time listening for the phone
to ring with any information about her brother, Pfc. Mark Wilson.
The last time she saw him was outside of their childhood home in
Hampton, Tennessee, on a chilly fall day in 1943. He walked off in
his khaki uniform "into the sunset," Eve recalls. "I was eight years old
and I thought he really looked handsome on that day." Eve says that
mental image of her brother is one of the few things she has left of
him. "You can't have closure on just that," she adds. There are other
mementos of her brother in the house, much of it military correspondence. One letter came from Col. G. M. Nelson, who replaced Lieutenant Colonel Peterson as commander of the 112th Regiment. In a

Am I Wounded Badly?

letter dated May 25, 1945, he writes of her brother: "He was a splendid soldier and was held in high regard by all members of this command. His loss is deeply felt by him [*sic*] many friends." While the Wilsons appreciated the words, they also rang hollow due to their nonspecificity. The letter, for instance, lacks the details of some of the other letters written by the colonel. In his letter to Ruth Lynn, the wife of another soldier in the same regiment who was also killed in that battle, he offers such details as the time and place her husband's body was found, the fact that he was buried by Germans, that a ring and a watch were found on his body, and that "he had been instantly killed by a bullet which penetrated on his left side."[19] Sometimes knowing particulars about the manner and circumstances of the death of a loved one helps with the grieving process. The Wilsons wrote many letters to a number of military officers requesting such information.

In an undated letter addressed to the quartermaster general, Mark's father, Ray Wilson, pleaded, "We are very much interested in knowing the details for they are important to us at this hour." There is no record of a response. Mr. Wilson died years later, wondering why the army didn't wait a full year before declaring his son dead, as is military protocol for MIAS. In February 2018 Eve finally received an answer. The soldier who saw Mark get killed was taken prisoner by the Germans and released six months later at the end of the war. It was only then—after the army had a chance to contact the American prisoner—that it learned of Private 1st Class Wilson's death. But the information was stashed away in Mark's Individual Deceased Personnel File (IDPF) in a repository in St. Louis hundreds of miles away, and not disclosed to the family until 2018, when Eve Cunningham attended an MIA family meeting in Florida. There an army official handed her she a copy of Mark's IDPF. In the file was a yellowed piece of paper, a "War Department Casualty and Missing Persons Questionnaire" that GIs released from prison camps in 1945 were asked to complete. A Dewey Falkenberry of Bonita, Louisiana, took the time to fill one out. To the question "Were you an eye witness to his death?" Falkenberry responded, "Yes." Based on this, the army sent a letter to the Wilsons on June 6, 1945, informing them that their son's MIA status had been changed to KIA. Had Eve not attended the meeting, the mystery would have continued to haunt her. But, even though Eve now knows that her brother was killed, she says "there still is no closure," because "they haven't found his body." All Eve can do now is "wait," she says. "I've been waiting since 1944."[20]

Even as details about the missing start to trickle out due to the army's new openness, there is still a great deal that the families do not know. For instance, the families of Pvt. Sydney Weaver, Pfc. Michael Loncar, Pvt. Joseph Merlock, and Pfc. Mark Wilson are not aware that these soldiers were all in the same company, in close proximity to each other in Kommerscheidt, facing a heavily armored German force on the morning of November 6, 1944, not one of them standing a fighting chance of survival. The information has been available in various government files ever since 1973, when a vast majority of military documents from World War II were declassified.

Am I Wounded Badly?

# 15

## It Had a Bittersweet Sound

As he hurled himself forward was born a love, a despairing fondness for this flag which was near him. It was a creation of beauty and invulnerability. It was a goddess, radiant, that bended its form with an imperious gesture to him.

—*The Red Badge of Courage*

In moments of loss, people react differently. Some cry, some scream, some get busy, some take up hobbies. Rosemary Farrell talked, to an invisible man. For more than sixty years. "Jack," she would say, "I'm going for a job interview today. What should I say? What do you think I should wear? Do you think this dress looks okay?"

Then, after the U.S. Army sent the Farrells of Arlington, Massachusetts, a granite marker, which they laid in a nearby cemetery, Rosemary went to stand at the memorial stone almost daily, even though there was no grave beneath it. A petite Irish girl—about five feet tall and weighing about 110 pounds—talking to a headstone under the oak and evergreen trees may have sparked the curiosity of a passerby or two over the years. But Rosemary didn't care. Unabashedly, she continued her stream of one-way conversations, regardless of who might hear: "Jack, where are you? What did you do to yourself? Talk to me. Say something. You need to help me. Okay? I really mean that."

The man she spoke to had light brown hair, a straight nose, a high

Fig. 15. Jack Farrell's 1940s residence as it looks today. Courtesy of the author.

forehead, and a twinkle in his eye. A photograph of him hung on a wall in her apartment. His gaze was trained right at her wherever she stood in the room. Rosemary liked that. It was a photo of Jack, her brother, five years her senior, with whom she had spent more time than anyone else while growing up in Arlington, until the day he left for the war. For twenty-three months Rosemary waited for Jack to come home. Then a Western Union man—that unwelcomed specter of a uniformed figure the neighborhood hated—rode up on his bicycle one fall day in 1944 to darken the Farrells' front door like an angel of death. After he delivered the message, the swoosh of air when the door closed behind him snuffed the bond between sister and brother like a candle. Jack was missing, the telegram read.

All Rosemary had left was her unbounded mind, which became like a magic wand that could make a long ago seem just like yesterday. In one fell swoop, she could travel to a place tucked safely away in the recesses of conscious thought, to a time and a space untouched by guns and cannons and death. That place was Spy Pond, a body of water in the middle of town, as big as a university campus, where

It Had a Bittersweet Sound

the two would ride their bikes along its pine-scented shores in the summer and skate on its frozen surface in the winter. "I can just see him now, I can still see him walking with his skates hanging over his shoulder," Barbara Wilson, Jack's other sister, once said. "It seems like it was just yesterday."

The abyss that separated Rosemary from Jack could vanish with just a flick of a thought, Rosemary discovered. With transcendent timelessness she could still be "Murph"—the nickname she received when she was an infant and Jack was five years old and couldn't pronounce "Rosemary"—the best he could do was "Murph," and the name stuck. For the family it was a subject of amusement; for Rosemary it was the deepest expression of love a sister could receive from an older brother. Time passed. Barbara married, became a Wilson, and raised a family. Rosemary never married and remained a Farrell. No one in the Farrell-Wilson family questioned why not, especially Jack Wilson, Barbara Wilson's son and Jack Farrell's namesake. He sensed that his aunt had been profoundly affected by her brother's disappearance. One day Jack's life changed, too. As with Rosemary, it did so because of his uncle Jack.

The metamorphosis began with the mysterious appearance of a picture on his computer screen the morning of June 10, 2009, of a soldier's boot from World War II. From all appearances there was nothing unusual about the army-issued footwear; dozens like it had been photographed by journalists and posted online from time to time. But—at least to Jack—this boot was special. Inexplicably, he became obsessed with finding its rightful owner.

The story of Jack and the boot begins nine months earlier, on a clear autumnal day in September 2008. Five men huddled around a patch of dirt and peering down at it intently, dressed in protective overalls and rubber boots. Some wore work gloves. One carried a circular metallic disc with a long handle. The air was crisp; summer had started to make way for autumn in the state of North Rhine Westphalia, tucked quietly away in the heavily wooded recesses of northwestern Germany. Waves of yellow wheat fields, nudged by a gentle wind, rolled from the edges of the village to the dark green rows of Silver Fir that stretched as far as the eye could see.

The men were laboring near the outskirts of the village of Kommerscheidt, inspecting a plot of land prior to the construction of a home, when the metal detector suddenly started pinging. The electromagnetic impulses sent from the circular disc into the ground had met the electromagnetic field of another metal object about two feet beneath the surface, setting off the response. The men quickly stepped back. Most of their ground sweeps recently had been run-of-the-mill types, with little scanner activity. But, on this particular day—Wednesday, September 24, 2008—the team was overcome with eagerness to find out what lay below.

A far cry from the village it had been in 1944, Kommerscheidt today is an idyllic landscape, with picture-perfect pastures dotted with calmly grazing cows and horses, meandering streams, and tidy rows of homes for the village's approximately one thousand residents. Trimmed hedges and manicured lawns adorn the dwellings, and children's swing sets sit in backyards. Immaculately kept barns sprinkle the countryside. Wooden bridges arch over gullies and waterways, and a two-lane road winds upward for a few hundred yards at a gradual incline to a sister town, Schmidt. With a slightly larger population, a small shopping area, and a smattering of churches and schools, Schmidt serves as a hub to the surrounding communities. Built on the highest elevation in the area, Kommerscheidt and Schmidt offer a 360-degree view of the surrounding landscape, overlooking a peaceful scene of rivers, gorges, lakes, and inlets that spans for miles. In 1944 the twin villages provided an obstructed view of enemy positions. In place of the rustic serenity that envelops the land today, back then there was carnage and death, and that previous dark and somber world has not entirely disappeared. Remnants of it lie just a few feet below the backyards, sidewalks, and driveways of the towns, as five German excavators were about to find out that day in 2008. At the time they were observing a protocol required by German law: because both the German and American armies left behind many unexploded bombs and grenades, before the launch of any excavation the ground had to be checked and swept for explosives by a group known as an Explosive Ordnance Dispoal (EOD) team.

One of the men observing the team was Herr Ludwig Fischer, the

Bürgermeister of Schmidt, who typically accompanies such groups to document activity and assist in a supervisory role. "Because in Kommerscheidt the fights were so hard . . . always today if one will build a house, the Deutsch EOD team comes and looks for ammunition," Fischer says.[1] The men had come to expect finding an occasional bullet shell or unexploded grenade. But, on this particular morning, the explosives squad stopped working immediately to send a message to the Deutsch Kreigsgraberfursorge, the German War Graves Commission, about what they had just uncovered. A little more than the depth of two shovel blades below the neat layer of lush green grass, in the loosened claylike dirt, lay the remains of a man. Buried with his skeleton were a mud-caked collection of paraphernalia, including a rusted rifle, identification tags, a helmet broken in half, and a tattered plastic poncho.

The next morning, Herr Schneider of the Kreigsgraberfursorge commission arrived around 9:00 a.m. Schneider is responsible for the proper handling of the remains of any soldiers, their personal items, or artifacts. Despite a thick fog typical of the region for that time of year, the crew continued the dig. Schneider, dressed in a gray work uniform, rolled up his sleeves and began clawing the ground with his bare hands. The EOD team happened upon its second find not long after: the remains of yet another soldier, alongside where the other one had lain. Next to this soldier also lay an array of belongings, including web gear, boots, belt buckles, gloves, scabbards, gas masks, knives, grenades, entrenching tools, wallet, religious cards, a fountain pen, and a handful of local coins. Also among the disinterred items was an army canteen; amazingly, although the metal container was rusted and banged-up on the outside, preserved nearly intact for more than sixty-four years on the inside was the water the soldier had been drinking before his death.

When word spread that two soldiers had been exhumed, many of the residents from Kommerscheidt and Schmidt flocked to the excavation site. They wondered if the men were American or German. As the excavators went about their business, the town residents looked on, curious but not surprised. The area today is a living museum of that previous time; tour groups, led by green-uniformed guides, regularly walk through in the summer and fall months. Evidence of the battlefield is everywhere. On the western edge of Kommerscheidt, past the cultivated gardens and crop fields, a steep slope leads to a heavily forested area. There, dozens of foxholes remain largely undisturbed from World War II. Deep ruts in the ground created from the tracks of tanks are also ugly reminders of that violent period.

The identities of the newly exhumed soldiers weren't a mystery for long. Their dog tags and wallets revealed who they were. One of them, Sgt. Edward T. Jones, was discovered on September 24, 2008. The other, S/Sgt. Jack Farrell, was found the following day. They were placed in separate, temporary coffins and driven to the nearby German veterans' cemetery in Hürtgen, another village in the forest. Both men belonged to the 112th Regiment of the 28th Infantry Division.

Schneider immediately notified the U.S. Army of the human remains. The army in turn alerted a team from the Department of Defense, formerly known as the Joint POW/MIA Accounting Command (JPAC). As it so happened, the JPAC team was in the vicinity of the Hürtgen Forest, looking for the crew of a plane that went down in 1944. They arrived the next day to conduct a brief inspection of the recovery site before heading to the German cemetery to claim the two Americans.

On September 26, 2008, the story of the discovery of Jack Farrell and Edward Jones was published in the daily *Aachen Zeitung* newspaper. The article named both soldiers and identified the Twenty-Eighth Infantry Division in which they served. (The information was taken directly from their dog tags and wallets.) Along with the article, the German paper ran a picture taken by a photographer at the scene, of a boot, mud-caked and battle-worn. Nine days later the remains of Jack Farrell and Edward Jones arrived at the Central Identification Laboratory, an MIA research facility, in Hawaii.

The *Aachen Zeitung* article, which is published in German, did not make it immediately into the English-speaking world; nine months later the photo taken by the German photographer was made available to the U.S media. However, the names of the two GIs was not included in the caption. In fact there was nothing in the article about

It Had a Bittersweet Sound

GIs being discovered with the boot. The caption was brief and vague: "More U.S. Army Artifacts from WWII Found in Germany."

Here's where the story gets interesting. Some would call what happened a stroke of coincidence; Jack Wilson, coauthor of this book, prefers to attribute it to divine intervention. When he logged on to the internet on June 10, 2009, and saw the photo of the boot on the website of the *Boston Globe*, there wasn't any way for him to know that the boot belonged to his uncle, because there was no accompanying article listing the names of the two disinterred U.S. servicemen. Yet a question flashed in his mind: "Could that be my Uncle Jack's boot?" The obvious answer at that moment was, "Impossible." His uncle fought in the Battle of the Bulge in Belgium and not Germany—at least that's what Wilson thought. Nonetheless, he resolved to learn the identity of the owner of that boot.

Even though the U.S. Army knew the identities of the two American GIs from their dog tags, it didn't make the information public right away. At the time it hadn't yet been able to notify the two soldiers' surviving relatives. Families often no longer live in the same geographical location these days, and, because of their mobility, it can take years before the military locates a next of kin. The army, however, didn't have a hard time finding Farrell's family, thanks to his nephew. Jack Wilson had made himself quite well known at various army departments. He called the Department of Defense Information Office in Washington, DC, the U.S. Army Information Center, also in Washington; the National Archives and Records Administration in College Park, Maryland; the American Battlefield Monuments Commission in Arlington, Virginia; and the U.S. Army Human Resources Command Past Conflicts and Repatriation (HCPCR) office, now in Fort Knox, Kentucky. He made sure that each of those departments took down the names and addresses of his uncle's two sisters, both of whom were still living. One of those agencies, the HCPCR, was interested; it sent the sisters DNA sampling kits. DNA tests come in handy when all that the army has of a soldier's remains are his or her skeletal bones. Forensic specialists take a DNA sample from a bone part and compare it to samples taken from surviving family members; when there's a match, they can theorize that the skeleton belongs to the soldier from that family. Genetic testing, though, wasn't necessary in the cases of Farrell and Jones, since the soldiers were buried with their identification tags. Also, their teeth were still well preserved (teeth take hundreds of years to decay), enabling MIA investigators to identify them both with the aid of their dental records. A few months later, in the fall of 2009, Jack received a phone call from the U.S. Army Past Conflict and Repatriation Office (APCRO), which is charged with contacting the families of fallen soldiers after they have been recovered and identified. An APCRO representative then made arrangements to meet with the Farrell-Wilson family.

Saturday, April 3, 2010. The day started off unseasonably warm, with the mercury having risen more than twenty degrees overnight. Following a long, blustery winter, it was indeed a new day in New England, with the temperature now headed into the seventies. Under a sunny sky, a plain, unmarked rental car arrived promptly at 9:30 a.m. in front of Barbara (Farrell) Wilson's home in a tree-lined, neighborhood of single-family dwellings in Norwood, Massachusetts.

"They're here," Wilson informed his family.

Farrell's two sisters, Barbara Wilson and Rosemary Farrell, had been waiting sixty-six years for this moment. They were about to learn what happened to their brother. Barbara, age eighty-six, and Rosemary, eighty-five, both had serious health problems, but they were prepared to endure whatever it took to get all the details about their brother. Many family members had thought the two sisters—who, in recent years, had been in and out of hospitals and doctor's offices—would never live to see this day.

Due to its importance, the family has come to dub this date "Notification Day." The excitement in the room was palpable. Rays from the springtime sun poured in through the double-paned windows overlooking the front lawn, and, through the large picture window, they could see two men approaching. One was dressed in a dark business suit, the other in a green U.S. Army Class A Officer's uniform. Looking straight ahead, both walked with an upright gait typical of men in the military. Each carried a cardboard box, one box slightly bigger than the other. With three generations of Farrell and Wilson men having served in the army, they knew that military protocol is not to bring a fallen soldier's remains on visits like this. The boxes were a bit of a mystery.

The doorbell rang. To Jack Wilson it had a bittersweet sound. He had eagerly awaited this day, too, but he had also developed a strong resentment toward the military. The U.S. Army was disorganized, frustratingly slow, and annoyingly bureaucratic, in Jack's opinion. He was notified about this visit in September of the previous year. It had taken the Army more than six months to make good on its promise. As he opened the door and looked the men in the eye, he could not muster the enthusiasm to say, "It's great to meet you." Instead, he said, "I'm glad that this day has finally arrived."

Eight members of the Wilson-Farrell family were there for the presentation. The two military guests were Michael Mee, a retired major in the U.S. Air Force, who was now identification section chief of the U.S. Army's Past Conflict and Repatriation Branch, and Capt. Andrew D. Parris, executive officer and casualty affairs officer in the Massachusetts Army National Guard. The family had rearranged the furniture to allow everyone to be able to see. In the center of the room were a sofa and a chair for the two guests. Around them were chairs for everyone else to sit. On a coffee table alongside the guests a family photo album and a college yearbook from Jack Farrell's Boston College days. The family asked Michael Mee to sit on the sofa with Barbara and Rosemary on either side of him. Captain Parris sat in an armchair directly across from them.

Michael Mee was the senior government official, and he took the lead conducting the meeting. He thanked everyone for their patience. The department was understaffed and underfunded, he said. As a result, the staff had to work on numerous repatriation cases at once, so that army representatives could combine multiple family visits on their trips around the country. In fact, Mee said, they had visited a family in southeastern Massachusetts the day before, to deliver a report on a recovered World War II Army Air Corps soldier. His remains had been found in the Mediterranean region.

Mee, who appeared to be in his late forties or early fifties, was trim and stood about six feet in height. He explained that he had grown up in Ohio. After joining the U.S. Air Force, he spent a good part of his time in the service stationed overseas and in Alaska. He had a friendly Midwestern disposition. When he spoke it was with the slow deliberation of a reflective man. His job wasn't an easy one. He had to explain to families how the parachute of their loved one failed to open, or how a plane carrying a crew of airmen crashed into the side of a mountain on a reconnaissance mission. Now he was about to tell this family how S/Sgt. Jack Farrell died. Conducting meetings in an orderly fashion is a practiced art—something Mr. Mee was apparently versed in from his days as a major in the Air Force. He paused to entertain any questions. There were none at this point.

First on the agenda were the two cardboard boxes. This grabbed everyone's attention. Mee said he had some articles attributable to Sergeant Farrell that he wanted to present. Captain Parris rose from his chair and walked over to the larger of the two cardboard boxes that had been placed on a table nearby. Lifting the cover, he reached in to remove a triangular mahogany case, which he handed to Rosemary Farrell. It contained a folded American flag along with the battle ribbons and medals that Jack Farrell had earned. Then came a true surprise. In the smaller cardboard container was a small, rectangular mahogany box. Captain Parris opened it slowly and removed a silver linked chain, which was attached to a dirt-encrusted identification badge: Jack Farrell's dog tags. There was silence, then excited exclamations. These small silver metal plates were put around Rosemary Farrell's neck, and she wore them for the rest of the day, constantly touching them. In some indescribable manner, it was as if Rosemary felt that her brother was back with her. Captain Parris also delivered to the family eight separate certificates, each identifying the service medals and awards that Jack Farrell had earned, among them the Purple Heart award, for battlefield wounds, and the Bronze Star Medal, for "heroic and meritorious achievement in military operations against an armed enemy."

Michael Mee now moved to the most difficult part of the presentation. He stood up to secure a large black leatherette book and returned to his position on the sofa between Barbara and Rosemary. Before opening the book, he provided a brief preamble. After looking around the room at each family member, he said he would present the story in as complete or as abbreviated form as they wanted. There was unanimity among those present that they wanted all the details, with nothing left out. This book is perhaps the most precious gift the military can give to a fallen soldier's family—a painstaking effort by a team of researchers, historians, and forensic experts within the Department of Defense that details the final days and death of a heroic soldier.

The book Mee was holding was a hefty volume, the size of a schoolboy's binder, 111 pages thick. It had been prepared by the JPAC Central Identification Laboratory in Hawaii. The book also contained photographs of dental records from Jack Farrell's stateside training, reports of efforts by the U.S. Army Quartermaster Corps's American Graves Registration Command's attempt to locate all the missing soldiers from the Hürtgen Forest after the War, and written communications to the Farrell family from the U.S. Army Adjutant General's office in 1951 on the final announcement of his death and nonrecoverability.

Now came the most graphic part of the report: photographs of the remains of Jack Farrell. He cautioned the family that the pictures, which were in digital color, might be difficult to view, and, if so, he would omit them from the presentation. No one knew how the two sisters would react; their last memories of Jack were of him as a college undergraduate, in the prime of his life. At the time he was a strong athlete with a square jaw and a full head of golden brown hair. They motioned Mee to proceed.

When he turned the page, everyone present audibly gasped. In a color photograph was the image of an entire skeleton, from head to foot. To most people it looked like an X-ray of a human's anatomy. But, to those in the room, it was Jack Farrell—the person they knew as a brother, uncle, and great-uncle. The skeleton had a life and a personality, with a halo-like aura, visible only to those who missed him and longed for his return. The emotion in the room was indescribable. Finally, Jack Farrell was back with his family. "Home at last, home at last," Rosemary said, breaking out in a big smile. The refrain would be repeated over the course of the day. Collectively, the family breathed a sigh of relief. After sixty-six years of not knowing, they now knew. The single regret was that Jack's parents were not there to see their son return. The visit lasted five hours.

About three weeks later, a Delta Airlines flight departed Honolulu, where S/Sgt. Farrell's remains had been stored for nineteen months at the DPAA's Central Identification Laboratory. U.S. military regulations require that a fallen soldier be accompanied to his home by a soldier of the same rank. S/Sgt. November Cuadra performed this duty. The transporting airline typically upgrades the accompanying soldier to a seat in first class. Before take-off, the pilot addressed the passengers on the intercom and explained that a special passenger was aboard the plane: a missing soldier from World War II was coming home to Boston after sixty-six years. He named the soldier and asked for a moment of prayer. All of the passengers stood and applauded. About fifteen minutes before the plane landed in Boston, a procession of police cruisers, funeral limousines, and a hearse appeared at the airport, almost magically; a welcoming honor guard displayed an American flag. Members of the Massachusetts State Police, a contingent from the U.S. Army Honor Guard, a number of Logan Airport officials, and the Delta ground crew all stood at attention as the casket was rolled out from under the plane. As the hearse turned off a busy road, all traffic stopped. A young man in his twenties jumped off of his bicycle in the middle of the road, stood at military attention, and delivered a crisp salute.

Approximately two hundred people attended the funeral mass, including two veterans who fought in the Hürtgen Forest. One of them was Pvt. Irving Smolens, a member of the 29th Field Artillery Regiment of the 4th Infantry Division, which relieved the 28th after its retreat from the forest. The other was Pvt. Anthony Grasso, who was a member of the 112th Regiment of the 28th Infantry Division. He was wounded by an artillery shell in the same battle that took the life of S/Sgt. Farrell.

The discovery of his uncle's remains didn't diminish Wilson's zeal. He feared that waiting for the army to contact the family of Sgt. Edward Jones Jr. could result in critical delays. World War II veterans are dying at a rate of about 350 a day, according to the U.S. Department of Veteran Affairs Statistics, and, with them, many of their siblings.[2] Shortly after his uncle's funeral in April 2010, Wilson tracked down a relative of Jones in upstate New York, about a half hour's drive from West Pawlet, Vermont, the GI's hometown. The nephew, Charles Pecue, contacted the army. Five months later, in September 2010, the family of Sgt. Edward Jones laid him to rest in a New York cemetery.

Since his uncle's repatriation, Wilson has made three trips to the Hürtgen Forest to discuss with town officials a financial incentive plan. He offered to pay local residents $100 to $200 for a sit-down interview for information on other American MIAS. The idea behind the community outreach is that some of the townsfolk may have grandparents or great-aunts and great-uncles still alive who may have knowledge of buried GIs in the area. One Kommerscheidt town official had tentatively agreed to permit Wilson to visit with the residents in the summer of 2016, but withdrew the invitation at the last minute. An explanation wasn't given. Wilson says he's been told that there could be as many as a hundred American soldiers buried in the area. "I just want to find one body," he says.

# 16

## Zwei Amerikanische Soldaten

He was sore and stiff from his experiences. He had received
his fill of exertions, and he wished to rest.

—Stephen Crane, *The Red Badge of Courage*

Traveling to the Hürtgen Forest and interviewing townsfolk
is one way of getting information about a lost soldier. But
it has its risks. Like Jack Wilson, you may end up eating the
cost of a plane ticket. Politics, a language barrier, and bureaucratic
red tape are potential deal breakers. And there is another problem—
the passage of time. Eyewitnesses from that era have died, for the
most part, taking to the grave their memories of the war and the soldiers who fought it in that forest.

Dr. Stanley Farrior, a retired dentist from North Carolina, found
another way to investigate the death of his older brother Julian, a
first lieutenant with the Twenty-Eighth Infantry Division, who perished in a flash of light at Vossenack in November 1944. His method
did require some travel, although not across an ocean.

His story started one morning in the late fall of that year. Stanley's father, David, drove down to open his clothing and dry goods
store in Burgaw, North Carolina. He noticed a man whom everyone in town dreaded to see, walking up right behind him with a telegram in his hand. "Mr Farrior." That's all he needed to say. David
immediately turned around and exclaimed, "Oh my God, Julian

is dead." Having just lost his wife, Lela, a few weeks prior, his grief was overwhelming.

Stanley was not with his dad at the time. He was a young boy and at school; he learned of his brother's death after he got home later that day. "I handled this terrible news about Julian by totally rejecting it as the truth," Stanley recalls. "As an eight-year-old boy, I did not grieve for many, many years." During that time, he was convinced—or he convinced himself—that the army had made a mistake, and that Julian would walk through the door at any time.

The parenting norm in those days regarding matters related to death and dying was "the less said the better." So Stanley continued to live his life as usual. As a teenager he became occupied with typical adolescent issues: friends, girls, sports, and what what he wanted to be when he grew up. In time Stanley graduated from high school, attended college, and received a degree in engineering. He dated, met his future wife, got married, changed careers, went to dental school, became a dentist, and raised a family. Then, in 2006, a thought he had managed to keep suppressed for all these years suddenly surfaced. Stanley had turned seventy; some of the responsibilities of parenting, marriage, and career were behind him, and he realized that he hadn't come to terms with his brother Julian's death. That older brother of his, who, at age twenty-seven, left home to go overseas, was now, in Stanley's mind's eye, younger than either of his sons. The feeling was the same as losing "a son who never had a chance to live out his life." At that moment he understood that he hadn't found closure. But how was he to deal with this loss? Farrior has been an intellectual all his life; once again he would turn to his intellect to solve a problem. He knew he needed to find out everything he could about his brother's death—but how could he find sufficient information about a battle that occurred long before the dawn of the information age?

He decided to do what U.S. government historians do to help the DPAA: get themselves to a library. It didn't matter that his home in North Carolina was a six-hour drive from Maryland, where one of the two main U.S. libraries for World War II documents is located. He was determined.

It took him about three weekend trips to the National Archives and Records Administration in College Park, Maryland, to collect all that he needed to get started. In the records he found the name of an eyewitness to his brother's death: a James A. Condon. Now the question was how to find him; all Stanley had was the name, with no state, city or street address. Typing the name into the Google search field called up more than twelve million results. He started dialing. His sixth call was to a man in Florida. Anxious to get to the next James Condon on the list, Farrior got right to the point. In his North Carolina drawl he asked, "Were you a soldier in World War II?"

The man said, "Yes."

"Did you fight in Germany?"

The man said, "Yes."

"Were you with the Twenty-Eighth Infantry Division?"

The man said, "Yes."

"Did you fight in the Hürtgen Forest?"

The man said, "Yes."

At that point Farrior knew he had the right number and identified himself.

"I'm Stanley Farrior," he said. "Julian Farrior is my brother."

From that point on, Stanley Farrior and James Condon developed an email relationship, which continued for months.

In October 2007 a smiling Stanley Farrior took his cap off to pose for a photo about fifty yards west of the Roman Catholic Church in the town of Vossenack: the spot where Julian died on November 9, 1944. Today it is a picture-postcard scene of immaculately kept lawns, shops, and homes, bushy gardens, maple and oak trees dipping their boughs gently over a finely paved road that stretches up to a tall gothic steeple with a six-windowed belfry. A photograph of the same location taken by an army photographer around the time that Julian died depicts a stark and apocalyptic war zone bearing little resemblance to its present setting. Lt. Farrior was killed instantly on that fateful evening and buried a few days later.

After reading everything about the fighting in which his brother was involved and traveling more than four thousand miles to the spot where he died, Stanley could rest at last. At Julian's gravesite in

Henri-Chapelle American Cemetery and Memorial, he left a small stone. Engraved in chalk white, it was set against a ribbon of rainbow colors—brown, blue, orange, purple, and pink—in concentric circles, in the center a bright shining light. The engraving reads: "Julian I love you, Brother Stan, October 2007."

"Once I started searching for information I had a continuing thirst for knowledge and discovery about Julian," Farrior says. Today the eighty-three-year-old spends most of his time working long hours in his garden, and he whiles away summers by the ocean along the Carolina coast. "I'm done finding out everything I need to know about Julian," he says. "I'm finally at peace."[1]

Among the many documents researchers rely on are two types of files, both archived in federal government repositories, known as the National Archives Records Administration (NARA). One is in St. Louis. It stores files kept on deceased soldiers, known as Individual Deceased Personnel Files (IDPFs). They contain a serviceman's dental records, death certificates, personal correspondence, and information regarding the military training camps they attended, the lengths of time they were there, and an assortment of other pieces of data, such as the military units in which they served.

The other type of file is kept in a government repository in College Park, Maryland. These files contain postbattle interviews with military generals, colonels, lieutenants, and sergeants, who recount actions taken during engagement and analyze the reasons for them. The death of soldiers or their absences at the time of roll call are also recorded, and the names of eyewitnesses, if any, are noted. These so-called after-action reports—or combat interviews—are sometimes sketchy, but at times full of detail: troop movements (e.g., advances and retreats), casualties, unit deployments by the hour, foxhole positions, enemy strength, radio messages, company morale, and weather conditions.

The reports are often written at the end of the day, when the soldier is hungry and exhausted, or in the early morning hours, after little or no sleep. They are hurriedly put together and rarely read as breezily as a novel. For the lay researcher today, the work can be painstaking and will most likely require an understanding

Fig. 16. In 2007 Stanley Farrior stands on the spot where his brother Julian died in 1944. Courtesy of the Stanley Farrior Family.

of military jargon, such as a BAR (Browning Automatic Rifle) or a "draw" (sloped gully), definitions of which aren't available in most civilian dictionaries. By weaving together information from multiple documents and recorded interviews, a researcher may be able to recreate a scenario or put together a cohesive narrative of what exactly happened to a group of soldiers or an individual GI at a given time.

Maps and drawings sometimes accompany the reports, including old pencil maps, drawn up by postwar recovery teams. Such teams conducted exhaustive searches for six years in the Hürtgen Forest. The U.S. government spent more than $2 billion in today's dollars searching for MIAs in Europe and the Pacific islands and left records of some of the work that was done. Often NARA historians will overlay an old recovery-team map with a Google Earth map, using new computer design software, to pinpoint the location where a soldier may have disappeared in the cartography of today. In other words, a

Hürtgenwald von Krieg zu Frieden, 1944 - 2004
Das zerstörte Vossenack

Remains of a Catholic Church in the center of Vossenack, Germany. It changed hands several times during the Hurtgen Forest Battle. This picture was taken November 7, 1944. The person standing in the road was very close to the loction of Julian Wade Farrior when he was killed on Nov. 9, 1944

Fig. 17. The place where Julian Farrior died in 1944.
Courtesy of the Stanley Farrior Family

World War II soldier may have been killed in a wheat field seventy-five years ago on the outskirts of town that is today a recreational park, a cemetery, a monument, a building, or someone's backyard.

DPAA historians and researchers face an additional challenge in the Hürtgen Forest. More than one battle was fought there. Between September 1944 and February 1945, more than a half dozen major battles were waged within an area of twenty-five square miles, with many regiments and divisions entering the forest at different times to launch offensives at the German Army. In the Vossenack area, for instance, both the 112th Regiment of the 28th Infantry Division, as well as the 121st Regiment of the 8th Infantry Division, engaged the enemy at different times about two months apart. The 28th attacked in November 1944, and the 8th came through in January 1945. Take also the Raffelsbrand area, one and a half miles away: both the 110th Regiment of the 28th Division and the 309th Regiment of the 78th Division forayed into the area—one in November, the other in January.

By narrowing the kill zone, historians can gradually eliminate potential candidates from fifteen to ten to five. Once the circle of candidates is reduced to five, the agency will start considering disinterment. Much of the work done by the DPAA today is focused on identifying the remains of approximately 150 soldiers who fought in the Hürtgen Forest and are buried as unknowns in three nearby cemeteries. Two are in Belgium—Henri-Chapelle American Cemetery and Memorial, and Ardennes American Cemetery. The third is the Netherlands American Cemetery in Margraten.

The military calls the tomb of the unknowns "X-files"—X being the unknown factor. After reducing the field of possible disinterment candidates, historians turn to the old recovery-team maps from the 1940s to see which X-file burials would yield a better than 50 percent chance of a positive identification. Exhumations are expensive, and, in order to keep costs down, the DPAA likes to make sure that the odds of a match are 25 percent or higher.

DPAA investigators were able to identify more than 35 X-files from 2017 to 2020, using the troop-movement-on-the-battlefield methodology (see table 3).

## Table 1. X-file recoveries

| Name | Regiment | Division | Date recovered | Cemetery |
|---|---|---|---|---|
| Shirley Bailey | 8th | 4th | November 2017 | Margraten |
| William Delaney | 22nd | 4th | December 2018 | Henri-Chapelle |
| Marvin Dickson | 110th | 28th | December 2008 | Margraten |
| Kenneth Farris | 22nd | 4th | April 2018 | Margraten |
| Leo Husak | 309th | 78th | February 2018 | Henri-Chapelle |
| John Walker | 18th | 1st | April 2018 | Margraten |
| Melvin Anderson | 803rd Tank | | April 2018 | Margraten |
| Floyd Fulmer | 110th | 28th | November 2018 | Neuville |
| Eugene McBride | 311th | 78th | June 2017 | Margraten |
| Lewis Price | 109th | 28th | November 2018 | Margraten |
| Harry Wilder | 110th | 28th | November 2018 | Margraten |
| Oscar Sapington | 309th | 78th | June 2018 | Henri-Chapelle |

Zwei Amerikanische Soldaten

| | | | | |
|---|---|---|---|---|
| Leslie Shankles | 60th | 9th | July 2018 | Margraten |
| James Park | 26th | 1st | June 2018 | Margraten |
| Robert Fitzgerald | 311th | 78th | September 2018 | Henri-Chapelle |

Soldiers whose identities were not known at the time they were buried but who have recently been identified. Table created by the author, compiled from NARA and DPAA statistics.

The DPAA has been under pressure from Congress to step up the pace, and the recovery rate has improved in recent years. In 2012 an internal investigation uncovered a series of scandals within the POW/MIA Accounting Command and Defense POW/Missing Personnel Office (JPAC), the agency's former incarnation, including fabricated retrieval ceremonies in Hawaii, boondoggles to Europe, the use of inaccurate databases to conduct searches, and deception by the North Koreans, who buried laboratory specimens in battlefields to make them look like fresh discoveries belonging to U.S. veterans killed during the Korean War. To make matters worse, the agency paid the North Koreans hundreds of thousands of dollars for their phony recoveries. Embarrassed, the army tried to suppress the results of the internal investigation. The Associated Press, however, received an inside tip, acquired a copy of the report under the Freedom of Information Act, and published a story on the cover-up attempt in July 2013.[2]

After the story appeared, the army was made to answer to Congress, and the Department of Defense was subsequently tasked with reorganizing the agency, renamed the Defense POW/MIA Accounting Command (DPAA) in 2015. A goal of two hundred identifications a year was set for the DPAA—more than three times the annual discoveries it had been averaging prior to 2013. The agency's budget was also increased: for fiscal year 2018, it received $131.3 million, up from $112.7 million for fiscal year 2017, considerably much more than the $80.8 million it was allotted in 2010.[3] The DPAA likes X-file cases: they yield a higher productivity rate than other forms of agency searches. With X-files, the DPAA already has a body. In cases involving searches for individual soldiers where there is no body, the work could take years. First they have to find remains, and then find out to whom they belong. With remains that have no identification tags or teeth, DNA testing and comparing results with the DNA of families who have provided genetic samples is perhaps the agency's only recourse. In DPAA terminology such cases are informally called "isolated graves," and searches for them take much longer. Still, the agency has hopes of finding them. It has targeted Kommerscheidt as a good place to look, partly because it is suspected there are a number of soldiers still buried there.[4] History buffs also theorize that there may be families in the area that go back three generations.

On a hunch that he would find the kind villager who buried his uncle more than seventy years before, Jack Wilson traveled to Kommerscheidt in the summer of 2012, accompanied by his wife, Mary. Wilson's cross-Atlantic journey was a bit of a risk. Four years before that, a construction crew had accidentally discovered the remains of Wilson's uncle, S/Sgt. Jack Farrell, and another soldier buried next to him, Sgt. Edward Jones, both of whom were repatriated in 2008. In the four years since, a building could have been erected over the gravesite; after all, a construction crew had found the burial place. Still eager to find out everything he could about his uncle, Wilson was willing to take a chance. He pitched the trip to Mary as a wedding anniversary celebration. "Oh, great," Mary said. "We've never gone away for our anniversary and now you want me to walk through battlefields and cemeteries in Europe." Wilson sweetened the deal with stops in London and Brussels.

An army report had provided an address of the home where the remains were found: 153 Kommerscheidter Strasse. Upon arriving at the address—a pretty white house—Wilson rang the doorbell. Several cars were parked in the driveway, but no one answered the door. He rang again and again and again. Still no one came to the door. But, after traveling more than four thousand miles, Wilson was not about to turn around. He tried the doorbell of a neighbor. A man with a friendly smile emerged from his house.

Wilson had come prepared. He had made sure to rent a Volkswagen for the trip to Kommerscheidt; driving up in a Citroën or Peugeot may not be in good taste, he thought. The Volkswagen was parked in plain view. Also, he'd memorized a smattering of German to sprinkle in with his English in case he encountered a language impasse.

The man at the door said, "Hallo."

Zwei Amerikanische Soldaten

Wilson responded, "Guten Tag. Mein name is John Wilson von Boston. Sprechen Sie Englisch?"

The man said, "Nein, mein Bruder sprechen sie Englisch," and called for his brother, who came quickly.

After telling the brothers that he was from America, Wilson said, "Mein onkel was eins of zwei Amerikanische soldaten who had been discovered here drei jahr ago."

They both smiled, and the English-versed brother said, "Ja, the zwei boys were out back here." He invited Wilson to step into his backyard and pointed to a spot about forty yards away. "They were found there near the new haus," he said. Wilson perked up. His new German acquaintance didn't say "under" the house, but "near" it. "Kommen, I will show you," the brother said.

Wilson and one of the brothers crossed to a small fence that separated the property from a neighbor's. The brother stepped over the fence and walked to the edge of the neighbor's yard. He stopped and said, "Here, this is where they were found."

This was the moment for which Wilson had flown over the ocean. "My heart skipped a few beats," he recalls. "I was now standing at the location that had eluded my family for sixty-eight years. It was one of the most memorable moments of my life." He felt a strange combination of excitement and reflectiveness. "I thought about how my uncle was here all by himself for so many years, and I thought about my grandparents who never knew where he was." Wilson was overwhelmed; his heart was beating fast. As he and the brother walked back to their house, Wilson kept repeating, "Vielen dank." It was then that one of the brothers made a remark that, Wilson says he "shall never forget. 'You know, Mr. Wilson, there are many other Amerikanische soldaten still remaining here.'"

That also happens to be the belief of the DPAA. The agency's theory is based on simple math: an MIA-count to X-files ratio. There are more than thirty-six MIAs in the vicinity and only four X-files.[5] Total immolations of bodies are rare, even in plane crashes.[6] Besides, among all the towns in the Hürtgen Forest, Kommerscheidt, Vossenack, and Schmidt have had the highest numbers of isolated burial discoveries, made over the decades by souvenir hunters, construction crews, tourists, and local farmers. In addition to those of S/Sgt. John Farrell and Sgt. Ed Jones, nearly ten other isolated graves have been found in the last decade in the Vossenack-Kommerscheidt-Schmidt area.

### Table 2. Soldiers once lost

| Name | Regiment | Division | Date found | Place found |
|---|---|---|---|---|
| FOUND BY | | | | |
| 1. Paul Peternell, by German citizen | 121st | 8th | 1981 | Burg Berg |
| 2. Lemuel Herbert, by local farmer | 112th | 28th | 1988 | Kommerscheidt |
| 3. Robert Cahow, by two German citizens | 311st | 78th | 2000 | Vossenack |
| 4. Ernest Martin, by construction crew | 109th | 28th | 2000 | Vossenack |
| 5. James Turner, by citizen | 112th | 28th | 2005 | Vossenack |
| 6. James Konyud, by construction crew | 121st | 8th | 2007 | Vossenack |
| 7. Jack Farrell, by construction crew | 112th | 28th | 2008 | Kommerscheidt |
| 8. Ed. Jones Jr., by construction crew | 112th | 28th | 2008 | Kommerscheidt |
| 9. Julian Rogers, by souvenir hunter | 112th | 28th | 2009 | Vossenack |
| 10. Henry Marquez, by souvenir hunter | 112th | 28th | 2009 | Vossenack |
| 11. Gerald Wipfli, by telecom crew | 112th | 28th | 2010 | Schmidt |

Soldiers who were once thought to be lost but have been found. Table created by the author, compiled from NARA and DPAA (Defense POW/MIA Accounting Agency) statistics.

The area has more unknown isolated burials than other battlefields for two reasons, one of which stems from the nature of this particular battle. When the Twenty-Eighth Infantry Division retreated from the Germans in early November 1944, it did so in a hurry. The fleeing soldiers had no time to take their dead with them, and many of the fallen were left behind. The Germans, moving into the

Zwei Amerikanische Soldaten

territory after the Americans withdrew, did bury a number of GIs; these burials had to be done hastily, however, always with a lookout for long-range shelling by the Americans. There was little time, as a result, to scour the grounds for dog tags and other items such as wallets that would have aided search teams later in the identification process. But bodies must be buried for sanitary reasons, and out of respect for the dead.

The second reason for the high number of isolated burials in the area was the result of a disconnect between the village residents and the Bürgermeisters. At the end of the war, when German families returned to their villages, they found the area filled with the dead bodies of soldiers from both armies. The Germans were taken to a nearby cemetery for burial, and the Americans were interred in town, in many cases not far from where they were found. The delicate task of removing and burying them was the responsibility of the Bürgermeister and his crew. But, due to the high body count, the task was so overwhelming that the villagers couldn't wait for the caretakers to get to their neighborhoods; they began burying the bodies themselves without telling officials that they had done so. Therefore, the list of burials made by the Bürgermeister's crew was incomplete.

When the U.S. recovery crews later asked German municipal officials if there were any more American graves in the area, the Bürgermeisters mistakenly told them that there weren't any. The discrepancies between the U.S. Army's list of its KIAs and MIAs and the German lists of burials posed a problem for the supervisors of the search teams when they filed their reports to the army's graves registration unit. How were they to explain why the list of missing soldiers from the after-action reports do not square with the Bürgermeisters' recovery lists? Why weren't the bodies of the MIAs found? Cognizant of the well-touted high mandate of the U.S military—"no soldier left behind"—the report writers had to show that they had done everything they could to recover the bodies of their comrades. To placate their superiors, the graves registration teams made the Bürgermeisters sign affidavits vouching that they had conducted an exhaustive search of the area for American bodies, not once but multiple times.

The army graves registration detachment operation incorporated those affidavits into its final report on November 20, 1950, stating that the only places that had not yet been searched were areas still heavily mined. "These mined areas, according to local officials and demining team personnel, will not be completely demined or considered safe for entry for four or possibly five years from this date," wrote Hellmuth E. Willner, one of the group's principal investigators.[7] Willner noted that, "in view of the forgoing, it is concluded that further investigation in those areas not mined or those already demined would not result in the recovery of any of the subject unresolved casualties. It is further concluded that any attempt to conduct a thorough search of the mined areas would be costly, timely and above all extremely dangerous. Recommend Non-recoverable action be initiated."[8] In other words, the recovery group concluded that it would be futile to continue the search in the areas inhabited by the villagers.

Apparently Willner was wrong, as the remains of GIS continued to be disinterred in the coming decades. Because of the subsequent recoveries, in the fall of 2012 JPAC contracted a Florida-based archaeological dig team, Southeastern Archaeological Research (SEARCH), to conduct a study assessing the likelihood of finding MIAS in Schmidt, Kommerscheidt, and Vossenack. Contradicting Willner's report, SEARCH concluded that there was a "high probability" of finding a good number of GIS in the villages themselves, far from the mined fields referred to in the American Graves Commission's 1950 report. These "high probability" areas were identified in a 2014 SEARCH report.

This SEARCH report was not made available to the public, but we received a copy after filing a request for access to it, under the Freedom of Information Act. We discovered that most of the soldiers identified in the "high probability" locations were from the 112th Regiment, which had to retreat from the frontline more quickly than many of the other regiments. A number of those soldiers in the "high probability" category were from Company A of the 112th Regiment. As the Germans descended on their defense positions on the morning of November 6, 1944, in overwhelming numbers

Zwei Amerikanische Soldaten

and armory, the Americans had to retreat in a matter of minutes, with no time to take their dead with them. We examined a battlefield map from that morning in Kommerscheidt and overlaid it with a Google Earth map from today, to identify the neighborhood in its current configuration. We noted the property addresses where the remains of three other Company A servicemen—S/Sgt. Jack Farrell, Sgt. Edward Jones, and Sgt. Lemuel Herbert—were found. The maps indicated that all three men were buried not far from where they were believed to have been killed on the morning of November 6. Based on after-action reports of that battle, Company A unit members were located close together in foxholes in the western part of town, right in the path of a platoon of advancing German Tiger tanks. Flanking them were hundreds of Wehrmacht troops. Company A, armed merely with rifles, simply had no chance.

We believe that's where four MIAs were killed: Pvt. Sydney Weaver of Spirit Lake, Iowa; Pfc. Michael Loncar of Weirton, West Virginia, Pfc. Mark Wilson of Hampton, Tennessee; and Pvt. Joseph Merlock of Dorothy, New Jersey. These men and their families have been profiled in this book. We've talked at great length with their sisters, daughters, nephews, and nieces. During our conversations, we made it quite clear to the families that our research project has to some extent overlapped with that of the army, and that the information we have uncovered about the possible burial sites of their loved ones might best be delivered to them by representatives of the army, which, after all, is designated as the official bearer of news from the office of the adjutant general and the Department of Defense's DPAA. The families told us they didn't care who delivered the information. After all these years of not knowing, they just wanted to know, as soon as possible. This posed a problem for us. What was the ethical thing to do? Should we wait for the DPAA to find these soldiers, whenever that might happen? Time is of essence. A handful of surviving family members are in their eighties and nineties. Others are in their seventies.

The United States sent a search team to Kommerscheidt in the spring of 2016, but German nationals note that the search left much to be desired. Lt. Col. Mario Cremer, a German Army officer who lives in Kommerscheidt, assisted in that search, as well as in others. In an email on November 14, 2019, he wrote me this: "We had several investigation teams of JPAC or DPAA in Kommerscheidt over the last years. We showed them several spots where local inhabitants told us about that they knew there were remains of soldiers waiting to be recovered. But DPAA did not take big efforts to solve those cases."[9] The DPAA has been focusing their recovery efforts on cases in the surrounding towns and says it plans to return to Kommerscheidt for more recovery work. Ian Spurgeon, a DPAA historian, says the names of the men from Company A are specifically marked in their computer files—meaning their cases are still open and under investigation.

Like S/Sgt. Farrell and Sgt. Jones, Pvt. Weaver, Pvt. Wilson, Pvt. Merlock, and Pvt. 1st Class Loncar held their positions to the very end. There were probably moments when the thought of climbing out of their foxholes and running from the approaching Germans crossed their mind. They didn't. Instead they chose to be brave and pay the price on that cold November morning with the first flakes of snow of the season gently falling from the sky.

IT WAS A WARM DAY IN JUNE 1945. THE WAR IN EUROPE WAS over. Anthony Grasso was still alive. The private of the 112th Regiment of the 28th Infantry Division was thankful for that. But it was a bittersweet moment for the twenty-year-old from Needham, Massachusetts. Many of his buddies were dead, and he had become someone he wasn't proud of. "In war, you do things that you would never ever do anywhere else," he says. Ever since he was blasted into the air by an artillery explosion on the very first day of battle in the Hürtgen Forest, he had been recuperating from his wounds in various hospitals—first in Paris, then in London. From there, he was put on a hospital ship that sailed from Wales to Boston.

Once he had healed, Grasso realized he was no longer the same person who left for Europe in 1943. The prewar Grasso was a smart, happy, and easygoing boy. The new Grasso was angry, bitter, and afraid. He was a broken man. It took him six months to recover from his wounds. His only happy moment during that time was a chance meeting with his brother in London; Frederick Grasso was passing through town on his way to the Battle of the Bulge. Anthony was in a hospital bed, his head completely bandaged. One morning after waking up, he noticed a uniform hanging nearby; it said 11th Armored Division on it. He told an attendant, "I got a brother in that division." The attendant told his superiors, who contacted the division officers. They located Frederick, who happened to be in London along with his unit, and the army let him borrow a jeep to visit Anthony in the hospital. "We were like two ships passing in the night," Anthony says. The two brothers had a Thanksgiving meal together and reminisced about the old days when they were wild and carefree. Then they said goodbye. Grasso didn't know if he would see his brother alive again. Frederick went to the frontline, and Anthony was shipped to the U.S. Army base at Camp Edwards on Cape Cod in Massachusetts.

After months of rehabilitation, Grasso was finally cleared to go home. The army said he was okay, but he didn't feel okay. Something had changed in him. He knew it, but he couldn't explain it. For years after the war, Anthony visited a VA hospital in Boston. Doctors there told him that he was "shell-shocked." Later they started using another term: "post-traumatic stress syndrome" (PTSD). He preferred "shell-shocked." That was the nickname his friends gave him for a long time: "Shell-Shocked Tony." The once calm and happy guy got into fights at the drop of a hat; it would happen a lot in bars. After a while he just stopped frequenting them. He never liked drinking anyway.

Grasso went back to high school to get his diploma. The thought of playing varsity baseball—his one big dream as an eighteen-year-old senior—didn't even enter his mind now. He had no interest in sports anymore. Life looked different. The war had made him restructure his priorities; things that once had value had lost meaning. Most of the students in his classes were returning veterans, like him. Even though many of them were in their early twenties, they behaved like much older men. Grasso says, "We just went to school and went home. It wasn't like high school no more. We were in adult education."

After completing the twelfth grade, Grasso signed up for electrician school. At first he thought he could complete the program. The old Grasso—spunky, full of energy and wit—definitely would have; that Grasso was eager to accept any intellectual challenge. But he wasn't the same person now. The new Grasso withdrew from electrician school and got a job driving a truck for an ice cream distributor. A younger brother, Joseph, who was too young for World War II, went to medical school and became a dentist. Anthony drove a truck for forty-six years, until he retired.

During that time he continued seeing a therapist at the VA hospital in Boston. He experienced pangs of guilt. The lieutenant that was with him the morning of November 2, 1944, took the shrapnel for Grasso. If it wasn't for him—1st Lt. Frank DuBose—Grasso most likely wouldn't be alive. Following his discharge from the army, Grasso also suffered from headaches and dizziness. He didn't feel like himself. One day the therapist asked him, "Mr. Grasso, do you have suicidal thoughts?"

It's a wintry day in February 2019. The snow that fell last week is still thick on the ground. Inside his neatly kept three-bedroom home, Grasso sits across the kitchen table from me. He is wearing a thick New England Patriots sweatshirt, a baggy pair of blue jeans, and a misshapen pair of sneakers that are at least five years old. I am interviewing him for this book. He grimaces whenever he shifts his weight; his body is wracked with pain. I wait for him to finish his sentence. He looks up from the table to see if I heard what he just said. I continue looking at him, waiting for his answer. I don't mind the silence. It is uncomfortable, but I can wait. Grasso is uneasy. I can tell. I remain silent. This is my eighth visit with him. Each time I've spent at least a couple of hours with him, chatting. Once we spent nearly the whole day together. We sat. He talked. I listened, asking a question now and then, mostly when he stopped talking. We drove around the multiple neighborhoods where he'd grown up. He showed me his grade school, his middle school, his high school, the card shop he hung around as a teenager, the home he lived in before the Great Depression impoverished his family, and the sec-

**Fig. 18.** Anthony Grasso (*back left*) and his family.
Courtesy of the Anthony Grasso Family.

ond, more modest home the family moved into after that. We drove
to the station where he'd taken the train to boot camp with a young
man who had just signed with the New York Yankees. He showed me
where his father had dropped him off and told me how he looked that
morning: distant and preoccupied. Grasso has a pretty good memory. I think I have come to know him fairly well, after all these trips.
He has been very generous with his time, always obliging, never for-
getting an appointment. He has answered all my questions candidly
thus far. There is one more question before him now. He knows it.
I didn't have to verbalize it. He has gotten to know me so well. We
have developed the understanding that when he stops talking and
I remain silent, it means that I know he has more to say. He looked
at me and read my mind. *What was your answer to the therapist when
she asked you, "Have you had suicidal thoughts?"*

"Yes," he whispers with the raspy voice of a ninety-year-old man
and nods his head. "I told the therapist. Of course." Grasso doesn't
have to say anything else. Over the months, we've grown comfortable with each other. We don't have to keep talking all the time. I

Fig. 19. A memorial stands one block from where S/Sgt. John J. Farrell once lived. Courtesy of the author.

think about his bucket list and his wish to travel to South Carolina to stand by the grave of Lt. Frank DuBose.

Anthony knows that I know why he hasn't taken his life. He doesn't need to spell it out for me. I see it in his light brown eyes: his family. Three daughters and eight grandchildren. There are pictures of them everywhere in his house. They have made him forget about the war.

Zwei Amerikanische Soldaten

## Table 3. Those still missing in the Hürtgen Forest

*Here, then, are the still missing soldiers from the battles in the Hürtgen Forest. They are listed by name, rank, army serial number, and the county and state where they lived prior to enlistment.*

| Name | Rank | Serial No. | County/State |
|---|---|---|---|
| Akers, Joseph (NMI) | Cpl. | 35 432 212 | Wayne WV (R) |
| Anderson, Melvin C. | Sgt. | 37 153 333 | NE (R) |
| Anderson, Ralph J. | S/Sgt. | 14 007 737 | Oconee SC |
| Andrews, Charles (NMI) | Pvt. | 42 090 478 | Rochester NY (R) |
| Aprilante, John R. | Cpl. | 32 633 083 | Kings NY |
| Archambeault, Francis (NMI) | Pvt. | 31 375 778 | Manchester NH |
| Asero, Matthew M. | Pfc. | 32 118 414 | Kings NY |
| Bailey, Shirley E. | Pvt. | 35 772 887 | Kanawha WV (R) |
| Banks, Cecil (NMI) | S/Sgt. | 33 659 950 | VA |
| Barabas, John J. | Cpl. | 36 608 854 | IL |
| Barker Cecil (NMI) | Sgt. | 35 448 651 | Huntington WV |
| Barney, Harley E. | Pfc. | 36 630 176 | Vinton OH |
| Barrow, Pearl F. | Pvt. . | 37 731 632 | Sedgwick KS (R) |
| Bates, Lawrence J. | S/Sgt. | 32 039 349 | NY |
| Beliles Otis E. H. | Pvt. | 35 720 385 | Evansville IN |
| Birek, Martin L. | Pfc. | 33 400 535 | Allegheny PA |
| Blair, Walter E. | S/Sgt. | 32 207 611 | Chenango NY |
| Blanchard, Daniel C. | T/4 | 34 230 718 | LA |
| Blanton, Raymond C. | S/Sgt. | 33 644 965 | Henrico VA (R) |
| Blatnik, Joseph A. S. | Sgt. | 33 036 419 | Pittsburgh PA |
| Bradshear, Walter L. | Pvt. | 38 661 059 | AR |
| Brooks, Sturm W. | Pfc. | 13 018 085 | Sumter SC (R) |
| Brotherton, Clarence W. | Pfc. | 36 756 847 | IL (R) |
| Brown, Jack W. | 2/Lt. | 0 545 163 | PA |
| Brown, Raymond L. | Pfc. | 34 871 646 | Lauderdale MS |
| Buskirk, Jack L. | T/5 | 39 315 080 | OR |
| Cahow, Robert T. | Pfc. | 36 206 366 | Barron WI (R) |
| Campbell, Charles A. | Pfc. | 33 233 001 | Harrisburg PA |
| Cannon, Leo L. | S/Sgt. | 35 475 235 | Louisville KY |
| Cansler, James J. | Pvt. | 37 744 699 | Polka MS (R) |
| Canup, Grady H. | Sgt. | 34 093 884 | Pickens SC |

| | | | |
|---|---|---|---|
| Carson, Joseph (NMI) | Pvt. | 33 716 276 | PA |
| Centen, Donald R. | Pfc. | 36 293 976 | WI |
| Chernko, James (NMI) | S/Sgt. | 6 896 994 | Fayette PA (R) |
| Cicconi, Salvatore J. | Pfc. | 42 121 145 | Binghampton NY |
| Cobb, George F. | Pvt. | 33 727 066 | Baltimore MD (R) |
| Cooke, Kenneth H. | Pfc. | 36 417 255 | MI |
| Conklin, John M. | S/Sgt. | 32 080 716 | Orange NY |
| Conner, W. D. | Pfc. | 38 089 907 | Martin TX |
| Coppola, Charles, Jr. (NMI) | Cpl. | 32 687 493 | NY |
| Countryman, Arthur W. | T/Sgt. | 20 602 751 | Will IL |
| Cuellar, Leonard (NMI) | Pfc. | 36 626 049 | IL |
| Cuozzo, Michael (NMI) | Pfc. | 42 068 233 | Kings NY |
| Daly, William J. | Pfc. | 32 309 120 | Newark NJ |
| Delaney, William F. | Pfc. | 34 492 989 | Kingston TN (R) |
| Dempfle, Francis N. | Pfc. | 32 833 115 | Erie NY (R) |
| Dennis, Jack K. | Pvt. | 34 792 444 | Polk FL |
| Derflinger, James M. | Pvt. | 33 546 320 | Warren VA |
| Detloff, Leonard J. | T/Sgt. | 36 105 267 | MI |
| Dickson, Marvin E. | Pfc. | 35 147 414 | Marion IN (R) |
| Di Iorio, Liberato (NMI) | Pvt. | 11 111 688 | RI |
| Dobson, James L. | Pvt. | 36 442 107 | DeKalb IL |
| Dorsey, Carl G. | Pvt. | 37 736 829 | Sumner KS |
| Dougherty, Calvin C. | Pfc. | 16 088 853 | Charlevoix MI (R) |
| Drabecki, Anthony T. | Pfc. | 35 555 353 | St. Joseph IN |
| Dumont, Edward C. | Pvt. | 31 456 753 | Essex MA (R) |
| Edwards, Herbert W. | Pvt. | 15 336 969 | Mingo WV |
| Edwards, John R. | Pfc. | 34 788 808 | Walton FL |
| Farrell, John J., Jr. | S/Sgt. | 11 099 534 | Arlington MA (R) |
| Farris, Kenneth D. | Pvt. | 38 607 946 | Collingsworth TX (R) |
| Faulknor, Roland P. | Pvt. | 36 960 336 | MI |
| Feidler, Charles B | Pvt. | 33 884 654 | PA |
| Fernandes, Alfred J. | Pfc. | 31 447 143 | Newport RI |
| Ferrara, Vincent J. | Pfc. | 36 958 626 | WI (R) |
| Ferry, Edward W. | T/4 | 36 355 567 | Cook IL |
| Fleeman, Archie V. | Pvt. | 39 569 683 | Contra Costa CA |
| Fitzgerrell Robert J. | T/Sgt. | 18 160 898 | OK (R) |

Zwei Amerikanische Soldaten

| | | | |
|---|---|---|---|
| Foley, Robert W. | Pvt. | 12 130 830 | Monroe NY (R) |
| Frantz, Gerald R. | Pfc. | 33 611 532 | Wilkes Barre PA |
| Frazier, Lloyd W. | Pfc. | 37 168 092 | MN |
| Fugate, Albert C. | Pfc. | 37 189 417 | IL (R) |
| Fulmer, Floyd A. | Pvt. | 34 651 755 | Newberry SC (R) |
| Garcia, Joe A. | Pvt. | 37 702 625 | Denver CO |
| Garza, Rubie R. | Pvt. | 6 260 485 | TX |
| Gastelum, Richard G. | Pfc. | 39 578 698 | Los Angeles CA (R) |
| Gerdes, Woodrow F. | S/Sgt. | 37 378 050 | MO |
| Gervais, William A., Jr. | Pfc. | 31 140 372 | Bristol MA |
| Giles, William R. | Pvt. | 19 187 529 | WA |
| Givens, Jacob W. | Pvt. | 35 075 744 | KY (R) |
| Goldstein, Aaron (NMI) | Pvt. | 32 991 892 | Kings NY |
| Goldthwaite, Harry W. | Pfc. | 42 094 250 | Onondaga NY (R) |
| Grigaitis, Edward G. | Pvt. | 13 056 609 | Luzerne PA |
| Groh, William L., Jr. | Pfc. | 35 549 958 | Lucas OH |
| Guido, Carmelo B. | Pvt. | 32 030 036 | Chautauqua NY |
| Gunnoe, Joseph H. | Cpl. | 35 654 719 | Kanawha WV |
| Hager, Clarence W., Jr. | T/5 | 37 604 944 | St. Louis MO |
| Halbrook, Leroy F. | Cpl. | 36 436 206 | Macon IL |
| Hardin, Ira I. | S/Sgt. | 07 023 421 | VA |
| Hardy, Robert W. | 1/Lt. | 01 016 788 | IL |
| Harris, Dewey W. | Pfc. | 37 383 238 | St. Louis MO (R) |
| Harris, Melvin L. | Pfc. | 39 724 232 | Los Angeles CA |
| Harris, Preston (NMI) | Pfc. | 38 117 537 | Hunt TX (R) |
| Harvison, William C. | Pvt. | 06 397 020 | MS |
| Hathaway, Alevin A. | Pvt. | 31 339 130 | VT |
| Hautala, Waino (NMI) | Pvt. | 36 194 238 | Alger MI |
| Healion, Arthur J. | T/5 | 32 806 100 | Queens NY |
| Heelein, Nicholas J. | Pvt. | 36 635 646 | IL |
| Hekiman, George H. | Pfc. | 32 838 900 | NY |
| Hendricks, Wilder L. | Pvt. | 34 887 038 | Coffee TN |
| Hensley, George B. | S/Sgt. | 15 118 144 | Raleigh WV |
| Herbert, Lemuel H. | Sgt. | 33 023 842 | Lackawanna PA (R) |
| Herrera, Reyes (NMI) | Pfc. | 38 442 764 | NM |
| Heurich, William H. | Pfc. | 33 034 759 | PA |
| Hickey, Albert C. | Pvt. | 38 700 951 | Wilbarger TX |

| | | | |
|---|---|---|---|
| Hines, Walker (NMI) | Pvt. | 07 087 626 | NC |
| Hobbs, Clarence S. | Pfc. | 38 140 145 | Van Zandt TX |
| Hockert, Edward D. | S/Sgt. | 37 168 039 | MN |
| Hong, Quan (NMI) | T/4 | 39 003 371 | CA |
| Hornyak, Michael C. | Pfc. | 33 395 228 | Greensburg PA |
| Hug, Bernard R., Jr. | Pfc. | 36 215 760 | WI |
| Hurd, John W. | Cpl. | 39 900 606 | Bingham ID |
| Husak, Leo J. | S/Sgt. | 38 432 713 | TX (R) |
| Ibe, Raymond (NMI) | Pfc. | 36 291 288 | Sheboygan WI |
| Isken, Arthur C. | Pvt. | 36 902 422 | NA |
| Jackovich, Alex | Pvt. | 35 845 496 | Vermillion IN |
| Jacob, George A. | Pvt. | 36 906 896 | IL |
| James, John (NMI) | Pvt. | 07 022 080 | PA |
| Jeffers, Oliver (NMI) | Pfc. | 34 491 814 | Scott TN (R) |
| Jenson, Henri (NMI) | Pfc. | 37 159 295 | MN |
| Johnson, Jack R. | Pvt. | 34 872 691 | NA |
| Johnson, Robert K. | Capt. | 0 737 128 | IL |
| Jones, Curtis L. | Pvt. | 42 114 650 | Rensselaer NY (R) |
| Jones, Edward T., Jr. | Sgt. | 31 020 148 | W. Pawlet VT (R) |
| Judd, Charles R., Jr. | Pvt. | 35 793 716 | Ft. Thomas KY |
| Jurak, William | Pfc. | 36 903 125 | IL |
| Kaiser, Leo W | Pfc. | 38 567 342 | OK |
| Kallenberger, Edward | Pfc. | 37 554 577 | NA |
| Kautz, Arthur L. | Pvt. | 33 845 965 | Monroe PA |
| Kennedy, Joseph E. | Pvt. | 35 778 073 | Mingo WV |
| Kern, Herbert R. | S/Sgt. | 15 103 843 | Cuyahoga OH |
| Kime, Carl F., Jr. | Pfc. | 14 034 785 | Mt. Gilead NC |
| Kleese, Lloyd | Sgt. | 15 015 210 | OH |
| Knapik, Boles S. | Capt. | 01 288 241 | NY |
| Knecht, Charles H | S/Sgt. | 20 302 770 | Luzerne PA |
| Knoll, Gregory V. | Sgt. | 37 354 966 | Finney KS |
| Kokotovitch, Saul | Pfc. | 35 094 839 | IN |
| Konyud, James C. | Pfc. | 35 273 676 | Cuyahoga OH (R) |
| Krapf, Howard G. | Pfc. | 33 481 964 | Allentown PA |
| Kreigh, John W. | Pfc. | 33 764 399 | Clinton PA |
| Lacny, Stanley W. | Pfc. | 36 325 066 | Cook IL |
| La Fontaine, Arthur D. | Pvt. | 42 114 767 | NA |

Zwei Amerikanische Soldaten

| | | | |
|---|---|---|---|
| Langevin, Arthur T. | Pvt. | 31 431 740 | Norfolk MA |
| Lawall, Harold E. | S/Sgt. | 42 051 048 | Kings NY |
| Lawson, Johnson, Jr. (NMI) | Pvt. | 35 075 548 | WV |
| Legler, Leroy C | Sgt. | 33 147 241 | Berks PA |
| Lehman, Walter R. | Pfc. | 37 516 251 | MO |
| Light, Robert C | Pvt. | 35 224 513 | Richland OH |
| Linder, William R. | S/Sgt. | 14 053 580 | Greenville SC |
| Lochowicz, Eugene E. | Pfc. | 36 836 906 | WI (R) |
| Lockwood, Eugene A., Jr. | Pvt. | 34 606 050 | Guilford NC |
| Loncar, Michael (NMI) | Pfc. | 15 171 452 | WV |
| Loterbaugh, James G. | Pvt. | 35 738 624 | Mushingum OH |
| Luster, Sam (NMI) | Pfc. | 34 394 063 | Elmore AL |
| Lyons, Donald E. | Pvt. | 35 299 139 | Lucas OH |
| Maffia, Victor E. | Pvt. | 39 477 219 | Multnomah OR |
| Maier, Roy C. | Pfc. | 37 621 640 | NA |
| Marchesi, Joseph A. | Cpl. | 32 807 171 | Bronx NY |
| Maringer, George A. | Pfc. | 35 683 706 | OH |
| Marah, Joseph M. | Pfc. | 34 581 498 | NA |
| Marquez, Henry E. | Pvt. | 37 736 316 | Wyanndote KS (R) |
| Marsh, Joseph M. | Pfc. | 34 581 498 | AL |
| Mauck, James M. | 1/Lt. | 01 309 290 | VA |
| Marshall, James L. | Pvt. | 42 016 085 | NJ |
| Marsigleano, Frank (NMI) | Pvt. | 32 705 995 | NY |
| Martin, Douglass A. | S/Sgt. | 31 028 048 | MA |
| Martin, Ernest E. | 2/Lt. | 17 125 208 | MT (R) |
| Maurin, John F. | Pfc. | 36 675 393 | Whitehall MI |
| McCurley, Ballard (NMI) | Pvt. | 39 147 939 | CA (R) |
| McKeon, Matthew L. | T/Sgt. | 35 061 572 | OH |
| McMahon, Paul W., Jr. | Pvt. | 36 843 611 | WI |
| McNamara, Robert J. | Pfc. | 33 772 562 | PA |
| Meech, Richard A. | Pfc. | 32 939 009 | Monroe NY |
| Meier, Roy C. | Pfc. | 37 621 640 | MO |
| Merlock, Joseph C. | Pvt. | 42 080 273 | Atlantic NJ |
| Michaud, Raymond J. | Pfc. | 31 115 900 | Aroostook ME |
| Middlekauff, Raymond H. | Pfc. | 33 903 479 | Baltimore MD (R) |
| Mikala, Floyd J. | Pvt. | 36 193 865 | Manistee MI |
| Miller, George (NMI) | Pfc. | 32 970 110 | NY |

| | | | |
|---|---|---|---|
| Mingonet, Aime M. | Cpl. | 14 118 101 | FL |
| Mixon, James C | Pvt. | 14 005 291 | Wilcox AL |
| Moniz, Daniel (NMI) | Pvt. | 39 041 143 | Alameda CA |
| Moore, Edward L. | Pfc. | 32 251 526 | Niagra NY |
| Moore, Joseph R. | T/Sgt. | 20 320 603 | Henrico VA |
| Morrison, Bill (NMI) | Pfc. | 34 162 013 | AL |
| Moss, Thomas O. | Sgt. | 33 046 620 | VA |
| Mulder, John T. | 2/Lt. | 0 509 594 | OR |
| Murr, Albert (NMI) | Sgt. | 36 373 724 | Lasalle IL |
| Neumer, Robert F. | Pvt. | 35 631 196 | OH |
| Nelson, Joseph P. | Pfc. | 35 042 075 | Fountain IN |
| O'Bryant, James L., Sr. | Pfc. | 34 898 607 | NC |
| Orshan, Seymour | T/5 | 42 006 412 | NJ |
| O'Toole, Edward L. | Pfc. | 39 116 433 | CA (R) |
| Owens, David N. | Pfc. | 20 454 111 | Gaston NC |
| Pallik, James B. | Pvt. | 36 756 309 | NA |
| Paladini, Edward E. | Pfc. | 39 140 517 | Alameda CA |
| Panepinto, Salvatore S. | 2/Lt. | 01 822 306 | IN |
| Paoli, Albert J. | Pvt. | 36 673 053 | IL |
| Paris, Peter J. | Sgt. | 36 238 712 | Marquette MI |
| Park, James K. | Sgt. | 38 418 145 | TX (R) |
| Pawlik, James B. | Pvt. | 36 756 309 | IL |
| Paxton, Lyle (NMI) | Pfc. | 15 762 078 | WV |
| Peternell, Paul | Pfc. | 33 395 819 | Greenberg PA (R) |
| Phillips, Wendell G. | Sgt. | 36 122 842 | Detroit MI |
| Pitman, Bruce M. | T/Sgt. | 36 317 736 | Knox IL |
| Pitzer, Reginald A. | 2/Lt. | 0 766 681 | TX |
| Plasson, Victor P. | S/Sgt. | 31 424 392 | Suffolk MA |
| Potts, Benjamin T. | 1/Lt. | 0 1011 981 | VA |
| Pratt, George W.M. | Pfc. | 34 984 428 | TN |
| Price, Lewis E. | Pfc. | 31 495 809 | Jefferson TN (R) |
| Quick, Richard H. | Pfc. | 36 583 270 | Clarksburg WV (R) |
| Radanovich, John W. | Sgt. | 36 539 481 | MI |
| Rapp, Edward B. | Pvt. | 39 477 233 | Multnomah OR |
| Rassler, Victor J. | T/4 | 37 272 260 | MN |
| Retone, Anthony, Jr. (NMI) | Pvt. | 33 434 875 | PA |
| Reab, Lyle W. | Pvt. | 37 448 195 | NE |

Zwei Amerikanische Soldaten

| | | | |
|---|---|---|---|
| Reese, William R. | Cpl. | 33 489 584 | Berks PA |
| Reeves, Noah C. | Pvt. | 34 395 778 | Lawrence AL |
| Richardson, Earl H. | Pvt. | 42 108 909 | St. Lawrence NY |
| Riggspy, Billy D. | Pfc. | 35 638 774 | KY |
| Riley, Charles W. | Pfc. | 35 219 430 | Belmont OH |
| Roberts, George E. | 1/Lt. | 0 517 419 | TX |
| Rogers, Julian H. | Pfc. | 35 093 703 | IN (R) |
| Roussel, Martial J. | T/5 | 31 319 489 | ME |
| Sachnowski, Stanley (NMI) | Pfc. | 20 231 950 | Erie NY |
| Salas, Manual | Pfc. | 37 513 475 | KS |
| Sappington, Oscar E. | Pfc. | 38 592 456 | Tulsa OK (R) |
| Sargent, Kermit E. | Pvt. | 33 527 043 | VA |
| Schear, Robert L | Pfc. | 37 666 136 | Franklin IA |
| Schmidt, Herman A. | Sgt. | 39 177 817 | Snohomish WA |
| Schutt, Merle S. | Sgt. | 16 107 083 | IL |
| Schwartz, Emmet W. | Pvt. | 35 837 608 | Ft. Harrison IN |
| Seiler, Gustave J. | Pvt. | 32 891 167 | Kings NY |
| Shankles, Leslie E. | Pfc. | 37 241 407 | KS (R) |
| Shann, Paul (NMI) | Sgt. | 34 366 736 | Wayne TN |
| Shannon, Bernard E. | Pfc. | 20 312 426 | Erie PA |
| Shebelski, Thomas (NMI) | Pfc. | 33 511 757 | Northumberland PA |
| Sheffer, Howard F. | Pvt. | 33 902 861 | Baltimore MD (R) |
| Sheftic, Robert C. | Pvt. | 35 518 064 | Cuyahoga OH |
| Shields, Kennedy J. | Pvt. | 33 707 106 | PA |
| Simon, William L. | Pfc. | 36 823 444 | WI |
| Sitarz, John J. | Pfc. | 35 761 251 | Hancock WV (R) |
| Stackpole, James E. | Sgt. | 31 304 444 | Essex MA |
| Steckler, Clarence H. | T/5 | 37 322 484 | ND |
| Stehlin, William F. | Pfc. | 35 675 356 | Cincinnati OH (R) |
| Stevens, Bruce B. | Sgt. | 32 130 095 | Cattaraugus NY |
| Story, Leonard W. | Sgt. | 32 973 244 | Nassau NY |
| Sweeney, Bernard J., Jr. | Sgt. | 32 645 733 | New York NY |
| Taylor, James R. | T/4 | 33 132 506 | Bath VA |
| Terrano, Mario J. | Pfc. | 42 036 010 | Kings NY |
| Thalman, Norman E. | Pvt. | 39 710 556 | Los Angeles CA |
| Thans, George R. | Pvt. | 31 415 968 | Hampden MA |
| Thurston, Max W. | S/Sgt. | 36 588 775 | MI |

| | | | |
|---|---|---|---|
| Tomlin, Jack | 1/Lt. | o 537 795 | GA |
| Traudt, Walter | Pfc. | 32 869 889 | Queens NY |
| Trick, James I. | Pvt. | 33 873 738 | Lycoming PA (R) |
| Trotter, David H. | Pvt. | 31 218 300 | York ME |
| Turner, James W. | Pvt. | 39 579 498 | Altus OK (R) |
| Turner, Merlin F. | Sgt. | 39 405 336 | Contra Costa CA (R) |
| Valdez, Evaristo E. | Pvt. | 18 114 692 | Harris TX |
| Vallecorsa, Andrew (NMI) | Pvt. | 33 920 462 | Beaver PA |
| Verweire, Wade J., Jr. | T/Sgt. | 35 346 481 | Allen IN |
| Vinyard, Joe A. | Cpl. | 34 364 280 | Loudon TN |
| Wade, Henry C. | Pfc. | 35 499 024 | Russell KY |
| Wagner, James R. | Sgt. | 35 046 799 | Cuyahoga OH |
| Walker, John H. | Pfc. | 37 692 327 | Louisa IA (R) |
| Wall, Norman D. | Pfc. | 37 534 693 | MO |
| Wallace, Clyde M. | Pfc. | 33 842 132 | Lunenburg VA |
| Wallin, Paul W. | Pvt. | 39 203 147 | n/a |
| Walsh, James E. | S/Sgt. | 39 262 509 | San Diego CA |
| Waltz, Marison (NMI) | Pvt. | 36 983 847 | IL |
| Ward, Benjamin F. | S/Sgt. | 06 973 076 | GA |
| Ward, Richard L. | Pvt. | 35 897 549 | IN |
| Warren, Robert J. | Pfc. | 35 071 711 | Butler OH |
| Wassil, Larry S. | Sgt. | 32 245 879 | Essex NJ |
| Watson, Joe N. | Sgt. | 07 030 959 | IL |
| Weaver, Sydney E. | Pvt. | 37 691 327 | Spirit Lake IA |
| Wegner, Norman E. | Pvt. | 36 809 384 | WI |
| Welchel, Henry L. | Sgt. | 14 020 191 | Polk GA |
| West, Clarence E. | 1/Lt. | 01 299 341 | SC |
| Whipple, Milo O. | Pfc. | 35 665 804 | Darke OH |
| White, Floyd C., Sr. | Pvt. | 32 951 509 | Cumberland NJ |
| White, William E. | Pvt. | 32 944 455 | Ulster NY |
| Whitlock, Seals A. | Pfc. | 34 089 670 | Gwinnett GA |
| Whitman, Duane (NMI) | Pfc. | 14 007 887 | Lexington SC |
| Wilder, Harry W. | Pvt. | 37 706 411 | Denver CO (R) |
| Wildman, Walter G. | Pvt. | 33 589 024 | Bucks PA |
| Wilholt, Ernest | Pfc. | 35 812 899 | KY |
| Williams, Harry J. | Pvt. | 37 635 593 | St. Louis MO |
| Williams, Myron E. | Pvt. | 36 687 843 | IL |

Zwei Amerikanische Soldaten

| | | | |
|---|---|---|---|
| Wilmoth, Arnold H. | Pvt. | 35 771 977 | Huntington WV |
| Wilson, Alonzo H. | Pvt. | 32 046 223 | NY |
| Wilson, James O. | Pfc. | 31 066 571 | New London CT |
| Wilson, Mark P. | Pfc. | 34 725 164 | Carter TN |
| Winsch, Carl, Jr. | Pfc. | 32 073 153 | Middlesex NJ |
| Wipfli, Gerald F. | Pfc. | 36 267 007 | Wood WI (R) |
| Wittenberg, Melvin E. | Pfc. | 31 299 189 | Suffolk MA |
| Wolfe, Cliffe H. | T/Sgt. | 36 506 694 | MI |
| Wolfson, Hyman I. | Pvt. | 31 298 679 | Suffolk MA |
| Young, Gilbert | Pfc. | 33 792 532 | Philadelphia PA |
| Young, Robert V. | Pvt. | 35 285 338 | Lorain OH |
| Zaslov, Dave (NMI) | Cpl. | 35 266 828 | Cuyahoga OH |

Table created by the author. Compiled from NARA and DPAA. (R): Recovered since 1950; may not be complete list; finding party, location, and date mainly unknown. NMI: No middle initial.

# NOTES

## Introduction

1. Proceedings, Pvt. Eddie Slovik court-martial case 36896415, Department of the Army, Army Board for Correction of Military Record; William Bradford Huie, *The Execution of Private Slovik* (Yardley PA: Westholme), 231.

2. Associated Press, "In London Drive on Crime Wave: Comb City for 10,000 Army Deserters," *Chicago Tribune*, December 16, 1945, 21.

3. Interview with Michael G. Bradbeer, January 10, 2019.

4. Combat interview, S/Sgt. Nathaniel Quentin, T/Sgt. Harvey Hausman, S/Sgt. Stephen J. Kertes, Sgt. Travis C. Norton by Capt. William J. Fox, December 7, 1944, Siegfried Line.

## 1. Molly and Peggy

1. *Spirit Lake Beacon*, November 21, 1946, 5.

2. Interview with Peggy Robinette, January 30, 2019.

3. Susan Wiggs, *Map of the Heart* (New York: William Morrow, 2017), 24.

4. Phillip W. Stewart, "A Reel Story of World War II: The United News Collection of Newsreels," *Prologue Magazine* 47, no. 3 (Fall 2015): https://www.archives.gov/publications/prologue/2015/fall/united-newsreels.html (accessed April 23, 2020); "Through the American Newsreel (1942–1945)," Proquest News, Ann Arbor, Michigan, https://www.proquest.com/products-services/film/world-war-ii-through-the-american-newsreels-1942-19451.html (accessed April 23, 2020).

5. Interview with Linda Bepler, February 15, 2019.

6. Interview with Linda Bepler.

7. Wilson Farrell family collection.

8. Wil S. Hylton, *Vanished: The Sixty-Year Search for the Missing Men of World War II* (New York: Riverhead, 2013), 30.

9. Chris J. Hartley, *The Lost Soldier: The Ordeal of a World War II GI from the Home Front to the Hürtgen Forest* (Harrisburg PA: Stackpole, 2018), 209.

## 2. They Can't Find Jack

1. Interview with Amelia Messina, February 11, 2019.

2. Interview with Eve Cunningham, April 8, 2019.

## 3. Young and Strong and Male

1. Interview with Anthony Grasso, January 27, 2019.

2. Interview with Willie Fikes, January, 6, 2014.

3. National Radio Address given on October 29, 1940, from Washington DC, FDR Library, Marist, http://www.fdrlibrary.marist.edu/archives/collections/utterancesfdr.html (accessed April 23, 2020). The way the draft selection process worked: there were 6,500 local areas at which men between the ages of 21 and 36 registered for the draft. On October 16 more than 16 million of them did. Each registrant in each of those 6500 local areas received a number ranging between 1 and 7836.

4. On October 29, 1941, blindfolded secretary of war Henry Stimson pulled numbers out of a 10-gallon glass bowl and handed them to President Roosevelt to be read over national radio. "FDR at the Selective Service Draft Lottery, October 1940," YouTube, December 7, 2009, https://www.youtube.com/watch?v=19-8TY0LUdo (accessed April 23, 2020). See also https://www.criticalpast.com/video/65675046220_President-Roosevelt_Congressmen-standing_addressing-nation_American-youth (accessed April 23, 2020).

5. Vital Statistics Rates 1940–1960, Center for Disease Control, https://www.cdc.gov/nchs/data/vsus/vsrates1940_60.pdf (accessed April 23, 2020).

6. National World War II Museum, New Orleans.

7. Louis M. Lyons, "389 Cocoanut Grove Identified Dead," *Boston Daily Globe*, November 30, 1942, 1.

8. Interview with Sheila Peterson Helmberger, August 2012.

9. *Spirit Lake Beacon*, October 24, 1940, 11.

10. Weaver family collection.

11. Weaver family collection.

12. Sydney Weaver, letter home, March 9, 1944, Weaver family collection.

13. Sydney Weaver, letter home, March 7, 1944, Weaver family collection.

## 4. Under the Gaze of a Zen Master

1. "U.S. Military by the Numbers," National World War II Museum, New Orleans, https://www.nationalww2museum.org/students-teachers/student-resources/research-starters/research-starters-us-military-numbers (accessed April 23, 2020).

2. There were 119 army mobilization training camps during World War II, 66 of which were established during or immediately prior to the war; 48 of them are no longer in existence. See "World War II Army Mobilization Training Camps," Global Security, https://www.globalsecurity.org/military/facility/camp-ww2.htm (accessed April 23, 2020); and "Camp Croft, South Carolina," South Carolina History Net, http://www.schistory.net/campcroft/irtc.html (accessed April 23, 2020).

3. "Research Starters: U.S. Military by the Numbers," National World War II Museum, New Orleans LA, https://www.nationalww2museum.org/students-teachers/student-resources/research-starters/research-starters-us-military-numbers (accessed April 23, 2020).

4. Interview with Thomas G. Bradbeer, January 10, 2019.

5. "Camp Croft: ETV Update," Know It All (Spartanburg, South Carolina), https://www.knowitall.org/video/camp-croft-etv-upstate (accessed April 23, 2020).

6. Interview with Anthony Grasso, February 27, 2019.

7. Interview with Thomas G. Bradbeer, December 19, 2018.

8. Interview with Thomas G. Bradbeer.

9. Huie, *Execution of Eddie Slovik*, 72.

10. Julian Farrior letter home from Officer Training School at Camp Benning, Stanley Farrior family collection. The U.S. Supreme Court ruled in 1971 that IQ tests are a violation of Title VII of the 1964 Civil Rights Act. The army no longer administers such tests.

11. Julian Farrior, letter home, from Camp Benning, Georgia, Stanley Farrior family collection.

12. Interview with Thomas G. Bradbeer; Thomas G. Bradbeer, "General Cota and the Battle of the Hürtgen Forest: A Failure of Battle Command," *Army History* 75 (Spring 2010): 18–41.

### 5. The Stillness of a Predawn Hour

1. M. Bedford Davis, *Frozen Rainbows: The World War II Adventures of a Combat Medical Officer* (Elk River MN: Meadowlark, 2003), 32.

2. Interview with Stanley Farrior, March 19, 2019.

3. S-1 Report, 112th Infantry, 28th Infantry Division, November 26, 1943, National Archives and Records Administration (NARA), College Park, Maryland, 1st Lt. Robert C. Nelson, historian.

4. Rick Atkinson, *The Guns at Last Light: The War in Western Europe, 1944–45* (New York: Henry Holt, 2013), 1.

5. S-1 Report, 112th Infantry, January 12, 1944, 1st Lt. Robert C. Nelson, historian.

6. S-1 Report 112th Regiment, July 3, 1944, Capt. Richard A. Dana, historian.

7. S-1 Report 112th Regiment, July 3, 1944, Capt. Richard A. Dana, historian.

8. S-1 Report 112th Regiment, June 15, 1944, Capt. James Nesbitt, historian; Bedford, *Frozen Rainbows*, 124.

9. V-Mail from Wales, Loncar-Bepler family collection.

10. Associated Press, "In London Drive on Crime Wave: Comb City for 10,000 Army Deserters," *Chicago Tribune*, December 16, 1945, 21.

11. Interview with Lt. Col. Thomas G. Bradbeer, December 19, 2018.

12. Fred L. Borch, "A Deserter in France: The Strange Case of Private Wayne E. Powers," *Litigation* 41, no. 1 (Fall 2014): 7–8.

13. "A Happy Hidden Life Ends for an AWOL GI," *Life Magazine*, April 7, 1958, 28; Borch, "Deserter in France."

14. Loncar-Bepler family collection.

15. Interview with Anthony Grasso, February 20, 2019.

16. S-1 Report, 112th Regiment, August 12, 1944, Lt. Julian Farrior, historian.

17. Bedford, *Frozen Rainbows*, 138.

18. Michael E. Weaver, *Guard Wars: The 28th Infantry Division in World War II* (Bloomington: Indiana University Press, 2010), 170.

19. Omar Nelson Bradley and Clay Blair Jr., *A General's Life: An Autobiography by General of the Army Omar N. Bradley* (New York: Simon & Schuster, 1983), 287.

20. Bradley, *General's Life*, 287.

21. Maj. William Fellman, 2nd, "Report of Execution by Shooting," Pvt. Eddie Slovik court-martial case 290498, record of trial folder, exhibit A, APO 887; Benedict B. Kimmelman, "The Example of Private Slovik," *American Heritage*, September/October 1987, 38.

22. G Company History, August 1944, NARA, College Park, Maryland, Lt. Julian Farrior, historian.

## 6. The Autumn of Its Reign

1. D. K. R. Crosswell, *Beetle: The Life of General Walter Bedell Smith* (Lexington: University Press of Kentucky, 2010), 627.

2. Bradley, *General's Life*, 332.

3. Interview with Thomas G. Bradbeer, December 19, 2018.

4. Bradbeer, "Failure of Battle Command." In 2010 Bradbeer received the Army Historical Foundation Distinguished Writing Award for the article.

5. Gen. James M. Gavin, *On to Berlin* (New York: Bantam, 1978), 300–301.

6. MacDonald, *Siegfried Line Campaign*, 44–45; National World War II Museum/casualties.

7. Charles B. MacDonald, *The Siegfried Line Campaign: United States Army in World War II—The European Theater of Operations* (Washington DC: Office of the Chief of Military History, Department of the Army, 1963), 45.

8. "28th Infantry Division Siegfried Line September 1944," V. Corps Logistics Report, October 3, 1944, 1st Lt. John S. Howe, File 585.51, NARA, College Park Maryland; Weaver, *Guard Wars*, 179.

9. MacDonald, *Siegfried Line Campaign*, 44–45; 28th Division Unit Report No. 3, October 7, 1944.

10. Bradbeer, "Failure of Battle Command"; MacDonald, *Siegfried Line Campaign*, 45–49.

11. Interview with Thomas G. Bradbeer, December 19, 2018.

12. Julian Farrior family collection, October 8, 1944.

13. William C. Sylvan and Captain Francis G. Smith Jr., *The War Diary of General Courtney H. Hodges and the First U.S. Army* (Lexington: University Press of Kentucky, 2008), 127.

14. Bradbeer, "General Cota," 23; Robert A. Miller, *Division Commander: A Biography of Major General Norman D. Cota* (Spartanburg SC: Reprint Company, 1989).

15. Weaver, *Guard Wars*, 181.

16. Atkinson, *Guns at Last Light*, 73.

17. Joseph Balkowski and John C. McManus, *Beyond the Beachhead: The 29th Infantry Division in Normandy* (Lanham MD: Stackpole, 2005), 268–72.

18. Interview with Thomas G. Bradbeer, January 10, 2019.

## 7. Replacement Depot No. 15

1. Interview with Peggy Robinette, January 30, 2019.

2. Chris J. Hartley, *The Lost Soldier: The Ordeal of a World War II GI From the Home Front to the Hurtgen Forest* (Guilford CT: Stackpole, 2018), 98.

3. Index of crossings, World War Troop Ships, http://www.ww2troopships.com/crossings (accessed May 7, 2019).

4. Sydney Weaver family collection.

5. Julian and Stanley Farrior family collection.

6. Letter from Julian Farrior to Grace Farrior, October 17, 1944, from somewhere near the frontline in Germany, Farrior family collection.

7. Interview with Thomas G. Bradbeer, December 19, 2018.

8. Interview with Thomas G. Bradbeer.

9. United States v. Pvt. Eddie D. Slovik (36896415), Company G, 109th Infantry, Board of Review No. 1 CM ETO 5555, January 6, 1945, 159.

10. V-mail, October 9, 1944, Pvt. Sydney Weaver to family in Spirit Lake, Iowa, Sydney Weaver family collection.

11. Bradbeer, "Failure of Battle Command," 23.

12. Miller, *Division Commander*, 106; interview with Thomas G. Bradbeer.

13. G Company History, 112th Regiment, A.P.O. 28 U.S. Army, October 1944, NARA, College Park, Maryland, Benajah H. Brunner, historian.

14. Letter from Julian Farrior to Grace Farrior, October 25, 1944, Farrior family collection.

15. V Corps after-action report, October 3, 1944, NARA, College Park, Maryland. The author of this report was anonymous.

16. Weaver, *Guard Wars*, 181.

17. Bradley, *General's Life*, 342.

18. Martin Blumenson, *The Patton Papers, 1940–1945* (New York: Houghton Mifflin, 1974), 647–48.

19. Sylvan, *Normandy to Victory*, 161–62.

### 8. Tucked into the Alluvial Folds

1. Gavin, *On to Berlin*, 309.

2. Gavin, *On to Berlin*, 306; "The Battle of Schmidt," instructional aid produced by the U.S. Army Command and General Staff College for classes in "Fundamentals of Combined Arms Warfare," and designated by the numbers m3121–2/R3121–2.

3. John Gerrard, *Mountain Environments: An Examination of the Physical Geography of Mountains* (Cambridge MA: MIT Press, 1990), 13–16.

4. Atenstaedt, "Trench Foot," 282–89.

5. Davis, *Frozen Rainbows*, 182; Edward G. Miller, *A Dark and Bloody Ground: The Hürtgen Forest and the Roer River Dams, 1944–1945* (College Station: Texas A&M University Press, 1995), 12–13.

6. Gavin, *On to Berlin*, 309.

7. Combat interview, 1st Lt. James A. Condon with Capt. William J. Fox, December 14, 1944, Luxembourg.

8. Alexander "Sparky" Kisse, "Battle of the Bulge/Hürtgen Forest Recollections," You-Tube, January 10, 2007, https://www.youtube.com/watch?v=PTE9BPmiZNo (accessed April 23, 2020).

9. Jeffrey S. Bush and Simon Watson, "Trench Foot," StatPearls Publishing, Medical University of South Carolina, February 20, 2019, https://www.ncbi.nlm.gov/books/NBK482364/ (accessed April 23, 2020).

10. G Company History November 1944, NARA, College Park, Maryland, 1st Lt. Benajah H. Brunner, historian; Miller, *Dark and Bloody Ground*, 15–16; Russell Frank Weigley,

*Eisenhower's Lieutenants: The Campaign of France and Germany, 1944–1945* (Bloomington: Indiana University Press, 1981), 365–66.

11. Sylvan, *Normandy to Victory*, 153.

12. Daniel P. Bolger, "Zero Defects, Command Climate of the First Army," *Military Review* 71, no. 5 (May 1991): 71.

13. Bolger, "Zero Defects," 71.

14. Bolger, "Zero Defects," 70; Blumenson, *Patton Papers*, vol. 2, 479.

15. Bolger, "Zero Defects," 71.

16. Bolger, "Zero Defects," 71.

17. Combat interview, Maj. Gen. Norman D. Cota and Brig. Gen. George A. Davis by Capt. William J. Fox, December 13, 1944, Wiltz, Luxembourg.

18. Davis, *Frozen Rainbows*, 193; Charles B. MacDonald and Sydney T. Mathews, *Three Battles: Arnaville, Altuzzo, and Schmidt* (Washington DC: Center of Military History, United States Army, 1993), 255.

19. Davis, *Frozen Rainbows*, 194.

20. Combat interview, Maj. Gen. Norman D. Cota and Brig. Gen. George A. Davis by Capt. William J. Fox, December 13, 1944, Wiltz, Luxembourg; Cecil B. Currey, *Follow Me and Die: The Destruction of An American Division in World War II* (New York: Stein & Day, 1984), 43.

21. Bradbeer, "Failure of Battle Command," 17; Gerald Astor, *The Bloody Forest: Battle of the Huertgen, September 1944-January 1945* (Novato CA: Presidio, 2000), 356.

22. Letter from Sydney Weaver, October 31, 1944, from somewhere near the front in the Hürtgen Forest, Sydney Weaver family collection.

23. Davis, *Frozen Rainbows*, 194.

24. Bradley, *General's Life*, 343.

25. Combat interview, Maj. Gen. Norman D. Cota and Brig. Gen. George A. Davis by Capt. William J. Fox, December 13, 1944, Wiltz, Luxembourg.

26. G Company History, November 1944 Report, NARA, College Park, Maryland, 1st Lt. Benajah H. Brunner, historian.

27. Crane, *Red Badge of Courage*, 48–49.

28. Interview with Anthony Grasso, February 19, 2018.

### 9. Flashes of Fire

1. Bradley, *General's Life*, 342–43.

2. Bradley, *General's life*, 342–43.

3. Currey, *Follow Me and Die*, 6.

4. Atkinson, *Guns at Last Light*, 318.

5. Atkinson, *Guns at Last Light*, 317.

6. Combat interview, Maj. Gen. Norman D. Cota and Brig. Gen. George Davis by Capt. William J. Fox, December 13, 1944, Wiltz, Luxembourg.

7. Interview with Anthony Grasso, February 26, 2019.

8. MacDonald, *Three Battles*, 258–59; Combat interview, S/Sgt. Eugene Holden by Capt. William J. Fox, December 6, 1944, Siegfried Line.

9. Combat interview, Maj. Richard S. Dana by Capt. William J. Fox, December 1, 1944, Ouren, Belgium.

10. Currey, *Follow Me and Die*, 100.

11. Combat interview, 1st Lt. James Condon by Capt. William J. Fox, December 14, 1944, Malusmuhle, Luxembourg.

12. Combat interview, 1st Lt. Eldeen Kauffman by Capt. William J. Fox, December 8, 1944, Lieler, Belgium.

13. Combat interview, 1st Lt. James Condon by Capt. William J. Fox, December 14, 1944, Malusmuhle, Luxembourg.

14. Combat interview, 1st Lt. Eldeen Kauffman by Capt. William J. Fox, December 8, 1944, in Lieler, Belgium; MacDonald and Mathews, *Three Battles*, 262; Astor, *Bloody Forest*, 108; Miller, *Dark and Bloody Ground*, 260.

### 10. Like a Little Napoleon

1. Rudolf Christoph Freiherr Von Gersdorff, "The Battle of the Huertgen Forest, November–Early December 1944," National Archives of the United States, Foreign Military Service, A-Series—a-891, U.S. Army Military History Institute, Carlisle, Pennsylvania, 9–11; Edward Salo, "Final Report Hurtgen Research Support Services," Southeastern Archaeological Research for Joint POW/MIA Accounting Command, 2014, 55–56.

2. Albert W. Burghardt, "My Tour With the 28th Division: The Hurtgen Forest," unpublished manuscript, Pennsylvania National Guard Military Museum, Fort Indiantown Gap, Annville, Pennsylvania, 6.

3. Currey, *Follow Me and Die*, 103.

4. Combat interview, Maj. Gen. Norman D. Cota and Brig. Gen. George Davis by Capt. William J. Fox, December 13, 1944, Wiltz, Luxembourg.

5. Currey, *Follow Me and Die*, 106.

6. MacDonald and Mathews, *Three Battles*, 288.

7. MacDonald and Mathews, *Three Battles*, 289.

8. MacDonald and Mathews, *Three Battles*, 290.

9. Interview with Thomas G. Bradbeer, January 10, 2019.

10. Interview with Thomas G. Bradbeer.

11. Interview with Thomas G. Bradbeer.

12. Interview with Thomas G. Bradbeer.

13. Interview with Thomas G. Bradbeer.

14. Combat interview, S/Sgt. Nathaniel Quentin, 1st Sgt. Harvey Hausman, T/Sgt. George A. Lockwood, S/Sgt. Stephen J. Kertes, Sgt. Travis C. Norton by Capt. William J. Fox, December 7, 1944, Siegfried Line, Germany.

15. Combat interview, S/Sgt. Nathaniel Quentin, 1st Sgt. Harvey Hausman, T/Sgt. George A. Lockwood, S/Sgt. Stephen J. Kertes, Sgt. Travis C. Norton by Capt. William J. Fox, December 7, 1944, Siegfried Line, Germany.

16. Combat interview, S/Sgt. Nathaniel Quentin, 1st Sgt. Harvey Hausman, T/Sgt. George A. Lockwood, S/Sgt. Stephen J. Kertes, Sgt. Travis C. Norton by Capt. William J. Fox, December 7, 1944, Siegfried Line, Germany.

## 11. Like Caskets Tossed from the Deck

1. Combat interview, Maj. Richard S. Dana by Capt. William J. Fox, December 1, 1944, Ouren, Belgium; MacDonald and Mathews, *Three Battles*, 299–300.

2. Combat interview, Maj. Richard S. Dana by Capt. William J. Fox, December 1, 1944, Ouren, Belgium; Currey, *Follow Me and Die*, 120–22.

3. Davis, *Frozen Rainbows*, 198.

4. MacDonald and Mathews, *Three Battles*, 300.

5. Tom Brady, "Private Wipfli, 112th Regiment," email correspondence with Dave Barth, September, 2017.

6. Joint POW/Accounting Command (JPAC) Central Identification Laboratory, Forensic Anthropology Report, CIL —056-1-01, June 18, 2010.

7. MacDonald and Mathews, *Three Battles*, 306.

8. MacDonald and Mathews, *Three Battles*, 306.

9. MacDonald and Mathews, *Three Battles*, 306.

10. Combat interview, Maj. Richard Dana by Capt. William J. Fox, December 1, 1944, Ouren, Belgium.

11. MacDonald and Mathews, *Three Battles*, 306.

12. Sylvan, *Normandy to Victory*, 164–65.

13. Atkinson, *Guns at Last Light*, 320; combat interview, S/Sgt. Nathaniel Quentin, 1st Sgt. Harvey Hausman, T/Sgt. George A. Lockwood, S/Sgt. Stephen J. Kertes, Sgt. Travis C. Norton by Capt. William J. Fox, December 7, 1944, Siegfried Line, Germany.

14. MacDonald and Mathews, *Three Battles*, 327; Miller, *Dark and Bloody Ground*, 71.

15. Harold Denny, "With American Forces in Germany," *New York Times*, November 5, 1944, 1.

16. Combat interview, S/Sgt. Nathaniel Quentin, 1st Sgt. Harvey Hausman, T/Sgt. George A. Lockwood, S/Sgt. Stephen J. Kertes, Sgt. Travis C. Norton by Capt. William J. Fox, December 7, 1944, Siegfried Line, Germany.

17. Lt. Col. Carl Peterson, "Summary of Statements," after-action report, November 7, 1944, NARA, College Park, Maryland.

18. "Five German Tanks," *Xenia Ohio Daily Gazette*, July 5, 1945, 1.

19. Combat interview by Col. G. M. Nelson with fourteen sergeants who participated in the battle, November 13, 1944, Siegfried Line, Germany, NARA, College Park, Maryland.

20. Salo, "Final Report."

21. Combat interview by Col. G. M. Nelson with fourteen sergeants who participated in the battle, November 13, 1944, Siegfried Line, Germany, NARA, College Park, Maryland.

22. Combat interview by Col. G. M. Nelson with fourteen sergeants who participated in the battle, November 13, 1944, Siegfried Line, Germany, NARA, College Park, Maryland.

23. Combat interview by Col. G. M. Nelson with fourteen sergeants who participated in the battle, November 13, 1944, Siegfried Line, Germany, NARA, College Park, Maryland.

24. MacDonald and Mathews, *Three Battles*, 352; Miller, *Dark and Bloody Ground*, 83.

25. Bradbeer, "Failure of Battle Command."

26. Combat interview of Cpl. Joe Philpot by Capt. William Fox, Lieler, Belgium, December 15, 1944, NARA, College Park, Maryland.

27. Julian Farrior family collection.

28. "Summary of Interrogation of Master Sergeant Paul A. Wilson Relative to the Receipt of a Message Ordering Lt. Col. Peterson to the Rear of the 112th Regiment," document 735017, NARA, College Park, Maryland.

## 12. If I Leave Now

1. Army Board for Correction of Military Record, Transcript of Hearing in Case of Eddie D. Slovik, June 15, 1977, 62–63; Huie, *Execution of Private Slovik*, 162.

2. Benedict B. Kimmelman, "The Example of Private Slovik," *American Heritage* 38, no. 6 (September–October, 1987): 98; Huie, *Execution of Private Slovik*, 162.

3. Kimmelman, "Example of Private Slovik," 98.

4. "The Court Martial/Execution of Private Edward Donald Slovik," Court-Martial Case 2, 290498, War Department/Department of Defense, Office of the Judge Advocate General, 54.

5. Kimmelman, "Example of Private Slovik," 98; Huie, *Execution of Private Slovik*, 154–55.

6. Kimmelman, "Example of Private Slovik," 98; Huie, *Execution of Private Slovik*, 154–55.

7. Court Martial Case 2, 290498, 1052–53.

8. Court Martial Case 2, 290498, 1054.

9. Court Martial Case 2, 290498, 1049.

10. Court Martial Case 2, 290498, 1054–55.

11. Kimmelman, "Example of Private Slovik," 98.

12. Kimmelman, "Example of Private Slovik," 98.

13. Huie, *Execution of Eddie Slovik*, 169.

14. Huie, *Execution of Eddie Slovik*, 177.

15. Court Martial Case 2, 290498, 1166.

16. Court Martial Case 2, 290498, 1745; Kimmelman, "Example of Private Slovik," 104; William Bradford Huie, "Are Americans Afraid to Fight?," *Liberty Magazine*, June 1948, 79.

17. William Bradford Huie, "Are Americans Afraid to Fight?," 79–81; Elliot D. Cooke, *All But Me and Thee: Psychiatry at the Foxhole Level* (Washington, DC: Infantry Journal, 1946), 11.

18. Cooke, *All But Me and Thee*, 11.

19. Interview with Thomas G. Bradbeer, January 10, 2019.

20. Interview with Thomas G. Bradbeer, January 10, 2019.

21. Interview with Thomas G. Bradbeer, January 10, 2019.

22. Interview with Anthony Grasso, March 13, 2019.

## 13. Lower Levels of Dante's *Inferno*

1. Interview with William Snyder, May 20, 2019.

2. Davis, *Frozen Rainbows*, 198.

3. Currey, *Follow Me and Die*, 179.

4. Currey, *Follow Me and Die*, 179–80.

5. Combat interview, Maj. Richard Dana by Capt. William J. Fox, December 1, 1944, Ouren, Belgium, NARA, College Park, Maryland.

6. Robert D. Billinger Jr., "Enemies and Friends: POWs in the Tar Heel State," *Tar Heel Junior Historian*, Spring 2008, 28–29.

7. Chris J. Hartley, *The Lost Soldier: The Ordeal of a World War II* GI *From the Home Front to the Hurtgen Forest.* (Lanham MD: Stackpole, 2018), 220.

8. Gavin, *Onto Berlin*, 308.

9. Gavin, *Onto Berlin*, 309.

10. Gavin, *On to Berlin*, 306–9.

11. Henri-Chapelle, American Battle Monuments Commission, https://www.abmc .gov/cemeteries-memorials (accessed April 23, 2020).

12. Individual deceased personnel file of 1st Lt. Ernest Temper; interview with Ted Temper, March 15, 2019.

13. Report of burial, February 15, 1945, Ernest L. Temper, individual deceased personnel file; Atkinson, *Guns at Last Light*, 488.

14. After-action report no. 328.03.6508 for the Twenty-Eighth Infantry Division, November 1944.

15. Interview with Herr Ludwig Fischer, June 10, 2012.

16. Interview with Herr Ludwig Fischer, June 10, 2012.

17. Individual deceased personnel file of 1st Lt. Turney White Leonard.

18. Individual deceased personnel file of 1st Lt. Turney White Leonard.

19. Christoph Rass and Jen Lohmeier, "Transformations: Post-Battle Processes on the Hurtgenwald Battlefield," *Journal of Conflict Archaeology* 6, no. 3 (2011): 190.

### 14. Am I Wounded Badly?

1. Col. James R. Woodall, *Williams-Ford Texas A&M University Military History: Aggie Medals of Honor* (College Station: Texas A&M University Press, 2010), 91.

2. Jerry C. Cooper, "A Special Aggie Ring Comes Home," *Texas Aggie Magazine*, January 2001, 14–15.

3. Interview of Capt. Bruce M Hostrup by Capt. John S. Howe, 1st Lt. Raymond E. Fleig, 2nd Lt. Richard J. Payne, A Company, 707th Tank Battalion, November 14, 1944, at company command post, Roetgen, Germany; Currey, *Follow Me and Die*, 188–89.

4. Affidavit provided by German citizen Hubert Dohmen to the American Graves Registration Command, October 27, 1949; individual deceased personnel file, 1st Lt. Turney White Leonard, William Snider family collection.

5. Letter from Lt. Col. Carl Peterson to Maj. Gen. Edward Witsell, Adjutant General's Office, March 31, 1949, Washington DC, William Snider family collection.

6. Letter from Lt. Col. Carl Peterson to Maj. Gen. Edward Witsell, March 31, 1949, William Snider family collection.

7. Letter from Lt. Col. Carl Peterson to the adjutant general, March 31, 1949, William Snider family collection.

8. Woodall, *Aggie Medals of Honor*, 101.

9. Individual deceased personnel file of 1st Lt. Turney White Leonard, William Snider family collection.

10. Individual deceased personnel file of 1st Lt. Turney White Leonard, William Snider family collection.

11. Individual deceased personnel file of 1st Lt. Turney White Leonard, William Snider family collection.

12. Cooper, "Special Aggie Ring," 14.

13. Individual deceased personnel file, S/Sgt. John J. Farrell, Farrell-Wilson family collection.

14. Individual deceased personnel file of 1st Lt. Turney White Leonard, William Snider family collection.

15. Interview with Peggy Robinette, January 30, 2019.

16. Ed Tiebax, email, February 3, 2019.

17. Interview with Linda Bepler, March 16, 2019.

18. Robin Buehler, "A Family Remembers," *Weymouth Township*, December 27, 2001, 1.

19. Hartley, *Lost Soldier*, 228.

20. Interview with Eve Cunningham, March 19, 2019.

### 15. It Had a Bittersweet Sound

1. Interview with Herr Ludwig Fischer, June 10, 2012.

2. "WWII Veteran Statistics: The Passing of the WWII Generation," National World War II Museum, New Orleans, https://www.nationalww2museum.org/war/wwii-veteran-statistics (accessed April 23, 2020); U.S. Department of Veteran Affairs Statistics, https://www.va.gov/vetdata/ (accessed April 23, 2020).

### 16. Zwei Amerikanische Soldaten

1. Interview with Stanley Farrior, May 3, 2019.

2. Robert Burns, "MIA Efforts Risk Total Failure," *Associated Press*, July 8, 2013.

3. Fiscal Year Budget Estimates, 2010 and 2018, POW/MIA Accounting Agency (DPAA), https://comptroller.defense.gov/ (accessed April 23, 2020).

4. Interview with DPAA historian Ian Spurgeon, February 12, 2019.

5. Interview with Ian Spurgeon, February 12, 2019.

6. Interview with Ian Spurgeon, February 12, 2019.

7. Hellmuth E. Willner, "Narrative of Investigation," Headquarters 7887 Graves Registration Detachment Operations Division APO 757 (Liege) U.S. Army, November 20, 1950, NARA, College Park, Maryland.

8. Willner, "Narrative of Investigation."

9. Email from Lt. Col. Mario Cremer, November 14, 2019.

# INDEX

Index 245

Printed in the USA
CPSIA information can be obtained
at www.ICGtesting.com
LVHW091218151223
766489LV00004B/319